TELLING ME MY STORIES

TELLING ME MY STORIES

FRAGMENTS OF A HIMALAYAN CHILDHOOD

KUNZANG CHODEN

BLOOMSBURY
NEW DELHI • LONDON • OXFORD • NEW YORK • SYDNEY

BLOOMSBURY INDIA
Bloomsbury Publishing India Pvt. Ltd
Second Floor, LSC Building No. 4, DDA Complex, Pocket C—6 & 7,
Vasant Kunj, New Delhi, 110070

BLOOMSBURY, BLOOMSBURY INDIA and the Diana logo
are trademarks of Bloomsbury Publishing Plc

First published in India 2025

ISBN: PB: 978-93-61313-97-4; eBook: 978-93-61315-23-7
2 4 6 8 10 9 7 5 3 1

Typeset in Adobe Caslon by Manipal Technologies Limited
Printed and bound in India by Thomson Press India Ltd

FSC www.fsc.org MIX Paper | Supporting responsible forestry FSC® C010615

To find out more about our authors and books visit www.bloomsbury.com and sign up for our newsletters

For sale in the Indian subcontinent only

For my mother and father, whose lives were too short, and to my uncle *Akhu* lama, who became my parent and my teacher

Contents

Prologue

Ogyen Choling, my ancestral home, was turned into a museum more than twenty years ago. The decision to turn my private home into a museum for public viewing was to keep it alive. I wanted to honour and remember the more than twenty generations who lived here over nearly six hundred years. The shape of the land on which the house stands is said to resemble the crown of an elephant's head. The elephant in Buddhist iconography is considered an auspicious symbol for longevity and strength. The first settlers, my distant ancestors, chose to establish their home on this very spot, on a hilltop shaped like the crown of an elephant's head. The landscape has not changed, and walking up the valley and looking towards the hilltop, the shape of the hill does, with some imagination and belief, still resemble the crown of an elephant's head. But over the centuries the householders occupying the *nagtshang* or manor have endured major transformations. There was once a time that the household enjoyed political stability and economic prosperity and commanded respect as an honourable establishment of economic, social and religious influence. The buildings themselves have undergone alterations due to the forces of nature that allowed or deterred the occupants of the household from living according to their accumulative karma or the lack of it.

For as far as the village collective memory goes, I know that the entire complex was destroyed by the earthquake of 1887, and it was rebuilt by my great-grandfather and completed in 1902. The new structures were said to have been reconstructed using the previous structures as a model. Although written records are scant, the oral records are more comprehensive and even detailed from this period onwards. I have had the opportunity to meet elders who remembered the earthquake first-hand or heard about it from their parents. I have relied on their memories and my own when setting up the museum.

Today, without any conscious effort, I can make the mental shift of once having lived in the house to guiding visitors through it as a museum; the emotional shift is always more troublesome. All the buildings in the complex and every room holds special memories for me. Every artefact displayed in the museum is laden with memories of how and when and who used it. As I walk through each room, I immediately become immersed in reminiscences of my parents, my brothers, relatives, visitors and attendants, their lives and mine, their stories and the stories of those who lived there before us. Lives from the past can be invoked in each room and through each artefact, but what always overwhelms me is the silence of the untold stories that I yearn to hear. Sometimes, when I am alone the rooms feel filled with unspoken words, and I find myself unconsciously yearning for those long gone to appear and speak to me.

While many of the previous generations are long gone, there are still living beings that have stood the test of time – the three giant oak trees in the compound. Like faithful guardians, these trees, weighty in appearance and strategic in location, were brought here and planted as saplings by the women who were brought into the house as brides from afar. The oak saplings travelled with these women for more than three days over a high pass until they found their destined spot. This species of oak is not endemic to our temperate region. They came from the subtropical regions where these brides were born. It must have been with loving care and attention, the trees flourished into impressive old age, not only as landmarks but also as repositories of my ancestors' histories. I feel a strong affiliation with the trees and find much solace and comfort in being in their presence, especially the one that is next to the temple. It is this tree I turn to daily when I circumambulate the temple and interact with my colleagues, the elders and the old people of the village.

The bare and brittle oak tree on the east side of my family's temple trembles and rattles as the cold winter wind shrieks through it. The air is crisp; it's the height of winter. The village elders who are gathered around the temple draw their scarves tighter around their faces and pull down their sleeves to cover their hands against the chill. Now, only the prayer beads which dangle from their hands are visible as they walk the merit-making circuit around the temple, again and again. The circular route takes them from the left to the right. They retrace their steps repeatedly. It's time for me to join these elders who are circumambulating the temple. This has been my daily routine since I returned to live in my ancestral home in 2013.

The elders know that spring is approaching when the tips of the bare branches swell with quiet, new life. The swelling tips will thicken and grow heavier by the day. The elders will continue counting their prayer beads, counting the days to spring. These tips will burst into pale, tender, almost translucent, green leaves. These will sprout on the knotty branches until the entire tree is dressed in new life. When the gusty winds from the south blow persistently, the elders will feel the warmth caress their cheeks which have been weathered and roughened by the harsh winter.

Later, streaks of flashing lights will cut across the sky and thunder will rumble, closing in on them. Then they will know that the monsoon rains have arrived. Soon, the tree will be full of shiny dark green leaves and rain will drip from every leaf tip, drops falling in a symphonic cascade on the ground below, causing tiny rivulets to trickle down the slope. The elders will take shelter under the overhanging roof of the prayer wheels attached to the base of the temple. They will emerge from the shelter as the drops cease; they will not be deterred from their daily merit-making walk. Once the rain has lessened, they will hear the light rustle of the drying leaves as the north wind defiantly screeches through the branches. The yellow, golden and brown leaves will float down in flurries and litter their path to redemption, but they will walk on, holding steadfastly to their beads and prayer wheels, believing that they are on the right path. They will shuffle through the fallen leaves of autumn. Each step marked by a crunching sound, and someone will quietly remark that winter will be here soon. They will watch the dark branches turn bare and brittle and see them tremble and rattle in the cold winter wind.

As I join the elders, they greet me with smiles and welcoming gestures. Now I am in the honoured procession, privileged to have earned a place with the elders by my own increasing age. As aged members of the community, we are allowed and expected to be here, saying 'we are here to gather our *jag* (food rations) for the journey onwards', a euphemism about praying for our afterlife. We know we are at the final phase of our journey in this lifetime. Our measured steps will lead us on to the path to our next life, of which we know little, but faith moves us on. What we do know is that we must prepare ourselves by chanting mantras and make the repeated circumambulations around the temple through the changing seasons.

Aged as we are, and mindful as we strive to be, we are still not free of grasping and clinging to the remains of our lives. We talk and ask each other about our everyday concerns. We wonder why there is no smoke rising above the house of our neighbour, the old man who lives by himself. Is he all right? We cannot ignore the cows which have wandered into *Aum* Pema's wheat field; the cows are grazing leisurely for all of us to see.

Unseen are the sentiments of resentment, anger and regrets that we hold on to, which can suddenly arise in our chest even as we try to concentrate on chanting our prayers.

Under our greying and white hair and our fumbling steps, we are still humans. Some of us have just a few teeth, others have none. 'How can you eat?' asks a curious novice to the group. 'Just push the food around your mouth and send it down your throat,' advise the experienced. *Aie* (grandmother) Dechen grins and points to the only two remaining front teeth in her mouth. One's age is ever present in our appearances and thoughts. Many of the elders have discovered the age-defying magic of hair dye. But they have yet to acquire the art – the tell-tale streaks of hair dye running down their faces show that they have dabbled in the magic.

In our shared thoughts, we pray that none of us will die at the tabooed age of eighty-one years, for the body of an eighty-one-year-old cannot be cremated until the sun turns. This is our custom and sometimes the wait for the solstice could stretch into many days and weeks. This would cause such anguish and inconvenience to the loved ones who live to see off the dead. *Ap* (father) Pema is hard of hearing, but he smiles as if he has heard every conversation and approves of everything. He does not want to feel left out. When he is not adjusting his newly acquired eyeglasses, which sit precariously on his nose, he is intently recording his circumambulations. Even with the glasses, he must bring his face close as he etches sharp lines with a small piece of stone on to the surface of the flat stones in the walls to keep count of the circumambulations he has completed. Others keep count with pebbles. They place heaps of pebbles on the ledge of the alcoves of the prayer wheels. Each complete circumambulation is marked by a pebble which is moved to make a new heap. Each pebble represents a full circuit around the temple.

We have time to talk, drink tea from our flasks and share the snacks we bring to our gathering place, to reminiscence and laugh together. A little chatter cannot hurt. Aie Lhamo, widowed for more than ten years now, is teased about her young lover who visits her occasionally. We have nothing against that. We are only amused, and some apprehensively ask, 'Haven't we had enough of men in our lives?' I once saw Aie Lhamo sitting quietly behind the *chorten* speaking to her lover on her phone held close to her mouth. Her face flushed with the promise of a secret romance and there was an audible tenderness in her voice, lowered to a whisper. Some of us can handle our smartphones quite deftly. As soon as we speak into the machines our normal voice changes into a sing-song tone, recognizable as our distinctive style of speaking into these little devices. These devices which keep us connected but distracted.

Some of us stop frequently to rub our aching limbs, sometimes a moment in the sun stretches into hours. That's all right, we have time, we have made time for ourselves. Our conversations invariably turn to those who have died. For example, we speak of the man who had shifting eyes that watched everything and everybody so he could offer advice to all. The man was so wicked and colluded with bureaucrats and muddled up all our land boundaries, leaving us to live through endless quarrels and heartaches. Worse still, remember that woman who fought with her sister and plotted to have her sister's entire family deleted from the national census record? These cruel and malicious legacies still haunt the victims and curtail their lives. Remember the woman who wove the best textiles but died from loneliness and alcohol after her husband passed on? Her four or was it five children were orphaned, and we wonder where they are now.

The mention of children reminds Aie Wangmo of the baby she lost in a miscarriage. Miscarriages were so frequent those days. It was during the dreaded days of labour tax obligation which lasted right into the 1950s and 1960s. Every family had to render service to the government as a form of labour tax. They had to work on constructions or carry loads from one place to another. Aie Wangmo was twenty-six at the time of the miscarriage. Now she is seventy-seven years old. We look at each other and agree that if it was within our lifetime, it could not be that long ago.

Aie Wangmo was all alone. Her companions had to leave her behind to grapple alone with the debilitating womanly pains she began to experience. Her companions had a rendezvous they could not miss in fear of harsh punitive actions by the overseers. When her baby came too soon, she was two days away from home and a day away from where she had to report. After a series of thundering pains, the baby came months too early. A sudden gush of fluid flushed through her body. She lay on the ground as her whole body convulsed in pain in a thicket of wormwood plants. She later wiped the blood on her thighs and legs with the tender leaves of the plant. Then she buried the mass of what looked like large clumps of blood clots in a hole she dug with her hands. That was her baby. The sharp pain in her fingertips from digging the hard ground merged with the dull pains in her body after the expulsion. Afterwards she found shelter near a solitary house in an unfamiliar location. The inhabitants of the solitary house did not know who the sick woman was, but they let her take shelter in their cowshed. She slept curled up in her bloodied clothes for two nights and two days, sipping the water from a bamboo container placed near her. Today she has six children, all grown up and some even waiting and hoping to go to places far away from Bhutan. Well-informed Aie Yeshi casually notes, must be to Australia, not a question but a statement.

Aie Dolma looks up from the prayer beads in her hands and says, 'To faraway places, where? We never imagined that people would go off to places beyond the first motorable roads we built.' She recalls her own labour tax days and the motorable roads she worked on. 'We worked on the first roads in the country,' she asserts without rancour. 'Do any of you remember working on the road from Phuentsholing to Thimphu?' she asks. 'It took us seven days or more to reach Thimphu from Ogyen Choling and even more days to Phuentsholing. We had to carry our own rations.' Creases of concentration appear on her forehead, but she does not remember the name of a certain place where she started her work. It was somewhere close to Phuentsholing, she recalls. Looking at all who listen, she is encouraged to continue her reminiscences. She was walking along a foot trail through a thick jungle when she suddenly heard someone hoarsely whisper, 'lepers'. As if in a trance she saw a group of people who looked neither this way nor that, their heads bent forward, their eyes fixed on the ground as they walked past. They didn't want to show their disfigured faces. In those days there was no cure for leprosy and no motorable roads. The people were going somewhere but they must have lived in an isolated leper colony, hidden in the jungle. Where was she? In that jungle somewhere between Phuentsholing and Thimphu. That's all she remembers. She recollects that she and her companions moved away from the path to make way for them. She was leaning against the hillside, that she remembers well, and seeing the shafts of light piercing through the dark canopy of the jungle treetops. That's all I remember, she states and looks blankly at us.

I delight in the stories I hear from my companions. I learn much about their lives and my own in the telling of their stories. We trace beyond our own lives, reconnect with others before us. We look at the vagaries of our lives that we have shared, endured and embraced. These sporadic stories remind me that my memory too will decline and become fragments. Right now, I feel a sense of comfort and self-confidence as

I ease into old age in good company. For me, seventy years is no small feat. I have been blessed with a long and mostly happy life. My life was not spectacular or extraordinary, but it is mine. I am fortunate that I can tell the stories of my life in writing, unlike my companions who regretfully ask, 'Who will listen to the stories about our lives? Who will believe our stories, so different from today's generation. Nobody will ever know our stories fully.' Writing down my own stories is a commitment I feel: to share them with those who care to listen. My stories chronicle my childhood in Bhutan during the 1950s and 1960s, a time before the transformations that altered the nation and every individual Bhutanese life.

I write as my memories come to me in a stream of free-flowing thoughts. My stories come together, linked randomly. A particular stimulus in the telling of one narrative can lead to another without a planned link, and may appear disjointed and muddled. I write of the people and events which made impressions on me and created memories. The incidents and encounters that appear, both small and big, have amplified my life. Most of the stories detail my lived experiences as a child, but my thoughts and remembrances are layered by the stories I later heard in my adulthood.

As I recollect my childhood, my heart aches for all the emptied spaces that were never filled. Sometimes I try to accept that the untimely deaths of my parents were a consequence of cumulative karmic debts. My brothers and I were taught to believe in karmic debts, the influence of past lives shaping the present. So, maybe we were destined to navigate our lives without parental guidance and support, while facing the constantly shifting unchartered path to our country's modernization. I write my story as a footnote to the larger history of my country.

In my more composed and unbiased state, I console myself by reasoning that perhaps my parents would have had a hard time adapting to changes from their place of privilege as members of a landed family cushioned in their historical and religious entitlements. They lived in the comfort of high societal regard. My parents were steadfastly grounded in their established world view and lifestyle. They knew no other life. The abrupt changes would have wrecked their sense of self.

In the winter of my own life, living again in my ancestral home, the fragments of my childhood, when my parents were in their prime, feel vivid again. My idyllic memories are so different from my present life, but everything I recount here happened in my lifetime. So it can't be that long ago.

1

Thresholds

WHILE MY MOTHER WAS in labour for my birth, she had to use the toilet. As she was crossing the threshold from her bedroom to the toilet, I was born. I like to think of myself as being born literally and symbolically on the threshold. I was born at the end of 1952 when Bhutan was also on the threshold of a new era. Around the time of my birth, the third King of Bhutan, His Majesty Jigme Dorji Wangchuck, ascended the throne. The third King, who is known in our history as the father of modern Bhutan, ushered in immense changes, bringing Bhutan into the twentieth century. Many lives, including my own, were irreversibly altered within the larger context of Bhutan's development and modernization.

Bhutan's visionaries had decided that if the country was to change from an inward-looking, self-isolated kingdom to a forward-oriented member of the global community, a modern, western-style education was the most crucial foundation. They, in earnest, began the task of building a nucleus of educated people in the country. Children were recruited from all over the country to be sent to schools in India. Until then, Bhutan was largely an oral society with only a small group of literate people who were mostly from the religious community and the elite. Naturally, there was a general reluctance and a quiet resistance against such a sudden move to educate all. Parents did not want to send their children to a country they did not know, for an education which they considered alien. There were incidents of parents hiding their children and bribing the officers who came to recruit children for the scholarship programme to spare their children. In extreme cases some parents even declared their children to be suffering from a physical or mental disorder and incapable of learning.

In my case, my parents were not just favourably inclined but quite openly enthusiastic. They were both literate and knew something of the value of modern education. They had travelled to India and had seen for themselves the idyllic scenes of neatly uniformed and seemingly happy children going to the schools in Kalimpong, in the Indian state of West Bengal. They reasoned that a western-style secular education could not be so bad. More importantly, the Prime Minister at the time, Jigme Palden Dorji, had personally asked my father to send two of his sons (my older brother Rinzin Dorji and my younger brother, Sonam Wangchuk) to study in India. Father probably took this to be a gesture of honour. But my parents decided, for some reason unknown to me, to send me in place of my younger brother. I suspect that they felt that my younger brother, who was a year younger than me, was too young to go on the long journey. Or perhaps father did not want to part with his favourite son. Although parents in general are quick to deny that they have any favourites among their children, even as a nine-year-old, I instinctively sensed who was the more favoured in the family. Father loved Sonam best, and I accepted it in a very grown-up way as something quite normal. So, I was going in place of my brother. With this parental decision, I was made to cross the most significant threshold of my life, leaving my home, parents and country for a foreign education.

Sometime in my adulthood, I heard from my aunt Kunzang Wangmo that the Ogyen Choling villagers were shocked and bewildered when they heard that my parents had decided to send my older brother and me to schools in India. How could our parents jeopardize the religious and genealogical lineage of Dorji Lingpa (1346–1405) which has been so carefully preserved for hundreds of years? Because education and religion were perceived as being *choe-younten* (synonymous), theirs was a sincere and logical concern. A *chipa* (foreign or outsider) education as opposed to a *nangpa* (insider) might mean the end of age-old beliefs and traditions. Armed with gifts of eggs and home-brewed alcohol, and loaded with apprehensive fears, the villagers united and came to confront my parents. The bolder and more vocal ones scolded my parents, and the others joined in. 'We have looked up to your family and have been led by your ancestors and parents for generations in Ogyen Choling. Now you are sending your children to a foreign land for a foreign education, and you are making us into *goyung mulai shron*g [headless worms]. Who will look after this manor? You cannot leave it empty. Who will carry on with the religious traditions? And who will see to our needs?' they had chorused in mournful tones. I have no doubt that the villagers were genuine in their concerns for my family, but they were also concerned for themselves, for they saw themselves as inseparable from us. It is ironic to think that although in the equation of landlords and tenant farmers, with the farmers on the losing side, it was they who were truly alarmed by any potential disturbance in the status quo. They were seemingly secure and comfortable with the conditions with which they were familiar. They feared the unknown. Any change in this insulated society was seen as a threat. For my parents, too, although they appeared to be not only willing but eager to send two of their children to India, it could not have been easy. With hindsight I think they must have had an emotional quandary which was outweighed by logical and objective considerations. They must have felt the dilemma of change versus continuity. While they valued continuity, they opted for change, perhaps hoping that they would eventually find a balance.

By the early 1960s the waves of change were already touching insular and secluded lives all over Bhutan. Even without knowing the complexities, most Bhutanese had heard of the traumatic transformation taking place north of us in Tibet. Nobody could ignore the flow of the Tibetan refugees coming into Bhutan. These refugees had been displaced by change. While the ideology of *gongthren* (communism) was beyond people's comprehension, it was enough to know that it was causing drastic reconstructions of the society. In our own country, the recent social reforms emancipating the serfs were a huge transformation, impacting everybody's lives and reversing fortunes. That things were evolving was on everybody's mind, even if most lacked a full understanding of the causes and consequences of these alterations.

Change seeped into our lives slowly but surely, altering even my childhood. Until this point, my brothers and I had been trained, following the traditional system of learning, to read, write and chant prayers in our private home school. From obliviously chanting prayers, we now had to suddenly learn a new language in preparation for education in India. Father recruited a teacher to teach us English. We realized that there was more to education than being able to chant prayers at the top of our voices, swaying our bodies to the rhythm. The teacher was a cousin, a young man who knew some English. He taught us the alphabet, and when we finished learning A to Z, we could rattle it off like happy parrots. Father asked, 'Are there only twenty-six letters in the English alphabet?' He had been counting. There are thirty in *Choekyed* (classical Tibetan). Then he commanded our cousin, 'Teach them more!' but there was nothing more our teacher could teach, because that was all he knew. Father himself began to learn the letters and numbers in English, and he started to write Arabic numbers on the boxes in his stores. Many of the boxes already had Bhutanese numbering and letters for inventory records, but father wrote over them or beside the labels in Bhutanese. Father was open to change and eager to learn with us.

How did I take this new development? I cannot remember. I did not throw a tantrum. I did not resist and cry over being sent to school, of that, I am sure. But the rest of it is blank. I cannot remember anything. Maybe my parents did not even have to reason with me and coax me; they just decided for me, and I never questioned them. What I do remember is that just the fact that I was going to India awakened a new curiosity in me. I knew India was a big country, far away from Bhutan, but beyond that I knew very little. A sudden fear was planted in my mind when an aunt, who had recently gone to India, came back with horrific tales. She said she had travelled across immense rivers in boats which had sharp knife-like propeller blades under them. She told us these blades chopped up all sorts of water creatures until she was travelling in a river of blood. So, I gathered that India was not only far away but also dangerous. I later learnt that my aunt had travelled a short distance on the Brahmaputra river, which is naturally reddish in colour. Probably somebody had teased and frightened her with the story of the water creatures killed under the boat. But the image of the bloody river stuck in my mind as I began to compile information on India.

There were other aspects of the country I knew. Father had gone to India just the year or so before and had bought us some of the most exotic gifts, as well as clothes, toys and candies. We relished the candies, and long after they were eaten, even in the memory of those pink and green sweets, our mouths salivated, and we yearned for more. These candies were our introduction to sugar, so India was also the land of sweets. Among the other gifts was a large rubber ball. It was a source of wonderment to us. It was big yet so light and it bounced with such force. Father had bought it for us after he had seen children play with balls in Kalimpong. He had been amazed at the skill and dexterity with which they had handled balls. Another fact – children in India played with bouncy rubber balls! Father had been especially impressed by all the clever tricks they could perform. But we had never seen, leave aside handled, an uncontrollable bouncy rubber ball. It was a painful moment of humiliation when father openly expressed his shock and disappointment over our clumsiness. We could barely hold it when it was thrown at us, and we could not bounce it more than once. He kept telling us to do this and that with the ball, chiding us for our lack of deftness. Father could not believe how clumsy his children were. He shook his head and clicked his tongue in dismissive hopelessness. What a painful realization it was for him. Could our clumsiness with the ball have triggered some doubts in my father's mind: 'Will my children manage to live in India?'

After many fumbles with the ball, finally, one of the older children gave the ball one good kick, probably by accident because he immediately stuck out his tongue in regret and cringed as the ball flew on to the roof of the four-storeyed *utse* (central tower) of the manor house. Father did not permit us to go and retrieve it immediately, and when we eventually did go to get it a few days later, it was not there any more. Either the wind or a go-getter among our friends had made it disappear. That was the end of the ball, but the important thing was that we were now going to Kalimpong, the place from where the ball had come, where the children were clever and skilful.

However, I had no idea how the people in India looked. I knew that white sugar, colourful candy, father's cigarettes, bales of cloth, the cotton yarn my mother ordered for her weaving projects all came from India, but I had no idea how an Indian looked, dressed, behaved, or what they ate. My curiosity was aroused. I had some knowledge of the fact that India was a country just next to ours but beyond the Indian *jathang* (plains) there were areas vaguely called *gyamtsho phakha* (over and beyond the oceans). Sometimes, when my mind dared to go beyond these *gyamtsho thamed* (endless oceans), I imagined these were places of the *sinpos* (flesh-eating demons) that Guru Rinpoche had gone to subdue. In my desperate attempt to imagine what people outside of Bhutan may look like, I began to put together images from my own experience. Some rubber toys father brought us from Kalimpong, for example, conjured one set of possibilities for what people from beyond the ocean might look like. Were the Indians from beyond the oceans? Now looking back, I think these toys were some Disney characters, maybe Mickey Mouse or Donald Duck. Each of us had been gifted one; mine was a pink elephant with blue eyes. I wondered if Indians might look like these toys. I once took the toy with me when I had a bath in front of a blazing fire and, while I was made to soak in the tub, the toy, which was near the fire, melted and became a gooey mess, and that was the end of my imaginations.

Sometime after we were given these gifts from India, we were in our winter resort in Gorgan, in Lhuentse district. While we were eating breakfast, somebody informed us that an Indian forester was doing a survey of the forest nearby. We listened attentively. A mere glance in my direction from my older brother Rinzin was enough to tell me that we now had a secret joint mission. As soon as breakfast was over, we dashed off into the chir pine forest that covered the hill near our camp. We hoped to finally see what a real Indian looked like! We followed the trails, looking for any disturbed spots in the fallen needles that carpeted the ground and any other signs of where the forester may have gone. We stopped at the trees to look at the mysterious markings, notches and crosses on them, wondering what kind of tools the Indian had used. I even tried to dramatically sniff at the cut mark on the tree to get new information: Did an Indian smell different? We finally gave up, knowing that our parents would soon be looking for us. We had just wanted to look at an Indian person and tell him that we were going to his country soon.

I knew that the preparations for our journey were being made even during our time in Gorgan, but I have no memory of that either. My parents must have carefully packed the provisions for the long journey and the gifts for the various people we would meet. My days in Gorgan were spent with the small but constant realization that I would soon be parting with my parents. I continued to live my life as a young, privileged girl of nine, in the comfort and security of being part of my family. I was old enough to appreciate the warmth of the subtropics and the bounty of exotic fruits in a charming space carved out for us by our ancestors. Although we came every year to our eastern resort to escape the cold wintry conditions in temperate Tang, this time I grew more attentive and appreciative of everything around me because somehow, I knew that I would soon be removed from this perfect setting. I was never free from a niggling feeling of dread and anxiety of the impending journey.

While we were in Gorgan, I was overwhelmed by the number and kinds of people who came to meet my father and mother. All sorts of people were introduced to us as relatives. There were many different categories of relatives – *neywa tuk tuk* (close relatives), neywa *gnoma* (real relatives) and there was another category, *dangpoi* neywa or relatives of ancient times. Finally, there was a category of neywa *shak whay* or 'of course we are related'. I could feel myself becoming linked in one big circle of being related all around in some way or the other. The older relatives recited in unhurried detail the family trees and the lineages of how we were related. Part of my father's parentage was from Lhuentse, so there was a big network. Now how I wish I had listened more attentively and/or had a better memory of these relatives. Ironically, all the categories of relatives merged into the category of neywa *yasigaiwala* 'vanished relatives' when we became orphans within a few years of these introductions.

We must have been in Gorgan for about three months. We would have normally gone back to Ogyen Choling in time for *losar* (the lunar new year) which usually falls sometime in February or March. But the year we were to leave for India was very different. That year losar was to be celebrated in Gorgan and we were to leave for India a few days after the new year celebrations. Although I was not fully aware, father had been ailing. But that did not stop him from preparing for the construction of a new house which was to be his dream house. There was a frenzy of activities around the construction. My memories of those last few days are confusing with father not being well, the preparations for the construction and overwhelming everyday worries, tinged with the strange sad fear that I would soon be parting from my parents. We could have travelled following the eastern route, through Mongar, on to Trashigang and entered India through Samdrup Jongkhar and then on to Kalimpong. That would have been the normal route, but we were being sent back westward to

Ogyen Choling, an extra three days of travel, because our parents were convinced that since we were to begin such a significant journey, we should begin it from our permanent home in Bumthang.

Losar was celebrated, but I cannot remember anything of it. On the second day after Losar, I was called to say goodbye to my father. He was in bed, I remember. He wanted my brother and I to come to him separately. While I was saying goodbye, I was intensely conscious of the game of archery that was going on near our camp. I could hear the men shouting and cheering. It was a surreal backdrop for a sad farewell. I later learnt that father insisted on the game continuing for days, even after we had left, to distract him from the unhappiness and loneliness he felt at our departure. When I entered his room, I saw that he was sitting up in bed, leaning against piled up pillows. He embraced me and held my hands as he spoke, like he would speak to an adult, and that unnerved me a little. I was confused. I felt heavy inside, but my body felt light and disoriented. The uneasiness of the feeling made me want to flee from this strange situation. He did not look ill, and he did not look happy or sad. He just looked very serious. He told me to study hard and then said that I must never marry a foreigner. What could a nine-year-old girl know about marriage and foreigners? I think I said, 'all right', as if it was as simple an instruction as 'wash your hands', without realizing the enormity of his last statement. I never saw Father again.

This gloomy parting with my father was the beginning of my journey into the unknown. This was to be the journey that would test me and shape me, as the old world which I was born into and just beginning to know, gradually fell apart. As a guileless young girl, I travelled along a trail that was thrust upon me. During the rest of my journey, I tried to seek a path for myself amidst the confusion of separation, unimaginable distances and alienation. The journey that began in 1962 is ongoing as I continue to live my life, fording the changes that have propelled me to become me.

2

Remembering Mother

LIKE ALL WOMEN OF her generation, my mother's only thoughts at the time of my birth were probably of gratitude and relief that both she and her baby had survived. Pregnancy and birthing were dangerous in those days, and women believed that their 'lives had been halved' when they became pregnant. My mother had no idea how different my life would be from her own. Her life had been predictable, as a girl child. She was born into Chummey *Shelgno* (an aristocratic family) with social and economic privileges but heavy with expectations. She was to follow the traditional customs, to be groomed and nurtured to become a compliant and demure young woman who would fulfil the duties demanded by her station. In fulfilling her duties, she came to be the bride of a man of equal socio-economic status, my father, for a short time of fourteen years. During this time, she gave birth to five children. I was the second child. Unlike my mother, I have lived long enough to tell my story and glimpse into hers.

My mother died in 1964, at the age of thirty-two. Today statisticians show that the life expectancy of a Bhutanese in the 1960s was indeed thirty-three years, yet 'she was so young, she died prematurely', remarked all who remember her. Today the life expectancy for Bhutanese women is seventy-one years, so she did die at a relatively premature age. But in the 1960s there were no medical facilities and she, like her husband, died of an unidentified disease. She died quietly in a big and empty room on the third floor of the utse which has over thirty rooms. There were just a handful of people in the house at the time of her death. A man, who was attending to her, said that she was in such great agony that her body contorted with spasms of pain and her head was wet with sweat. 'A drop of sweat on every hair on her head,' he said, yet she uttered no sound of discomfort. He said that the end came quickly; she hiccupped three times and stopped breathing, her head tilted sideways on the raised pillows supporting it.

Three days before she died, she had said that she had a headache and lay down quietly in her bed without complaining. She was never one to complain. 'She died so quickly, there was nothing we could do for her,' lamented my Akhu lama Nuden, my father's younger brother, who was in Ogyen Choling at the time. There was nothing that could have saved her. I think she had a disease that nobody could diagnose. She had given up on life; her husband had died two years before, and three of her four children had been sent away from her to boarding schools in India. She had with her my youngest brother, Ugyen Rinzin, who was barely four years old at the time and in poor health. There was nobody else there for her. In my nostalgic view, based on the small hints that she gave, I think that in her fourteen years as a bride in Ogyen Choling, she never felt fully welcomed or accepted by the community. My mother was an extremely sensitive person with a strong sense of empathy. Although she herself had come from a landed family, she was acutely conscious of the inequality and hierarchy of her society, and she found herself in an uncomfortable place as the mistress of a large and unfamiliar landed household steeped in obsolete traditions. My father and her children were her only anchors. Now, with father dead and her children separated from her, she was mostly alone. Thinking back to the passing conversations we had and listening to what others said about her, I think she died of a broken heart.

Days before she had the fatal headache, she had climbed on to the roof of the utse, manoeuvring five flights of stairs as if to look across the mountains to the places beyond her physical vision. I think she wanted to reach out to us in our schools in India. Now, with hindsight, I suspect that the time my mother was trying to reach out to us was when I was repeatedly beset by incomprehensible and disturbing dreams. Night after night I dreamed of our house going down the hillside in landslides or myself looking helplessly amidst the rubble of our destroyed home. I had dreams of myself wandering alone in the utse, lost and frightened, desperately searching for something I had to find but did not know what or how to find it. In these dreams I was always accompanied by a great sense of panic and loss. I had lost something that I could not name. I would often wake up from such a dream with a pounding heart and a terrible sense of despair.

I heard later that some days before her headache, she had spent a whole day all by herself by the river Tang Chu. She walked up and down the riverbank alone, feeding the fish morsels of barley dough in which she had wrapped *damzay* (sacred relics). Feeding the fish in the river was not an unusual behaviour, for she often did that on holy days. I had been with her on such fish-feeding trips. But it was strange behaviour, nonetheless, for the mistress of a large household, abandoning her many duties on a seemingly ordinary day and being on her own without a companion. What was she thinking of as she walked along the riverbank all by herself?

Perhaps I am reading too much into the events before her death, but don't we all do that? Especially when you try to think of the events that have irreversible consequences on your own life. I think that my mother was seized by an inexplicable need to connect with the people she loved and yearned for. I think she hoped her message of love and longing would travel down with the water of the river, for it was she who often told us that all rivers in Bhutan eventually journeyed to the Indian plains before they emptied themselves into the gyamtsho thamed, a mighty ocean without boundaries. Hers was a desperate but powerful gesture. I wondered at the time what my dreams meant. When I narrated them to the great yogin master Lama Sonam Zangpo, he prophesied with a concerned look on his face, 'These dreams do not portend good things, there may be some obstacles in your home. I will pray for you.' The obstacle was that mother was dying or already dead.

That was in 1964, and I was in St Helen's Convent in Kurseong with Lama Sonam Zangpo's granddaughter, Chimme Wangmo. Chimme Wangmo and I were related through some ancient familial connection, and she warmly extended her kindness to me and invited me to spend holidays and long weekends with her mother, Tshering Choki, Lama Sonam Zangpo's daughter. She was staying in a house rented from some disciples of her father. The house owner's two sons, Lalit and Gyeltshen, were kind and tolerant of Chimme and me, even though we often played girlish pranks on them, especially when they were studying. During this period, we often visited Lama Sonam Zangpo and his consort Ani Dondup in their retreat in the pine-forested hillside somewhere in Kurseong. Each trip to the hermitage was a magical getaway from the perplexing atmosphere in the Catholic convent run by Irish nuns. Leaving the confinement of the convent and the noisy, congested and sooty town bisected by the railway tracks, to be in the quiet of the tranquil atmosphere, was something I looked forward dearly. We always walked to this place, climbing up the hill and entering the solitude it offered. Being here was like being at home. Even as a child, although I could not verbalize nor articulate the joy of this experience, I felt completely at ease and happy in this environment that was so like Bumthang.

I referred to the lama as *Meme lama* (grandfather lama) as Chimme Wangmo did and, whenever he was not in secluded meditation, we were permitted to meet him. Both he and Ani Dondup were always affectionate and kind. Perhaps the lama already knew that my mother was dead and felt sorry for me.

Years before my mother married my father, she had wanted to become a nun; I think I had heard her say this herself. But she was made to marry my father, someone she had never met or even seen. In those days, marriages for the landed families were alliances of economics, prestige, bloodlines and other considerations, and had not much to do with the feelings of the people who were getting married. My mother told me that at the time of their wedding she was eighteen and father was twenty-one. They were both so shy that they did not speak to each other throughout the wedding ceremonies. They spoke for the first time only after my father accidentally dropped the flashlight in their dark bathroom and had to ask her to help look for it. His first words were, 'I have lost the flashlight, I may have dropped it into the toilet.' The newlyweds were staying in a room on the second storey in the central tower. They looked for the flashlight together and fortunately found it by the side of the toilet. Had it really fallen into the toilet, it would have gone two floors down the wooden chute into a pit in the ground and would have been lost forever. The rooms in the utse at that time would have been lit with oil lamps, and a dry-cell flashlight in 1948 must have been such a rare and precious possession that it provoked my father to break the silence and enlist mother's help. This is one incident I heard about personally from my mother. Now I try to remember when and why she narrated this anecdote. But like many other little details and stories about my mother, this one too seems to float in a void, and I cannot put it into context, but I do recall a small smile playing on her lips when she told it to me. I suppose that the flashlight incident was an endearing moment for her, breaking the ice in the awkwardness of my parents' first meeting. Recovering the flashlight together was metaphorically the symbolic light in their marriage which lasted for fourteen years. Theirs was a union of commitment, understanding, mutual respect, and they were supportive of each other. I would like to think that they shared some happy times, despite father's occasional forays of infidelity, which most men of his generation and station took as an entitlement.

My mother's brother-in-law, Akhu lama, had unhappily and reluctantly stayed on in Ogyen Choling after he had come home from India to attend the death rituals of his elder brother, my father, who had died two years earlier. My mother suddenly had to live with Akhu lama who was caught between his aspirations to be a practising Buddhist monk and having to learn the intricacies of being the patriarch of a landed household. His life as a householder was marked by many practical responsibilities compounded by the fast-evolving changes brought on by the social reforms which shook the core of traditional landed households all over Bhutan. On the one hand, he had the honour of upholding the religious lineage, and on the other hand, he had to learn to negotiate the life of a layman in a period of historical transformation. Although she greatly respected him and never resented him taking over the household, I am sure it was a testing time for my mother. During our last meeting she did say with sad resignation that it was not easy to live in a household headed by a monk. One of her amusingly trivial complaints was how he never gave his dirty clothes to be washed – instead, he hid them behind boxes and on clothes pegs.

When my mother suddenly died, we were all orphaned. But her youngest son, Ugyen Rinzin, was catapulted from being a toddler to a totally abandoned child. He belonged nowhere and to nobody. The three of us older children, Rinzin, Sonam and I, at least belonged somewhere – we belonged to the boarding schools where we were cared for in a communal life of routine, without abrupt changes. In the days after my mother's death, everybody in the household was immersed in all the complicated and long-drawn customs of rituals and prayers that need to be done for the dead. I heard that my four-year-old brother was tied with his own belt to a window frame because the men in the household did not know what to do with him. They had no time for an inquisitive boy who asked silly questions and demanded their attention. So, they had found the perfect solution: tying him to a window frame that allowed him a radius of no more than five feet.

I had parted from my mother for the last time in early 1964 when I left home to go to back to school after my school break. It was during that winter holiday that I had shared some intimate time with my mother. Mother liked to sit in her bedroom veranda and enjoy the winter sun. Even today the afternoon sun hits that veranda until sundown. I sat with her sometimes but never for long. She often asked me to *sek-tay* (pick out the lice in her hair). She never had lice but 'picking out lice' was a turn of phrase for a head massage. I think she liked the sensation of my fingers going through her hair. Her hair was inky black, so black that it felt like the colour would stain my fingers. I used to part her short hair and press along the pale white partings I made with my fingers. This was a treat for her. The soothing sensation soon made her nod off and I would slink away to go and play with my friends. Now I wish I had stayed on, just a little longer, to gain a little more precious time with my mother, for every minute I deprived myself of time with her, I feel a despairing pain. Every time I have a head massage now, I think of my mother who savoured the sloppy and reluctant massages I gave her.

I have another enduring memory of time with my mother during the same school holiday. One evening after dinner, as usual we were all gathered around the charcoal brazier in a room in the utse holding our hands over the hot charcoal trying to warm them. As a distraction I took out my geography book and showed it to everyone. I thought Akhu lama and mother would enjoy the pictures in it. But they wanted more than the pictures; they wanted me to read the text. Everybody was eager for me to read. After all, I had been at school for two years now. I struggled, spelling out most of the words and asking my brother Rinzin to help me with the more difficult ones. The text was about a man called Pedro who was a rubber tapper in Brazil. There was a black-and-white picture of him working on a rubber tree. Both Akhu lama and mother were intrigued by the account of latex collection, 'So this is where rubber comes from,' and wanted to know more, as I continued to struggle. My older brother Rinzin had a dark frown and reprimanded me, '*Khai* [an exclamation of disgust], if you want to read, you can do better than this.' Our cousin, who had learnt to read on his own, began to read a few words he recognized in the text. After each word he read out loud, he looked around the room for compliments and appreciation. Rinzin's facial expression turned to fury, and he struck me across the face. It was a solid strike that caused my nose to bleed. My brother felt so humiliated on my behalf that he felt compelled to hit me. The blood spurted into the brazier and emitted the smell of charring flesh. In more shock than pain, I cried out and clung to my mother. When the situation calmed down and I had stopped crying and the smell of my blood was diffused by Akhu lama who threw a handful of incense into the brazier, it was time to go to bed. I refused to sleep in the room that had been prepared for the children in the utse next to Akhu lama's bedroom. We always slept in separate rooms from the adults, never with our parents, but that night I insisted on going to sleep with mother who was sleeping all by herself in the *shagkor*, the building enclosing the central tower on the east and south. She slept alone in the room where the family used to gather for our meals when father was still alive. It was a big cold room, but she had chosen it as her bedroom. Looking back, I have a pathetic image of her making her bed on the floor in one corner of this large room but, at the time, I only felt the warmth and comfort of being able to sleep with mother in her bed. It was the first time I shared her bed, such a rare privilege. I snuggled up to her and talked a little before I fell asleep, and she continued to count her prayer beads, leaning against the closed wooden shutters of the window. She must have had a good reason for choosing this room. There was nobody else in this building, which had ten rooms. It pains me to recall what a lonely, cold and desolate life my mother lived.

The last time we parted from mother, I noticed with envy and respect how she drew my elder brother, Rinzin, aside and whispered to him on the day we left home. She accompanied us to the outer gate of our house. My fourteen-year-old brother nodded seriously as she spoke to him like an adult. I never found out what she had whispered to him so earnestly, so urgently. Then, as we proceeded through the gate into the village compound, she stood at the gate and watched forlornly as we bade goodbye to the women from the village who had lined up to say their farewells. With an overwhelming sense of unease which must have been sadness, I looked back at mother several times, as did my brothers. She stood still, a lonely figure framed by the weathered and bleached wooden poles of the fence. I felt a numbing tug at my heartstrings. This last impression of my mother in that wooden frame is still the loneliest image in my mind.

The sense of unease was replaced by a hurried discussion among the adults on which was the best spot from where we should mount our horses. The adults encouraged us to ride our horses immediately. I stood on the mound near the chorten as I was helped on to my horse which was already saddled and impatient, snorting and pulling at the ropes held by the horseman. As the horses trotted away from the village, I looked back one more time. There was no one in the space within the wooden frame of the fencing. Mother had gone back to the empty house, taking her loneliness with her. I often wondered what she had told my brother. Even though we waved back to the women who were now standing on the ridge, waving their white scarves and singing the mournful goodbye song, *aloo*, I felt the confusion of sadness and uncertainty. I clutched the still-warm red boiled eggs in my pouch. On that portentous parting with my mother that was the only warmth I felt. As my horse trotted off, I held the reluctant lopsided smile that I had managed for the women of the village, but the poignancy of the parting with mother accompanied me for the rest of the journey.

The village continued the custom of welcoming and sending off visitors for a long time, maybe right into the early 1990s. Visitors and the family members of the nagtshang were always received and seen off with welcome and goodbye drinks. Women from every household would come with drinks, and the visitors had to drink some or at least offer some to the deities. While drinks were being offered, the women would chant their usual words of welcome or goodbye. When the visitors left, the women would line up with their drinks and farewell gifts, usually a boiled egg or two. Sometimes as a special gesture of favour or endearment, they cooked the eggs with madder, a plant dye, to make the eggs red. Eggs were rare and precious those days, so each egg was special.

I have yearned to know more about my mother, beyond the image of a quiet, gentle woman who exited my life without even a goodbye. She left so silently. I will never know all the things she was waiting to tell me when I grew older. The things that I should have heard from her died with her, and I must be content with hearing about her life from other people. I hear only about the events witnessed by others and conversations shared with others. I have just a few personal poignant memories, often in a vacuum, with only fleeting appearances of her.

How much can a mother tell her twelve-year-old daughter about her own life during the two-week school break? Now I have accepted the fact that I will never be able to fill in all the gaps to reconstruct my mother's life. I have over the years formed my ideas on how it would have been to have a mother for a longer time. I imagined that mothers and daughters bond and grow together. Their presence and interactions complementing each other's lives as they commiserate and celebrate together and understand each other. From the experiences of other mothers and daughters and my own experience as a mother of daughters, I can see that reality is much more complex than that. Often, mothers and daughters seem to share more disagreements and heartaches than understanding and joy. I often wonder how it would have been to have a mother in my adult life and for my own children to have a grandmother. Either way, I shall never know. But the one thing I know for sure is that, had my mother lived, my life today would have been completely different. Already as a child of less than six, I have a fuzzy recollection of a prominent family asking my parents for my hand in marriage for their son who was a few years older than me. I suppose this marriage would have been what we referred to as *chung nyen* (child marriage). I would not have had to go and live with his family but would have been reserved for him. I would have lived according to the prevailing social norms and customs, and lived my life as expected for a girl from a 'good family'. But this was not in my destiny. In fact, no customs and traditions prepared me for what was to become of me because I was orphaned so early. I know that I am not unique; I am just one of numerous motherless daughters in the global sisterhood of orphaned daughters who have had to forge their lives unguided.

3

That's Not You, It's Our Mother

I HAVE SOME PHOTOGRAPHS OF my mother. They are blurry and unclear, but I can see my mother's face in my mind as I look at them. There is a particular group picture taken in a studio in Kalimpong in the winter of 1963. All these years I believed that it was me in the photo and wondered why my younger brother, Sonam Wangchuk, who is only a year younger than me, looked so much younger. Just recently when I looked at the picture with my brother, he said, 'That's not you, it's our mother!' I was outwardly amused but deeply shaken inside because I had for all these years seen my mother as myself. Why had I done that? I asked myself many times since, but I had no answers. Perhaps I wanted to be like my mother and unconsciously become her. Could I have filled in for my mother to lessen the pain and emptiness her departure created? This inadvertent misidentification may have helped me to relate to and comprehend my world. Nobody believes me but I was surprised that I lived past my thirty-second year because I was sure that I would die when she died, at the age of thirty-two.

My mother, in all her pictures except the one taken in Kalimpong, is always dressed in a slovenly manner, and that is how I remember her. She tied her thick belt, *kera*, loosely, and her two *kiras* which she wore over each other, were never in alignment. Her *toigos*, jackets, made of heavy serge material, were either navy blue or black in colour. I do not remember her wearing any other colours. Her toigos were short and never fully covered her kera. Those days women did not have the typical under blouses, *wonju*, that we wear under our toigos today. I am sure that the wonju is a part of the Tibetan costume which we appropriated and made our own. During my mother's time, women wore different shirts under their toigo. The older women wore *guzum* or *atsa*, a sleeveless tunic-like garment which textile experts today label as a version of the celebrated archaic *kushung*. Mother also wore a guzum under her kiras. These garments were made of cotton and sometimes of soft flannel and served the double purpose of being a petticoat and a nightdress. She always wore simple kiras, mostly *mathra*, the red-patterned checks in wool, or *horthra*, the multicoloured horizontal bands, also in wool. She had better kiras, some beautiful, highly priced and exquisitely patterned ones. But I never saw her wear any of these. She allowed her weavers and maids to wear them on special occasions like archery matches or when they danced. I still have a few of these which look used and worn out although they were never worn by my mother.

I remember mother always wore embroidered cloth boots called *tsang lham,* footwear that alluded to the place of their origin, Tsang, in Tibet, I suspect. There is a photograph of her taken in a studio in Tibet where she is wearing western-style shoes with laces. However, in my memories of her, she always wore tsang lham, where the upper part was made of thick woollen cloth. This part came up to the knees and had to be fastened with small belts. The lower part of the boot was made of either red or green woollen cloth and delicately embroidered in silk thread. The soles were made into a platform of about thirty centimetres with layered twine. These boots were warm but had no profile or grip in the outer soles, so they were prone to slip. Mother, in her usual, careless way, never tied the boots at her knees and that part of the boots were loose and folded over her ankles. Mother often slipped on the worn-out, slippery stairs in our house, and I think one of these falls caused the miscarriage of what would have been my sixth sibling.

The first time I came home after mother had died, I imagined I heard her footfalls, soft and muffled walking across the planks in the house. I wandered around the now mostly empty rooms filled with memories and some mementos. I was looking for the special hat that father had bought me during his last trip to Lhasa. It was a Tibetan hat called *tshering kingkhor*. It looked like a top hat that was elaborately embroidered in gold thread with soft woolly flaps that kept my ears warm. The peg on which it used to hang in mother's bedroom was empty. Akhu lama said he had given away many of the items that belonged to mother and that my hat had gone with them. Although the hat was the focus of my loss, it represented all that had vanished from my life. For the next few days, I could not help looking at the village children and their headgear to see if any of them were wearing my hat. Of all that I had lost, physically and emotionally, I was totally fixated on a hat.

Mother rarely wore jewellery. She had one string of coral and turquoise and some *Dzi* (the prized patterned agate stones) that she wore every day. She always wore the same earrings, gold-plated silver rings with *suemetok*, a floral engraving. Because she showed little attachment to adornments, her jewellery became the target of thefts over the years. She kept losing her corals and other jewels to people who worked in the household. Her carelessness and non-attachment to material things, especially ornaments, were recognized even by our pet monkey Dendu, who once stole a string of corals from her bedroom and climbed up on to the roof. Everybody knew that the distracted monkey could at any time drop the precious jewels on to the stone slabs in the courtyard below. Only through complicated and patient manoeuvring, and after a long period of tense negotiations, did the monkey finally exchange the string of corals for some fruit. My father's cousin, Jigme Dorji, who had managed the delicate exchange, was hailed as a hero by all those gathered in the courtyard to watch the monkey business. I remember this incident quite clearly because after the corals were safe in my mother's hands, she showed them to me and let me hold them for a while saying, 'These are your corals which the Queen Mother has given to you.'

Looking back now I think my mother was the capable mistress of a large household of a landed family. She herself had grown up in a similar household so she did not have to be taught how to manage one, although there was no mother-in-law to show her the ropes. She was everywhere in the house and the compound, doing all sorts of things to keep the home and estate functioning smoothly. She spent long hours with the weavers, planning and designing looms for the fabrics that needed to be woven to clothe the family members, for gifts and for clothing the servants. Each of the servants received one piece of fabric for a garment every year. This was known as *logodth* or annual dress. I think she enjoyed this work most compared to her other responsibilities.

In the later years cotton fabrics were imported from India to supplement what the weavers produced. One year she had been commanded to weave two *ghos* for His Majesty, the third King. There was quite a bit of excitement and much research, as the royal command was to weave a *kathra* and horthra, traditional archaic woollen fabrics which were going out of fashion. The former was made from white wool with thin blue-and-red stripes, and the latter had a blue-green base with thin multicoloured stripes. Mother had to search for samples, for these kinds of fabrics were disappearing. After much asking around, she finally found them with an old man in a nearby village. Weaving these ghos was her priority project and she did much of the work herself. I often wonder if the King ever wore the ghos my mother made.

Most of the cloth woven in those days was produced on backstrap looms. These looms were attached to the walls. For practical use of space in our loom room, there were also large beams where two looms were placed back to back. The loom rooms were always noisy from the loud *tang tang* of beating the weft into the woof and the women talking and joking with each other. The *thri thag*, or horizontal frame looms, were introduced only later. I remember well when my mother invited a woman, Rin Dolma from Choekortoed, the northern part of the adjacent valley of Choekor, to teach some weavers to weave on this new kind of loom. Rin Dolma had learnt to use the loom in Tibet, or from Tibetans in Bhutan, I am not sure which. She stayed with us for nearly a year. I know nothing of the progress of the weaving lessons, but I do recall her being a good dancer and that she charmed us all by dancing with ankle bells, something new and exotic for us. She danced to Indian and Nepali songs played on our gramophone. Then she suddenly left us, and we never heard from her again. Some sketchy stories of her having run away to Tibet or Sikkim for some vague reason were circulated. The rumours about her unexpected flight floated around for a while and died just as suddenly as she had appeared and disappeared. I think the main reason was something about her being hounded by a powerful jealous wife whose husband had an affair with her. Thinking back now about Rin Dolma running away from somebody, I have a hazy memory of my mother hastily hiding her in a cupboard one day. I was witness to this panicked incident and drawn into secrecy when mother turned to me warning me not to tell anyone about what had just transpired. I felt so grown up and important to be included in this intrigue. There certainly was an air of urgency and secrecy surrounding that mysterious woman. The horizontal loom stayed on even after Rin Dolma disappeared, as more and more weavers began to use it.

Although the women in the village were good weavers, the art of knitting was not known in Bhutan until the mid-1950s. I remember mother inviting a Tibetan woman to come to teach knitting to some of the women from the village. Bamboo knitting needles were made and, as processed wool for knitting was rare, mother processed the wool from local sheep and knitted knee-length stockings for father. As black-and-white wool was used in the weaving fabrics, it was browns, greys and the off-coloured wool that was used for knitting. She quickly learnt quite complex patterns, and I recall father often wearing attractive stockings knitted by her.

Sheep wool was the main fibre we used for the manufacture of textiles. Our family had a herd of about a hundred and twenty to a hundred and fifty sheep. They were kept for wool, and caring for the sheep and processing the wool was something that mother enjoyed. I remember her hand-feeding the sheep with some helpers, on cold wintry days, especially when there was snow on the ground and the sheep could not graze easily. They were fed lumps of buckwheat flour made into a hard dough. I learnt to feed bits of butter to the lambs. I was taught to smear the butter into their mouths, and I watched them sucking the butter and sneezing into my face. I loved the lambs, the soft and woolly animals who bleated gently and nudged and pushed their snotty faces against my own. One year I received the gift of an ewe from Aie Kesang, a prominent woman in the village. The ewe was so fertile and reproduced so fast that by the time I left for school in India she had produced as many as five lambs. I recognized some of the lambs from my own sheep and was often partial to them, giving them bigger pieces of butter.

The sheep were sheared twice a year. Once in the spring and again in the autumn. A few days before the sheep were to be sheared, they were driven into a side stream to be washed. I remember watching the animals being bathed one time. The whole herd was guided into a tributary of the Tang Chu at the bottom of the valley. The bewildered and nervous animals were made to wade through the stream. Two people were needed to hold a sheep which was then given a thorough washing, reaching into the space under their flanks and brushing their coats by hand, scratching and combing them with the fingers until they were considered clean. I remember how some of my friends and I excitedly ran along the banks of the stream, not minding our feet sinking into the marshy soil to keep the sheep in the stream and stop them from jumping on to the banks and running away. After a very wet and chaotic manoeuvre, the sheep were clean enough for shearing in a day or two.

I always found myself trailing the women and trying to get involved in all activities related to sheep. Although the main shepherd was always a man, as far as I can remember, all the work related to processing wool was always done exclusively by women. I would be there on the grounds, adjacent to the temple under the oak tree, where the women laid out a large bamboo mat. The sheep would be allowed to spread out freely in the compound. The women would catch the animals, which furiously resisted, and bring them down on the ground to lie on the bamboo mat. Often the women had helpers to hold down the sheep who sent out pitiful cries of *mayheyhey mayheyhey.* Later in school I was taught that sheep made the sound 'baa-baa' (as in Baa Baa Black Sheep) but as a child I knew our sheep cried *mayheyhey mayheyhey.* The animal would be made to lie on its side with its head resting in the lap of the shearer. The tools the women used for cutting the wool varied from rusty knives and rudimentary shears to scissors. Once the animals calmed down and stopped kicking and crying, the slow process of harvesting the wool would begin. The women talked and joked among themselves as much as they talked to the animals, sometimes berating the uncooperative animal or coaxing it to settle down. Every now and then sounds of shock and pain would erupt and drown the conversations of the women. An accident had taken place. A piece of skin had been cut or sometimes a deep cut in the flesh of the sheep had been made. It would be the woman responsible for this casualty who would sound her misdeed in shock and pain; the sheep rarely reacted. At the times I was present it was my duty to pass the *ngagmar* (healing salve), that my mother had handy. The ngagmar was butter imbued by healing mantras from a religious personality.

Mother liked working with the sheep, but she also had to deal with a herd of unruly and noisy goats. She had received a herd of rowdy goats as a present from Her Majesty the Junior Queen Ashi Pema Dechen. The only use of these goats was to provide manure for the fields. They were kept near our fields in the bottom of the valley where most of our wheat fields were located. Once there was some short-lived excitement when my father heard on the radio that Mahatma Gandhi, or Gandhi Raza as we referred to him, drank only goat milk. The entire herd of over a hundred goats was brought into the courtyard and a team of men led by my father identified the goats in lactation. What chaos there was, as the goats were not used to being caught and milked. They scrambled bleating and crying at various decibels and creating a discordant orchestra with the laughter of the onlookers. I joined my mother and some of the bemused women who watched from the sidelines. There were terrified goats everywhere, on the ledges around the utse, on the wooden steps leading to our apartments, and groups that huddled together in fear and dread in the corners of the courtyard. The men had managed to collect a small amount of milk after the massive effort. But it was decided that it was not worth all the struggle, as the milk had such a strong and unpleasant smell. 'Mission Goat Milk' was abandoned immediately and the goats continued to do what they could do best: provide manure for our fields. In the years that followed the deaths of our parents, the family's domestic animals began to dwindle in numbers and the goats were the first group of animals to disappear from our inventory.

Mother liked gardening. I remember both she and father making a big garden in the space east of the house in front of the stable and the kitchens. They planted rows of flowers along the bamboo fences enclosing the vegetable beds. Watering the garden was a big effort and everybody – the weavers, the servants, the stable boys and, sometimes, even the visitors, had to carry water from the communal waterspout to the garden when it was watering time. One year mother received vegetable seeds from the Queen Mother Her Majesty Ashi Phuntsho Choden. Some of these seeds were new and foreign, and eating one of the new products caused some anxiety, for we thought we were bleeding. I had never eaten beetroot before and, after I had eaten it for the first time, I proclaimed exaggeratedly that all my insides were coming out. Beetroot did not find a place in our cuisine at the time; it was too sweet and did not go well with our cooking with chilli. That was the only time we had beetroot in my parents' garden!

Although my parents were enthusiastic and adventurous gardeners, Ogyen Choling at nearly 3000 metres above sea level was much too high for many vegetables. So, they grew their vegetables at a lower elevation, in a patch of land we owned adjoining the huge rock face of today's famous Tang Rimochen Temple. This space which was protected and warmed by the rock that retained the heat of the sun is called Brak Ra or Rock Base. Meme Pawa, a very special person, who was a retired servant of Her Majesty the Queen Mother Ashi Phuntsho Choden, was appointed as the gardener. Her Majesty was keen on gardening and Meme Pawa claimed he learnt to garden while in Her Majesty's service. I do recall Meme Pawa bringing us fresh cucumbers and other vegetables from that garden sometimes. After my mother died, this garden was forgotten and, finally in the 1980s, the land slipped out of our possession when it was given by my uncle Ugyen Wangdi, my father's younger brother, to one of his girlfriends. She later exchanged the land for a second-hand Maruti van. Happily, it was recently instituted that the land be designated as the space for the annual ten-day community prayers (chanting the mantra *Benza Guru* 100,000 times). My mother would have approved of this, for she was a spiritual person. Many of my mother's duties as the lady of the household were keeping up the time-honoured prayers and rituals in the temple. She and my father did not spare any effort or resources in continuing these religious observances. They saw these religious acts as their most important duty. Nearly every day there were prayers or rituals taking place in the temples.

Today, having lived well past the thirty-two years of my mother's life, my retired husband and I enjoy spending much of our time gardening and landscaping. I think of this work as a continuation of my mother's joys and endeavours, and we are fortunate that we are not distracted by goats or sheep.

4

A Perfect Matrimony

My mother married a man that her family had chosen for her, just as she had been expected to. It was to be a perfect matrimony. The groom was a good choice that ensured the alliance of two prestigious families in Bumthang. My father in the late 1940s would have been considered a highly desirable match for any girl. As the eldest son of a well-respected landed household who would inherit extensive lands, cattle and horses as well as substantial moveable assets, he would be an undeniable economic advantage to any girl's family. Perhaps more than the economics, my father's impeccable genealogical legacy with at least two well-known Buddhist masters in his ancestral stock, took him beyond desirable to irresistible. At twenty-one years of age, father was a handsome man and surely the most eligible bachelor on the east side of the Pele la! He was sought after rather fiercely by several families who had marriageable young girls.

My eighteen-year-old mother at the time was in the service of Her Majesty the Queen Ashi Phuntsho Choden of the second King of Bhutan, His Majesty Jigme Wangchuck. Mother was the daughter of the Queen's half-brother, *Dasho* Gempo Dorji, the *drungpa* (public administrator) of Chummey and a descendant of well-respected ancestry traced to the fifteenth-century saint Pema Lingpa's son, Dawa Gyeltshen. She enjoyed considerable socio-economic status. After my mother's own mother died, the Queen had taken my mother into her care, where she served as an attendant to the Queen. Now the Queen was marrying her off properly, a responsibility she had taken upon herself. I wonder if there was ever a negotiation with my father's family or whether the Queen just commanded my father's family to receive her niece as a bride for their son. I once heard that on a visit to Ogyen Choling, the Queen expressed her wish to look at all the rooms in the family's house. My paternal grandmother Keba unlocked all the doors to every room and opened all the boxes in the house for the Queen to see. The Queen went from room to room for a visual inspection. The inspection completed, the Queen is believed to have said, 'Dorji Doma will marry well.' Whether there is any truth to this, the fact is that the Queen chose my father for her niece. My parents' fates were, thus, sealed, and the matrimony of two esteemed households in Bumthang was to take place.

But the marriage was doomed from the beginning. Somewhere along my life's way, I gathered from whispered conversations and implied references that my mother was not ready for this marriage. She was more inclined to religion and even considered becoming a nun. But hurried astrological consultations were made and an auspicious day chosen for the wedding. Aie Kesang Wangchu, a woman who had been in the service of the Ogyen Choling household and who remembered the wedding, thought it took place in the fifth lunar month which would have been sometime in June, the beginning of the monsoon rains. Perhaps the date was not so auspicious, because many powerful remedies had to be conducted to negate the inauspicious influences that were foreseen. Ashi Kencho of Lame Gompa *dzong*, who is the great-granddaughter of the first King from his first Queen, once told me that her father, Dasho Phuntsho Wangdi, who was skilled in astrology, was alarmed by the choice of the wedding date and is supposed to have said, '*Daben kaysa kud warey, tsai wa gnyen bai zakar mey ra.* (They could have not chosen a more inauspicious date. Damage has been done.)'

Over the years I heard it being said many times by different people that the wedding was grand. The wedding procession consisted of a representative of the Queen, relatives, friends of the families, singers, dancers, riders who were privileged to ride alongside the bride, and pack mules loaded with gifts of every kind. Even some cattle and horses were included as gifts. The procession started from Domkhar Palace in Gyetsa valley, where the Queen was living at the time.

I was in the village of Domkhar more than fifty years after my mother's wedding. I was there for a day with my daughter in 2003 to assist her with the interviews that she was conducting for her Masters' thesis. An elderly woman agreed to let us interview her, rather reluctantly. I was to facilitate as a translator. My daughter went through her questions but suddenly she looked at me strangely and, growing rather impatient, said, '*Ama*, this is my research, and you are not allowed to talk about other things.' The other things that I was talking about was my mother, and I didn't even realize when I had strayed away from my daughter's questions to introducing myself as Dorji Doma's daughter. The woman immediately warmed up and said, 'Ama *mai* I remember watching your mother's wedding procession which started from Domkhar dzong.' My mind was immediately imagining my mother as an eighteen-year-old bride. She would have been seventy years old at the time of our interview, had she lived.

The elderly lady said that she was a young girl at the time, and she remembered joining the people who stood on the side of the road in curiosity and awe to watch the procession pass by. What she remembered most clearly were the bulls decorated with silken scarves tied to their horns and cloth tassels hanging from their humps, walking along with the singers, dancers, riders, packhorses and other animals and, of course, the beautifully dressed people in the procession.

I think the wedding procession spent a night in mother's own family home in Prah, Chummey. The next day they travelled another thirty kilometres into Tang valley and set up camp near the famous Tang Rimochen Temple. On the day the bride was to enter the groom's home at an auspicious time, it rained incessantly. To take shelter from the rain, the reception group from Ogyen Choling, which was waiting to meet the procession, had to serve the welcome tea in a bamboo shed for cattle. Finally, the bridal procession reached Ogyen Choling in the torrential rain, and all those in the procession were soaked to the skin. To make matters worse, the horse that my mother was riding on, usually a docile mare, was startled by something or somebody and stood up on its hind legs, whinnied loudly and refused to go into the inner courtyard through the main entrance. The horseman brought the horse under control and guided it, perhaps too forcefully, into the inner courtyard, for once in the courtyard, the horse rose into the air again, whinnying and snorting dangerously, but mother managed to alight it swiftly. My mother had reacted quickly and was spared the humiliation of a fall or a graver accident. After a series of three *marchang* ceremonies of offering libation to the household's deities, the young bride was ushered into the utse where the bridal chambers had been arranged and where more formalities were carried out. I wonder what this eighteen-year-old girl thought and felt after this near disastrous episode. She had barely enough time to recover from the trauma when she faced for the first time in her life the man she was marrying. I am sure she was totally shaken and frightened. I wonder what my father thought of her, seeing his soaking wet bride for the first time!

My aunt, Kunzang Wangmo, my father's cousin who was part of the reception party, remembered looking around at all the *Chumedpas* (people from Chummey). Everybody was wringing out their soaked clothes. It must have been a truly pathetic sight! Aie Kesang Wangchu, who was also part of the reception, said that she still felt the water dripping down her body whenever she recalled that day. She demonstrated a small shiver at the recollection. I am sure the embarrassment of both parties was partially covered by the solemnity of the rituals which were carried out to perfection under my grandfather's supervision. 'Where was my father and what was he doing at the time while the commotion was unfolding in the courtyard?' was the question I repeated many times to many people who were present on that day, but nobody seems to remember clearly. Some say he came outside the utse, at the entrance to receive his bride, and others say he was in the utse waiting for her to join him. The unexpected confusion and chaos seem to have jolted and distorted everybody's memories of the day. The one thing that everybody does recall is that the pouring rain stopped 'as if cut off' as soon as the bride entered the utse. How can such a sign be interpreted?

What people also remember is the bridal trousseau that the Queen had lavished on my mother. Everything came in horse loads. There were not just single items but loads of household and kitchen utensils, agricultural, woodworking and stone-working tools, bales of cloth and bags of grains of every kind. There were bags of chillies, butter, lard and even a load of dried fish. While the onlookers could not see the clothes and jewellery she may have brought with her, they talked about what they saw and remembered even years later. Feasting and archery, games and dancing, went on for three days. Nothing eventful or worth remembering, according to my aunt Kunzang, happened during those days, except that one of the visitors experienced the usual mishap resulting from the lethal cocktail of 'mixing archery and alcohol', and an archer's arrow pierced his calf. He survived and, after a few days, was able to limp away.

My mother never had the chance to tell me about her wedding, but she did tell me about the dried fish. Dried fish was a high-value commodity imported from Tibet. The fish was wind-dried in the frigid atmosphere of high altitudes and considered a rare delicacy. I don't think they were even salted but had a lot of fat when we ate them on special occasions. When I was home, I often accompanied my mother to the storerooms in the utse. One day she pointed to a whole piece of dried fish on a wooden peg and said, 'Fish for me symbolizes sorrow. This is a fish from the load of fish that was included among my wedding gifts. Fish is the symbol of sorrow for me, and I carried my sorrow with me.' What could a child of less than nine years understand of symbolism and sorrow? It never occurred to me to ask her more about her wedding or her sorrow. Uncannily, forty-eight years later, in 1996, when I was cleaning the rooms in the utse in preparation for the museum, I clearly recalled the exchange between my mother and me in that room so many years ago. I looked at the wooden peg on the wall. A disintegrating but still recognizable form of a fish was still there. I took down the sorrow and had a cleansing burning ritual all by myself. This was a symbolic ritual that should have been done a long time ago. As I watched the fish burn, I thought of my mother and her sorrows. I had the vision of the permanently down-turned mouth of the fish. Fish never smile, do they? Perhaps because of my mother's belief about fish symbolizing sorrow, I have always had an aversion to fish symbols. Some years ago, a friend presented me a fish windsock from Japan. I could not bring myself to hang it in my veranda or even re-gift it to anyone, for fear of it being a harbinger of sorrow. Now I have convinced myself to overcome this jinx, and today the pink synthetic cloth fish with silver eyes hangs on my veranda in my house in Jakar, hopefully blowing away any potential sorrow. Every time I look at it, I deliberately imagine a smiling mouth on its face.

Unfortunately, unlike me chasing potential sorrows away, my mother had to live through her sorrows which began to unfold within days of her wedding. While the festivities were going on, her father-in-law, Jigme Dorji Wangchuk, suddenly became seriously ill and took to bed. His only complaint was an overwhelming sensation of heaviness on the nape of his neck between his shoulders, 'I do not have any pain except this heavy weight on my neck,' he is believed to have said. He died soon after he fell ill; he was in his mid-fifties. The atmosphere of celebration and festivities immediately gave way to one of bereavement and mourning, marked by sorrow and death rituals. The situation was exacerbated by the fact that my grandmother, Keba, was shocked into unconsciousness by the death of her husband and she too never recovered. Every time she regained consciousness, the pain of her loss and mourning was so intensely unbearable for her and her near ones, that her family members and attendants sedated her with *ara* (alcohol). She died before her husband's body could be cremated, even though she was a few years younger than him. My mother's in-laws were cremated together in the courtyard of the nagtshang complex. I cannot imagine the trauma of pain, shame and bewilderment that my eighteen-year-old mother must have suffered at this tragedy. I still feel a lingering ache for her. Mother was a stranger in a new household with unfamiliar people and a husband she had known just for a few days. And yet there she was in the centre of tragic double deaths. I have heard from those who remember that she was so disturbed and humiliated that she kept on attempting to run away from the disastrous situation for which she blamed herself. The idea that she might have brought these misfortunes to her new household is not an unusual Bhutanese way of explaining sudden fluctuations in fortune, and this was the source of her shame.

Her old maid, Aie Nektong, who had accompanied her from her village, had to physically restrain her from doing something drastic. '*Wai wai*, I don't know what to do with my mistress,' she is remembered to have bemoaned in desperation.

Although I did not hear it from my parents or relatives, I heard from other sources that following the disastrous consequences of the ill-fated wedding, the astrologers were held responsible for the colossal mistakes they had made in their calculations. Dasho Phuntsho Wangdi's alarmed concern was truly prophetic. I cannot confirm whether the Queen Mother met the astrologers and expressed her displeasure to them, but I heard that one of the main astrologers fled the country and stayed in hiding in Tibet for some years until the impact of these unfortunate happenings had become a distant memory – except for those whose lives had been so drastically affected by it. I often think about this catastrophic event and am left wondering: Can astrology really predict so accurately what is to come?

How I wish that my mother's sorrows would have ended with this monumental event. But no, her sorrows followed her for the rest of her life until her own death. Although my mother was a concerned mistress and a gentle and compassionate person who never wished harm to anybody, she never really felt completely accepted by the people of Tang, especially the village of Ogyen Choling. Sometimes the villagers resentfully referred to her as 'the Chumedpa'. Such statements of exclusion immediately alienated her and made her feel like an outsider. My mother should have known that it was not just one or two gestures directed at her that caused her to feel the hostility. She should have recognized that it was the accumulation of animosity built up over generations between the overlords and their allegedly submissive workers that had manifested in obvious forms of daily behaviours. My mother was just too sensitive. Even as a small child I could feel her agony. I recall a particular incident in 1964, two years after father had died. We were home for the winter holidays. Mother was nursing a big swollen black eye and was in a miserable condition. The cause of her affliction was a village woman calling her 'Chumedpa' under her breath but deliberately within my mother's earshot. My mother was so disturbed by this explicitly harmless but implicitly hurtful term of alienation, she became hasty, did not look where she was going and banged against a chair, toppled over it and hurt herself. Why I carry this sad image of my mother is perhaps that at twelve years old, I felt her pain and loneliness which were transferred on to me and stayed deeply imprinted in my memory. She was keenly aware of the disparities in the social system of her time. One of the daily realities she had to live with was the daily food distribution for the family and the workers. Meals were different for the various categories of people based on their position in the hierarchy. The high altitudes of Tang were not conducive to paddy cultivation, so rice was a rare and highly valued grain. This coveted grain, rice, was eaten only by the privileged few – family members, guests, and some of the older and more favoured persons in the household. All the others were given mostly buckwheat dishes. Although it was mother's duty to measure out and allocate all the food to the two kitchens every day – the family's private kitchen and the common public kitchen – the discrimination pained her. Whenever an opportunity arose, she reminded us that every grain of rice represented a drop of sweat, and that we should appreciate it and not waste even a single grain. She would repeatedly tell us that rice was brought to us after it was produced by our tenant farmers and carried for over three days by people and animals before we could eat it. Every so often I saw her quietly exchange her share of rice with a buckwheat dish in the common kitchen.

Maybe she preferred buckwheat or perhaps it was her quiet demonstration against the prevailing disparity. What I most clearly remember is her saying, more than once, that her earnest prayer was that she should not be reborn in a landed family where she would have to supervise workers in an unequally structured society.

While being introduced to Ogyen Choling, she should have already realized that she was not just entering an unequal economic structure but that she was also entering a patriarchy that valued men more than women. The welcome song that the women of the family and village had composed should have warned her. Rather than greeting her, the song was in fact trying to impress upon her that the household she was entering had three perfect and precious men. This song is still remembered by some older women in the village who sing it without hesitation or doubt.

Bey yul Tang chong lung pa lu
Nye Rimochen gi hang wog lu
Nye Thowadrak gi ay chok lu
Tsawa tsangchu youn chap sham sha yud
Key pa tonshing shemo sham sha yud
Tsemo zangdokpalri sheng sha yud
Chi chari kor sha yud
Nang Menzi yola chang sha yud
Zimchung lay bai kachen dongshing
Yab Dorji Lingpai densa lu
Say Sangye drawai puensum thrung
Yab ku yi rang wai say sum thrung
Yum thuk ye rang wi say sum thrung
Say chwai tsan ni choku zer
Say barmu tsan ni long ku zer
Say chung wai tsen ni trulku zer
Choku longku trulku sum

In the hidden land of Tang
On the pillow of the sacred site of Rimochen
To the right side of the sacred site of Thowadrak
The river is like a water-offering laid out at the base
The middle is adorned with blue pine trees
Like a copper-coloured heaven built on the peak of a mountain
The outer space is enclosed by a wall
The inner space is decked with brocade
In the rooms with pillars and wooden facades.
This is the centre of the father, Dorji Lingpa.
Three Buddha-like sons were born
Father of the sons is satisfied
Mother of the sons is content.
The eldest son is Choku
The middle son is Longku
The youngest son is Trulku.
The three jewels Choku, Longku and Trulku.

Had I been in my mother's place and listened to the lyrics carefully, I would have shuddered. From the words of the song, one can see clearly that the new bride was being thrust into a patriarchy where the male lineage was revered. The praise for the males in the family sounds intimidating. There is not a word of welcome for the bride, not a gentle word of comfort for the bewildered and frightened girl.

5

My Father and the Men Who Came Before Him

As schemed by the elders, my mother was married into a formidable household. She must have had some idea of its economic and social status, but she would have known nothing about the man she was to marry. In the absence of photographs or portraits in those days, I wonder if she dared to conjure up an image of her future husband. Could someone in her family have told my mother about the man she was going to marry? What sort of a man was he? Was he kind and handsome or was he a cruel man who cared little for the people he oversaw? She was certainly told something about the assets, both tangible and intangible, that my father represented – his carefully preserved historical and religious lineage – because that was what was important. But it was not important to consult her and ask whether she wanted to marry this man that they had chosen for her. So, although she knew nothing of the man, she faithfully followed the established custom and became his bride. She would have to help him manage his household and estate, bear his children and, most importantly, ensure the posterity of the genealogical lineage that was valued above everything else.

After their marriage, my parents shared a period of fourteen years together and, surely, got to know each other well. As for me, I knew my father for the first nine years of my life, and that was not enough time to really know him. It was only later in life, and long after he was dead, that I began to find out about who he was and where he had come from. It was in retrospection that I understand how he carried the burdens of history and how he tried to live up to the expectations as the patriarch of his family in compliance with tradition.

The continuity of Ogyen Choling's patriarchal lineage had survived over eighteen generations when my father had to assume the role of the nineteenth *Choeje,* lord of religion, in 1948. This title denoted a line of nobility that descended from religious figures. In the case of our family the title of 'Choeje' was combined with the term '*dung*', an honorific term for 'bone', referring to the secular paternal family line.

When I think of my father, the visual image that comes to mind is that of my younger brother, Sonam Wangchuk. But my brother in his late sixties is a much older version of my father whom I last saw at the age of thirty-seven. My brother is leaner, with sharper facial contours; he has a habit of slouching, while my father stood erect, tall and dignified. My brother was a lifelong civil servant until he retired. My father was never a civil servant even though he was commanded once or twice by the third King, His Majesty Jigme Dorji Wangchuck, to join the civil service. His duty to his ancestral home was the reason for his inability to join the government. I know this enigmatic pull to Ogyen Choling, our ancestral home, that he may have felt, because I felt the same force that drew me to live here again against all odds.

I think anyone who had seen my father would not easily forget him. He was a powerful yet attractive personality. Throughout his life he was known as Dasho Kunzang Dorji. The title of 'Dasho' has, in modern Bhutan, become linked to high-ranking officials of the civil service and is conferred upon deserving individuals by the King for outstanding service, but father had inherited his title, so he was what people referred to as a 'born Dasho'. He had a distinguished aristocratic bearing. As the eldest son of Dasho Jigme Dorji Wangchuk, the eighteenth Dung Choeje of Ogyen Choling and Keba of Chusa in Lhuentse, he took on the responsibility of the nineteenth lineage holder after the death of his father. He assumed the post uncontested, as his two younger brothers had already left home. His second brother, Dasho Ugyen Wangdi, had been sent to serve in the Royal Court of the Second King, His Majesty Jigme Wangchuck while the youngest, *Trulku* (the title for a reincarnated religious personality), Nuden Dorji, whom we referred to as Akhu lama, had opted for the religious path and gone to Tibet to join the reputed Nyingmapa monastery of Mindroling.

This coincidence of three sons being born into the family seems to have been an unplanned pattern for some generations. My grandfather as the eldest had become the Dung Choeje and lived in Ogyen Choling, managing the estate until his death. His brother, Gyurme Pema Kunzang alias Thubten Gyeltshen (1906–1939/40), was recognized as the ninth reincarnation of the fifteenth-century saint Pema Lingpa's reincarnation, Thugse Dawa Gyeltsthen, and was sent to head the monastery of Lhalung in Lhodrak, in southern Tibet. Because the post of the Thugse had prominent religious significance and some regional influence, I often heard interesting details about his life, even more than of my own grandfather's life. Since I know very little about my own grandfather, I will, instead, recount a story about my granduncle, an important family member about whose life there were often repeated but whispered tales of conspiracy that ended in humiliation and sadness.

I never met my granduncle, but stories about him were circulated even after he had died. I heard that Thugse was a man of hot temper. His temper was hot enough for the top

Tibetan management of his monastery to act. It appears a plot was hatched to calm down his temper with medical intervention. The indigenous doctors prescribed burning the vital points on his body. This practice was prevalent at the time, so it was nothing out of the ordinary. The vital spots on his body were identified and a tiny kindle of dried and softened plant material was placed on these spots and lit with a burning incense stick. The doctors repeated the treatment until they had completely disabled him and rendered him immobile; they had crippled him. He could not walk, nor could he use his fingers. He had to be carried from place to place. I heard this story from my granduncle's own reincarnate, the tenth Thugse Thegchog Tenpai Gyeltshen (1951–2010). He told me this story when I visited him, at his command, while he was very ill. He passed away soon after this meeting. While he was telling me this story, Thugse Thegchog Gyeltshen became animated and emotional. He said that the Tibetans who were assigned to carry him refused to take him to the places he wanted to go. He told me, 'I used to bite into their long hair and pull their pigtails until they took me to where I wanted to go.' He even demonstrated how he pulled their hair with his mouth. I was truly shaken by this information but more by the surreal experience of the gentle tenth Thugse transforming into the volatile, hot-tempered ninth in recounting this story.

It must have been the humiliation, isolation and helplessness that made my granduncle Thugse Thubten Gyeltshen seek affection from a Tibetan woman. The woman, Kuencho Lhamo, was not a beauty, according to the elders who had met her. She was an ordinary, humble woman who even had a goitre at the base of her neck. She outlived Thugse and later came to live in Tang and marry a Tibetan man, Ap Ningrela, a maker of barrels for fermenting grains for making alcohol. I remember Ap Ningrela, a small man with a scruffy face and untidy bristles of facial hair. He always wore a pair of worn-out Tibetan *bobola,* cloth boots, and was often in our house to make huge barrels for our alcohol processing.

Before the Tibetan government found out about Thugse's liaison with a woman, my granduncle wrote to the Dalai Lama's office to confess the breach of his celibacy. There is, in our family's possession, the written response from the Dalai Lama. The letter expresses aggravation, but it states that because of his honesty in confessing the crime, there would not be any punishment. Thugse was granted permission to leave Lhalung after handing over all the artefacts to the monastery. Thugse came home and lived in Ogyen Choling until he died.

During the 1800s, my great-great-grandfather, Wangchen Dorji alias Tshokye Dorji, the fifteenth generation of the family lineage, also had two brothers. Although nothing is very clear, there are hints of tension and unhappiness that led to a deliberate attempt to avert potential acrimony in the family. Tshokye Dorji, as the eldest brother, stayed on as the Dung Choeje and managed the Ogyen Choling estate until his death. He created a new estate in Binzibe, on a plateau north of Ogyen Choling, for his brother Choeje Namgay, and another estate in Tashicholing, west of Ogyen Choling, on the mountain slope to the west side of Tang Chu, for his other brother Choeje Wangdi. I suspect there was a fourth sibling, most probably a sister, whose name is now unknown, who was given as a bride to the house of Khangrab *Ponpo*, a local chieftain. She may have later become a nun. Some statues in the Khangrab *lhakhang* are still traced to Ogyen Choling. Interestingly, all three men took on the title of Choeje. Tshokye Dorji, however, later earned the better-known title of

'*Kushu*' or '*Penlop*' after he served as the governor of Trongsa in the 1840s and 50s.

There is little else known about my great-great-grandfather's two brothers who moved out of Ogyen Choling. Fortunately, there are some written as well as oral stories about Kushu Tshokye Dorji. I imagine my great-great-grandfather Kushu Tshokye as being like my father, a noble gentleman with an aristocratic bearing, a leader of men. Once I asked an unofficial but respected oral historian about him and was disappointed to hear what he had to say about my ancestor. With a dismissive gesture he said, '*Ayee*, that Tshokye Dorji became the Penlop of Trongsa not because of what he achieved but simply because his mother had offered the *gyaltsen* (the decorative victory banner) on the roof of Trongsa dzong and prayed that one of her sons would one day rule from the dzong.' What a letdown that was! Though I refuse to let this assessment be the conclusive evaluation of my ancestor. I also realized that this is how personalities in history can get sidelined when the narratives are made to suit the teller's political agenda.

I imagine my great-great-grandfather to be a special personality who achieved the coveted position of Trongsa Penlop most probably because of his leadership quality. He held it for the standard three-year term during one of the most tumultuous times of Bhutanese history. The Trongsa Penlops held considerable power and influence at the time. Of course, there is no denying that his mother's prayers must have helped. But I like to think of Kushu Tshokye Dorji as the crucial link between the troubled times of Bhutan and the beginning of peace, prosperity and stability under the Wangchuck dynasty, for it was Kushu Tshokye Dorji's chosen successor Jigme Namgyel who was the progenitor of the Wangchuck dynasty. My father never told us his genealogical and historical background. Perhaps he thought we were too young to understand such serious matters, or he thought he would tell us later. Only there was no 'later' for him.

I now possess a personal memento of my great-great-grandfather. It is a small piece of wood cut out of a window shutter on which there is a bit of grime. The stain is from Kushu Tshokye Dorji's head. He regularly leaned from his seat and rested his head against the window shutter. This piece of wood was saved when his winter home, our manor in Gorgan in Lhuentse, was dismantled in the 1970s. I have kept this relic among my precious possessions. In 2003, when my house in Jakar was burgled, the thieves went through my belongings and took all they wanted, but they thoughtfully left this piece of wood, which is wrapped in Bhutanese paper and labelled, for me.

Although my father never had a chance to tell us about his ancestors, he was fully aware of the fact that it was he who was fated to continue the nineteenth generation of religious nobility. His family was said to have descended from one of the most revered Tibetan treasure-discoverers, *Terchen* Dorji Lingpa. From a young age, although I was not sure of how or why, I knew we had a connection to Dorji Lingpa and his legacy, and accepted this as common knowledge. Although nobody sat down to tell me, just by hearing the often-repeated names and stories I was burdened by knowledge of my paternal line of descent, from which I could not easily detach myself.

Besides Kushu Tshokye Dorji who is also mentioned in the history books, there are two other ancestors who are historically significant. The first is Kushu Tshokye Dorji's own son Tsondrue Gyeltshen who went to fight the British with Jigme Namgyel, the father of the first King, who was at the time emerging as the most significant leader of the country. Tsondrue Gyeltshen accompanied Jigme Namgyel to Dewathang in 1865. There were as many as eleven battles between the British and the Bhutanese during the colonial era but the war of Dewangiri was the final and most conclusive confrontation. In his book *History of Bhutan*, *Lopon* Karma Phuntsho offers a last glimpse of my brave ancestor. The British had stormed the Bhutanese stockade, but the Bhutanese soldiers stood their ground until they were completely outnumbered by the enemy and forced to retreat. When others left the stockade and begged Tsondrue Gyeltshen to leave with them, he refused, saying, 'See you later.' After this there is no historical record of my ancestor. According to historical documentation, when the British stormed the Bhutanese stockades in the hills of Dewathang, 120 Bhutanese soldiers were indiscriminately butchered. Tsondrue Gyeltshen may have been among them. But his body was never found.

Five generations later, we, the family, still believe that it would have been easy to identify him. Our family claims, decades later, that he was said to be extraordinarily good-looking, possibly the handsomest man of his days! How could he not be recognizable? This gave room for a second narrative that says he was captured and treated honourably by the captors for his proven valour; the British had themselves witnessed his gallantry in the battlefield. Tsondrue Gyeltshen is said to have later married an Indian girl of some social standing. Many years later Bhutanese traders claimed to have met him in the jathang, a generic term for the plains of India. They are supposed to have said that he was riding on an elephant in a ceremonial procession and stopped to talk to the Bhutanese traders when he recognized them because of their attire. He was said to be mounted on the elephant in the style of a prince.

There were also some hazy stories of some correspondence from him being in our family's possession. At least two families in the village of Ogyen Choling were supposed to have descended from the plains people who were sent by Tsondrue Gyeltshen to work on his parental estate. He is also said to have sent plains people to work on the familial estate in our winter resort in Gorgan in Lhuentse. All these stories might seem too petty to even be footnotes to Bhutan's history. But I always feel curiously but warmly inclined towards people I see in the jathang, in the Indian state of Assam, to the south beyond Samdrup Jongkhar Dzongkhag. If Tsondrue Gyeltshen indeed married a local woman, any one of these people could be his descendants and be related to me as my long-lost cousin!

While this would-be scion of the lineage of Ogyen Choling was lost in mystery, it was his nephew, Ugyen Dorji, who became the seventeenth lineage holder. He was the son of Tsondrue Gyeltshen's sister Yeshe. Ugyen Dorji is most often referred to by his official title of Jakar *dzongpon*, the lord or governor of the Jakar dzong, which means that he was the legitimate ruler of Bumthang appointed by the central government. He is better known to us as Dzongpon *Drolpa*, or the former dzongpon, which implies that by the time he came back home, he had left the post. While we have no accounts of how he performed as the dzongpon, we have grounds to attest to his contributions and achievements in Ogyen Choling. It was he who rebuilt the structures after the devastating earthquake of 1897. The structures still stand today, and it is where I am at today as I muddle through the history of this place and its people. Dzongpon Ugyen Dorji not only restored the former structures but also expanded and improved the buildings. According to an established custom, the person who commissions the building of temples and the painting of the murals in them is acknowledged with a small portrait painted in the murals for posterity. In two of the murals in the present-day temple,

Dzongpon Ugyen Dorji appears. In one as a small, balding man making offerings to the Zhabdrung Rinpoche, and in another he is seen making offerings to the great treasure-discoverer, Terchen Dorji Lingpa. Although the temple paintings are generally executed following iconographic rules and not true representations of real-life humans, I feel that these images must have been inspired by the real person. We have at least two sets of Dzongpon Ugyen Dorji's ghos, now displayed in the museum, which were indeed stitched for a man of small stature. Although he was small in size, his legacy is large. Written records, like the *karchag* on the temple wall which details the expenditure for the building of the temple, state that Dzongpon Ugyen Dorji spared no effort or resources for the reconstruction and glorification of his ancestral home and its temples.

My father, the grandson of Dzongpon Ugyen Dorji, had an aura of being a person who knew who he was without being arrogant. Wherever he happened to be, he spontaneously took centre stage and things revolved around him. Thinking back now, father seemed to have enjoyed his position and executed his duties with efficiency and authority. In my earliest memory, Ogyen Choling was a place people respected, and there was always a lively and energetic atmosphere. The social reforms had been introduced in my childhood, but their full impact had yet to be felt. So, my father was still in control; perhaps one of the last of the legitimate reigning lords of the old social system.

My father had inherited sizeable landholdings, and many households in the immediate village and the neighbouring ones in the valley worked for him. Additionally, he owned cattle, horses and yaks which required effective stewardship. I remember the teams of workers assigned to work the fields, care for the animals and serve the family in various capacities including as servants and weavers.

Father supervised the workers with the help of a *lajab*, a supervisory assistant.

The most endearing image I hold is of him sitting cross-legged on a raised mat near a large cupboard with many drawers full of his documents. His stationery was in front of him on a small table – a pot of ink and a bamboo container with his bamboo pens inside. Later he used fountain pens. He wrote in the traditional Bhutanese style, with the paper folded and placed in the cup of his raised left hand against the forefinger, middle finger and ring finger and held in place by the thumb and the little finger. He paused often to think while biting on his pen. He was not writing religious scriptures or philosophical essays and commentaries; he was working on correspondence, records and inventories.

My father performed his religious duties without compromise. After all, this was one of his obligations as the Choeje but he was not an overtly religious man. In fact, I think he enjoyed the secular aspects of his position more. He was a passionate hunter, practised archery and loved horses. Father had a collection of guns and pistols and spent time cleaning and caring for them. In the same year he died, with the disturbance on the north of our borders, with the possibility of Chinese encroachments into Bhutan, the government collected all private guns and ammunitions saying it was a temporary precaution. My father's entire collection was taken to Jakar dzong. Maybe the government wanted to prevent any form of vigilante actions during the tense times in the early 1960s. The guns were never returned to us.

My father's love for his horses kept him busy every day. Every morning the riding horses would be brought in front of the eastern window and father supervised their grooming looking out of his window. The animals were brushed, their manes combed, and some were braided with ribbons and tassels. The old worn-off horseshoes were replaced with new shoes. I could never watch the men hammering the nails into the horses' hooves because I was so sure that it must have hurt the animals. Every evening the horses were taken for a run along the banks of the Tang Chu. Father sometimes went for the ride himself, but when he couldn't, he used to watch the grooms riding his horses through his binoculars.

My father loved life. He was full of energy and bursting with ideas and dreams. How could he stop living so suddenly? All that energy just extinguished. That is why it took me so long to accept his death. Could my father have died of diabetes? At the time that he died, nobody talked of the disease because we didn't know of it. But today it has become a common and dreaded disease, *buram gi naed,* the sugar disease. It took many years for my older brother Rinzin and I to talk about our father's death because neither of us witnessed his passing. We did not know how to even begin talking about something that felt unreal and confusing. When I later dared to ask those present at his death for details, they said my father suffered from constant thirst during his illness. I find myself thinking, yes, this is indeed a symptom of diabetes. I know because I have diabetes. Maybe I inherited my father's disease. In the two years after his death, mother never talked about his illness, or his death and I never could ask her about it. Finding it too painful to get rid of all reminders of her dead husband, during one of my visits home, I saw that mother had stored his bedding and some of the clothes he used in a rarely visited room in the attic. During subsequent school breaks, I noticed that father's belongings had been removed.

In 1962 there were no modern medical doctors or hospitals in Bhutan. It was not that my father died without getting all the care and attention that was available to him. The most sacred and precious religious relics, collected over many generations, were given to him orally or inhaled as smoke. The most elaborate and esoteric rituals and rites were performed on his behalf, but none of this could save my father. The best-known indigenous doctors attended to him using the curative methods known to traditional medicine. In fact, just like they had for my granduncle Thugse, the doctors burnt parts of my father's body to treat his ailments. I had watched doctors applying this method, so I had an idea of what my father was subjected to. I heard that they burnt him all over his body and the burnt areas became sore blisters. I heard that the doctors also let out the bad blood by making sharp incisions at crucial points on father's body, for they guessed that his illness had something to do with his blood. When his condition worsened and when there was nothing else to help him, Her Royal Highness Ashi Chokey Wangmo (the daughter of the Second King), who was married to my father's younger brother Ugyen Wangdi, requested her brother, the third King, for help. The King commanded an Indian military helicopter to have my father evacuated for medical treatment in India. My father refused to go, and he died the same day that the helicopter landed in Tang valley.

I later heard that at the time of his death, my father could not let go of life; he was not ready to die. He had one pressing worry that would not let him die in peace. As is customary, when the hour of death approaches, if the person is still conscious, someone, ideally a realized lama, is requested to read the book of liberation by hearing *Bardo Thodol* (a scripture that guides and directs the consciousness of the dying through its transition towards rebirth or liberation). The lama who was reading the book to him realized that father was having trouble letting go of his life, so he asked him, 'What is on your mind? Now you must let go of everything.'

My father is supposed to have replied, 'I am worried that my children are in a foreign country; they will marry the wrong people.' Although I heard about this from an aunt and not from my mother, I believe her, because this was so similar to his parting words to me two months earlier. Now I wonder if my father had a prophetic premonition. Less than twenty years after my father had expressed these fears, I did marry a foreigner. Not just somebody from across the border but someone from thousands of miles away: a man from Switzerland.

6

I Should Have Been a Boy

IT HAS BEEN SAID that there were rarely any girls born to the Ogyen Choling nagtshang family throughout its nineteen generations, beginning sometime in the 1500s. I am of the twentieth generation. Those rare girls who were born into the household did not live long or simply disappeared from our family tree. I have heard the elders say that the family had the tradition of bringing in brides but that there were only rare instances of giving away brides. Ours was a patriarchy that upheld the male lineage of direct religious transmissions and *choeju dungju* (bones – it was believed that only male children were capable of passing on the purity of the genealogical inheritance through their bones, whereas the female children only inherited the blood which could be easily tainted or corrupted). In the 1800s the only surviving girl was Ashi Yeshe, daughter of Tshokye Dorji, in the first half of the 1800s. She was said to have been beautiful and highly desired and was beleaguered by suitors. People still say that the face of the Tara statue in our temple was modelled after Ashi Yeshe. The fact that she was attractive and of an untainted genealogical lineage made her even more sought after. She was a firm believer in the purity of bloodlines and is alleged to have proclaimed that she would 'not mix milk with ink' by marrying a suitor of unknown genealogical descent. But her staunch standards for choosing a partner had their downside too. To escape from her suitors whose sentiments she did not reciprocate, Ashi Yeshe had to run away. She probably did this because she was afraid of any undesirable consequences for her family and household. Rather than bring shame and dishonour to her family she fled to the far east of the country and stayed in hiding for many years in self-imposed exile in Trashi Yangtse. She eventually returned, albeit secretly, and lived in hiding for the rest of her life in Ogyen Choling. She was secretly married to Choeje Thinley from Tamshing Choekor, who was a descendant of the fifteenth-century saint Pema Lingpa and a suitable husband by her own standards. Everything concerning Ashi Yeshe is blurry because the secrecy surrounding her life was so well guarded. But it is known that she lived in Ogyen Choling and had a son with Choeje Thinley, Ugyen Dorji. The story of her living in hiding in the new utse after the completion of the new complex suggests that she was alive right into the early 1900s, for the consecration of the new complex was done only in 1902.

As a small child, I remember being told that my great-grandmother Ashi Yeshe lived in hiding on the third floor of the utse. I even remember somebody pointing out the place in a room where her hearth was and above it an outlet for the smoke to escape through the attic. The opening in the ceiling was closed only as recently as 2018 when we worked on the room to expand the museum. It is only in this room that there is a hole in the wall facing the west. The hole looks very much like an arrow slit, a narrow vertical aperture for shooting arrows at invaders. It appears that the hole was made during the construction, and it was not for defence but for disposing of the wastewater from her kitchen. I assume this room and some others were used by her and feel a strong connection to them. Could the connection be because she and I were the two women who defied convention by being girl children born into this all-male household and surviving? I can hardly imagine how the family managed to keep up the guard and secrecy surrounding Ashi Yeshe. While I heard no other details of her life, what was often repeated as a fact was that her death was observed in secret. Death rituals are by custom long drawn and complicated, and I am sure her son would have observed the prayers and rituals in the best way he knew how. Her cremation was said to have been carried out in the forest north of Ogyen Choling, close to the river Shaykhay in a place called Apshigang near the leper colony. Her death rituals were performed secretly, disguised as other rituals. The ceremony of *gewa* or the ritual feast of giving for merit-making, observed on the twenty-first day after death, was masked as a party after a game of archery. I met an old man who remembered his grandfather recalling his participation in building the special crematorium in the forest. The rest of the secrets of her life died with her. What prevails today are the statues in the temple which were built in her likeness and in her memory.

The only living thread of association with Ashi Yeshe was a family in the village who trace their ancestry to the eastern part of the country where Ashi Yeshe had lived during her exile. Their ancestor had accompanied Ashi Yeshe as a maid when she returned from her exile in Trashi Yangtse. One of the last surviving family members whom I knew well used to worship the deity Ama Jomo, who is specifically associated with the east. This woman used to chant the litany of her worship in the language of the east, Zalakha, which was incomprehensible to all of us. She had learnt the words by heart but probably did not fully understand them as the chant was taught by the generations of women before her.

The life-sized silver statue of the female deity Dorji Phagmo (Vajravarahi) in a semi-ferocious standing posture was commissioned by Ashi Yeshe's son in her memory. This stunningly beautiful statue in the Tara altar of our family's temple is surely the most significant reminder that there was an extraordinary woman in the family who should not be forgotten. The statue is said to be made from all her silver jewellery. The statue was cast in Tibet and assembled here. Ugyen Dorji, Ashi Yeshe's son, ensured that the face was rendered beautifully. Even with her tongue curled in semi-ferocity in her mouth and eyes sternly focused on domination, she looks impressively feminine. Her posture of fierceness and grace makes me imagine that my great-grandmother was a beautiful feisty woman who was confident and courageous. Every time I gaze at her statue or merely think of her, I feel inclined to invoke some of her attributes so I might be blessed by her courage and determination.

Looking at the family tree covering twenty generations, there is another woman named Mogha Drolma, widow of Sangay Thinley, the seventh-generation patriarch who died young. Mogha Drolma is mentioned as not only being the head of the household of Ogyen Choling but also managing the estate of Guensar or Chungkyer in Lhodrak in southern Tibet. Ogyen Choling seems to have had familial links to the nobility in Guensar. It is likely that she came as a bride to Ogyen Choling from Guensar. The relationship between these two households survived over many generations. I have memories of the visits of the Guensar lama before the Chinese takeover of Tibet in 1959, so my recollections must go back to the mid-1950s. The links were maintained until then. Could the Guensar lama have been a relative of Mogha Drolma? Nothing more is known or recorded of who she was and how the male lineage was restored in Ogyen Choling. The same family tree records a Sonam Dorje as the eighth patriarch, which leaves me wondering whether he was the son of the mysterious Mogha Drolma. My informant, Thinley Dhondup from Guensar, who was ninety-nine at our last meeting, thought that Chogden Gonpo, the reincarnation of the fifteenth-century treasure revealer Dorji Lingpa, was closely associated with Guensar and that the main icon in the Guensar temple was that of Chogden Gonpo. Was the relationship based then on reincarnation and not on bloodlines?

Another woman who is rumoured to have been born into this family was a sister of Tshokye Dorji who is remembered to have been a nun later in her life and living far away from the house. She is not even referred to by name; she is simply known as 'the nun'. She is said to have lived and meditated in a cave not very far from Ogyen Choling. The cave is still referred to as *Animoi Khar Phang Phok*, the Nun's Cave of Echoes. Many people, and even we as children, had a vague idea of the location of the cave but I did not know anyone who had been to it. In 2014, when one of my daughters was location-hunting for her film which was about a nun, we set out to look for the cave. We had a guide, and we knew the general direction but not the exact location. We were told that once we reached the right locality, we should shout out 'khar phang phok' and follow the echoes that would resonate. Once we were in the area, we guessed was the correct one, we shouted out 'khar phang phok', and sure enough, we heard the echoes of our voices. But we could not locate the cave because the echoes seemed to come from everywhere. Perhaps it is the shape of the land that creates these echoes. The name is so apt because the whole area seemed to echo. Just when we were about to give up our search, our guide shouted out to a passing cow herder in the distance, asking him where the cave was. He did not know the location, but he asked another cow herder behind a ridge far away from us. From behind the ridge the voice of the other cow herder guided us to the 'white cave on the rock face'.

Thrashing and pushing through thick layers of brushwood and bramble, we slowly climbed the steep terrain and managed to climb up to where there was indeed a rocky outcrop around which stone walls had been erected on two sides. Inside this shelter there was just enough space for a person to sit upright but that's all one could do – sit upright and not move at all.

I sat in that space for a while, long enough to know that the person who lived there must have been a dedicated meditator who lived a stoic life. The small enclosure would have bound the person into immobility. The narrow valley at the bottom of the hillside is now under cultivation. But during the nun's days it was a lake. The cave must have been an idyllic place for someone meditating, for it would have offered a perfect view of the lake, fringed by blue pine trees on all sides. I wondered whether she had been a truly religious devotee or whether the male-dominated household had driven her to a life of isolated austerity?

One enduring account of this nun is of how she saved Ogyen Choling when it was besieged by enemy forces sometime in the 1800s. According to the legend, she drew a pig head on a stone and, after imbuing it with mantras of protection, threw it with a sling towards the enemy camp. The stone landed near the leader of the invaders who immediately saw this as a sign of displeasure of the deities of the occupied household and lifted the siege. Is this simply a legend that grew out the fact that the household was indeed under siege sometime after 1853?

My favourite story about this nameless nun is the one in which she is visited by a yeti who sought her help to extract a bamboo splinter from its foot. The nun had been living somewhere else, and it was after her encounter with the mythical yeti that she chose to relocate to the Cave of Echoes. I have not heard anything about her previous meditation site except that it was far away from home in a more isolated and solitary place. These two women sort of fade into history, shrouded in myth and mystery. But for the next four generations, there is no record of any women being born into the family.

So, I am an anomaly. Born in the year of the water dragon, in 1952, I have survived to tell my tale. But my survival was possible only through drastic measures. Aie Kesang

Wangchu, who looked after me as a baby and toddler, often recalled that on a number of occasions my mother had been ready to give up on me and take me for dead, because I had the habit of becoming unconscious, or 'dying' often. We use the word '*sethd*' or 'die' for one who loses consciousness or faints. Although the precise translation of fainting or losing consciousness is '*dremed*', we rarely used that term. The elders always used 'sethd' to refer to my fainting spells and as it invokes a more dramatic image, I will use the term 'die' rather than faint.

I would become unconscious for all sorts of reasons that I as a toddler imagined were worth dying for. At the back of my parents' minds, they were conscious of the curse that girl children would not survive in this household. On one occasion, my mother even handed over my lifeless body to a relative, announcing that the preparation for the dead be made, which meant placing my body behind a curtain to isolate me from the living. 'You would stop breathing, your lips would turn blue, and all signs of life would drain away,' Aie Kesang remembered. My 'dying fits', as they called them, first happened when I was barely a year old.

The first time I became unconscious was when my aunt Dechen Choden, my mother's elder sister, was looking after me. My mother was pregnant with my younger brother, and pregnant mothers do not breastfeed babies for the fear of poisoning them with 'rotten milk'. My parents had also planned a pilgrimage to India, and a breastfeeding baby and a pregnant mother were not ideal for a long pilgrimage, so I was kept with my maternal aunt in Prah, Chummey. Aie Kesang Wangchu was my nanny at the time; she was with me and cared for me during the entire time I was with my aunt. It was Aie Kesang Wangchu who often narrated when and how my first 'death' happened. For all practical purposes, leaving me with my aunt was a very good decision, especially because my aunt had her own baby daughter, Chimme Lhamo, who was the same age as me and was still being breastfed. Aunt Dechen Choden offered to feed the two babies together.

Travel to India in the early 1950s was not an easy undertaking. It was a long journey that had to be carefully planned, needing complex arrangements. As neither of my parents spoke any Hindi or English, the translator and guide, the remarkable Jog Phajo, was asked to accompany them. At the time he may have been the only one in the whole of Tang valley who spoke Hindi very well and some English too. He did not just speak English, but he spoke the language with a dramatic flourish, sounding like an actor in a Shakespearean play. How is it that he spoke this way? My guess is that he had used an outdated English textbook to study the language. Although he was older than my parents, he outlived them both. I still have a clear memory of him, this man who was a respected friend of our family as the great translator who had taken my parents on a successful pilgrimage of India and brought them home safe, sound and content. A small man with a long goatee, he was agile and intelligent. After we had attended schools in India and learnt some English, when we came home for our holidays, he always insisted on talking to us in English. That was then when we realized that he spoke a different kind of English from what we learnt in school. He greeted us with, 'How art thou, Sire.' Goodbyes were always, 'Fare thee well till the morrow.'

One of the most memorable times we spent with him was looking at a picture book of the Second World War, with him reading the captions of the pictures for us. Page by page, he scanned and scrutinized each picture as he explained what was happening. The whole family would sit around him spellbound. Later, when we were able to read by ourselves, we realized what a storyteller he was. He had been inventing stories, perhaps to appeal to us children. For instance, a picture of German soldiers going through the rubble of buildings in a bombed and destroyed city, he had told us, were schoolchildren looking for their lost books – that's how much children valued books and education in that country, wherever it was! Of course, it never occurred to us to question the great translator.

Confident under the guidance of Jog Phajo, my parents were gone for at least two months. During this time my aunt treated me no differently from her own daughter, Chimme Lhamo. She often chided me playfully, calling me, 'the bully from Tang' because it seems I was often so possessive of my aunt that I was resentful when she fed her own daughter. I do not recall aunt Dechen Choden at all, because she died a few years later giving birth to twins. But I have this endearing image of her as she breastfed Chimme Lhamo and me at the same time, one on each breast. Both, Chimme Lhamo and I were just beginning to crawl at the time, so we must have been quite a handful. One afternoon, when my aunt was breastfeeding Chimme Lhamo and me, I fussed and crawled off, sulking because I probably wanted my aunt all to myself. By then I was beginning to stand up by holding on to a support. That day, the adults watched me as I looked for a support to hoist myself up. I chose a wooden barrel and, as I groped for a hold on its circular top, I caught hold of a big piece of lac. The lac fell on my head, which is when I 'died' for the first time. Lac is a resinous substance excreted out of the body of a scale insect *(Laccifer lacca)*. The substance is collected and used for dyeing yarn in various shades of red. After the colour has been extracted, the substance is moulded into a circular mass which is later processed by heating to make sealing wax. Because it has adhesive properties, it is also used for fastening and fixing handles of knives, sickles and other tools and implements. Lac was very useful to have around the house. But on that fateful day, its sole purpose was to alter my life by falling on my head. That circular mass propelled my life into a series of dying episodes.

According to Aie Kesang Wangchu, everybody panicked as I lay lifeless in my aunt's lap. Pouring a little cold water on people who faint is a common practice to revive the unconscious person. So, everybody was calling out for water. My mother's elder brother *Ashang* Kunzang Dorji ran down a long flight of stairs to the water source at some distance from the house and filled a kettle of water, but by the time he came back I had 'returned'. But he insisted on pouring a little water on me anyway, since he had taken so much trouble to go that far to get the water. This made everybody laugh and brought some relief to the tense situation. The funny thing was that nobody had thought of using the water that lay in the seven bowls offered on the altar which was within an arm's length away from where I was. My poor uncle was teased constantly about his ability to fetch water so fast. From then on, 'dying' and not showing any signs of life for periods of time, *tozan youn*, as long as 'it takes to eat a meal' became part of my lifestyle. I still do not know what caused these fainting spells. Perhaps there is a physiological explanation. Or maybe there is a psychological one. Perhaps it was my strategy to get the attention I sought. Remember, I was a very precious girl child born after many girl-less generations. Whatever the explanation, I am told I persisted in dying quite often. I, however, can remember only one incident of dying rather well when I fell from an oak tree.

I may have been about five or six years old. We were playing one of our favourite games near the oak forest below the nagtshang. It was a sunny afternoon and the caretakers who looked after us were sitting on the ledge of the chorten not far from us. They were soaking up the afternoon sun, enjoying the rare time of quiet with the children busily engaged in playing. There are several oak trees that grow from a depression. The branches of a particular tree spread low enough for some of the older and taller children standing on the edge of the depression to be able to pull it down. They would pull the branches as far as possible and hold on to them, and then let the branches swing back with a great whoosh with one of the boys hanging on the branch. Holding tightly on to the branch, we would swing, along with the branch, high into the air and dangle from it. What an exhilarating thrill it was to go flying up and then dangle from the branch for a while until the older ones helped the littler ones to get down. The older ones, of course, could jump back to the ground. I loved this game and begged the older ones to help me again and again. They were getting bored and tired and needed a new twist to the same old game. I was not aware of this. They helped me to get on the swinging branch, I went whoosh up into the air, a few feet off the ground but they left me dangling from the tree and ran away saying, 'A bear is coming.' Bears love acorns, and every night and sometimes even during the day, they would come to eat the fruit. We never encountered a bear, but often saw their dung, sometimes very fresh, still hot and steamy, which meant they had been there not long before us. I must have fallen off the branch and landed on the ground. Whether it was the fall or the fear of a bear, I am not sure, but I did 'die'.

When I regained consciousness, the woman who was my caregiver was holding me tight in her lap, her tears falling on my face, questioning and besieging me, 'Why do you always do this? Now what will I tell your parents?' I must have shown some signs of returning because she said, 'Don't tell your parents that you had a fall.' Of course, I wouldn't because we were forbidden to play in that spot during the time when the acorns were ripe!

It must have been around that time that a lama from Kham in Eastern Tibet visited our family. In those days many lamas from Tibet visited our family. The lama stayed with us for a while, and my parents begged him to cure me of my 'dying illness'. I don't remember him, but I was cured after his intervention. The lama pronounced that I was never meant to be a girl; that I should have been a boy. It was as simple as that. And so, he turned me into a boy. He performed the powerful ritual of *kaggo*, and I was exorcised of the negative influences that caused me to 'die' so regularly. The ritual sometimes takes on a sinister aspect and the ritualist whips the victim to exorcise the evil influences. If I was whipped, I do not recall it and thank goodness for that. I was renamed Dorje Jigji. This name is not merely a boy's name but the name of one of the most ferocious protective deities belonging to the Gelukpa School of Tibetan Buddhism.

I have always looked for stories about my namesake. Recently I heard a story about the origin of this bull-headed deity. I heard it from a learnt scholar so I cannot ignore it. It is said that once a band of cattle rustlers somewhere in Tibet stole a bull and decided to slaughter it secretly in a cave. They took the bull into what they assumed to be an empty cave; they did not see a hermit meditating in its dark depths. Only after they had slaughtered the bull by chopping off its head did they notice the hermit. They immediately killed the hermit in the same manner as they had killed the bull. As soon as the hermit's head was severed, they took the bull's head and placed it on the hermit's body, creating a new manifestation with the body of a human and the head of a bull. This new manifestation became an angry and evil spirit that caused great harm to all other livings beings until it was tamed and subjugated by an enlightened master and made to become a protector of Buddhism. I had not realized until then that my name had such a long and complex story. I did not like this version of the origin of my name.

There is a painting of this deity in one of the chapels in Ogyen Choling. Even as a child, with a name like that I felt elevated to the level of deities, lifted out of the mundane drudgery of the human world. I had never paid any attention to the painting of this deity in the past. But after the painting was pointed out to me, I immediately and completely bonded with the image. Growing up, as we did, with no books to read and playing with only the toys we could devise and craft ourselves, we often went to the temples whenever they were open to gaze at the wall paintings of the various Bodhisattvas and deities. The temple paintings were like picture books for us. We were never tired of listening to the various stories and looking at aspects of the sacred and mysterious personalities represented on our temple walls. The concept of preservation of cultural heritage did not exist for us then. The paintings on the walls were like a favourite book, fingered and dog-eared. In the absence of adults, we naturally engaged in impassioned conversations and debate as we exchanged stories about various images. On occasions when we were in the temple in the central tower, I would go straight to the fearsome deity, put my hands possessively over Dorje Jigji's image and with confidence and familiarity announce, 'I am this one.' At the time it did not matter to me who this deity was; I was his namesake. It is only now that I have learnt that this deity is a derivation of the Indian god Shiva in his fierce form of Bhairava (Terrifier). This dark bull-headed figure was adopted into the Buddhist pantheon as Dorji Jigji, the Death-Slayer and, although he has a terrifying appearance, he is one of the many manifestations of Chenrizi, Avaloketisvara, or the deity of Compassion. I feel much better about this version of the origin of my name.

Even today, whenever I go into this chapel, years after I was given back my original name, Kunzang Choden, I find myself gravitating towards the painting of Dorji Jigji. When I am with visitors, and when I feel that they are interested in some personal anecdotes, I sometimes indulge in my story of how I was for a part of my life called Dorji Jigji. Some years ago, when I was narrating the story to some guests, my younger brother Ugyen Rinzin, who was present, matter-of-factly pointed to an even more terrifying image of Dorji Dragtro, the deity standing on a nine-headed pig on the opposite wall, and said, 'I am this.' I immediately challenged him, asking him why and he said, 'Because this is the image of my visualization when I pray.' And I was magically transported to the days of my childhood when we engaged in animated banter and challenged each other on our knowledge and familiarity with the images in the temples.

It was not only the change in my name, but the lama advised that I was to dress as a boy and not be treated any differently from my brothers. I was elevated to the position of a deity with the name of a deity but was to be treated no differently from my brothers. The psychological impact was immense, beyond common understanding, but the important thing was that I was cured of my 'dying' curse. From then on, for the next four or five years, I was a boy until I was sent to school in India in 1962. Within those years I did not see myself as being different from my brothers and their friends. I followed them and tried to gain their acceptance and approval. I joined in most of their games and tried to be like them. Although I tried hard to be like the boys, I was quite repulsed when they played typical male games of war and hunting. I became a stunned and passive onlooker when they killed a rat and pinned it to a *linga* (a spirit trap) and shot arrows at it. The stories of Mao Tsetung and communism as being the destroyer of Buddhism in Tibet had made such an impression on us that we saw communism as the common enemy. The boys shot arrows at the dead rat, imagining it to be communists. I did not want to join them when they caught a piglet, killed it and roasted it by burning it in a bush. I went to catch fish in the Tang Chu with them, employing a very primitive method that ensured that we hardly caught any, at least at the times I was with them. Standing in the shallows of the river water, we guided little fish under boulders and then smashed another boulder on top of the one under which the fish was waiting to be killed. The fish were smarter and faster; most of the time they swam away long before the boulder in our hand hit the boulder in the river. On very rare occasions I saw the white belly of a dead fish as it floated to the surface when somebody managed a kill. I seem to recall vaguely that the fish were baked on a flat stone and eaten. I don't remember eating any, although I remember the boys kindling a fire under a flat stone by the river.

One of the games we played regularly was jumping from the hayloft of the horse stable on to the pile of horse manure outside. The boys would jump from a height of more than three metres from the hayloft to the manure pile below to see who jumped the farthest. They allowed my friend Tshering and I to jump too, but we were never in the competition. The game often ended with each of the boys standing on the edge of the loft and urinating on to the manure to see whose urine reached the farthest. Not to be left out, Tshering and I mimicked them. They thrust their pelvis forward, held their penises and shot out jets of urine. If they could do it, so could we. We took the same posture and thrust forward our pelvis, nearly toppling over the edge, and urinated on to our thighs and legs. I thought I should be like them but felt naturally drawn to being a girl. I spent much of my time seeking women's company. Every day there were women in the loom rooms weaving fabrics; talking, laughing, teasing and sharing their stories, and that is where I spent many hours.

During the bureaucratic process of school registration, my name was changed back to Kunzang Choden because the Bhutanese officials thought Dorji Jigji was too unusual a name. I had to reorient to my new-old name, and my own relatives and acquaintances slowly shifted to calling me by my original name, while I had to make a special effort to answer to Kunzang Choden. The only two people who never stopped calling me Jigji to the end of their lives were Her Majesty the Royal Grandmother Ashi Phuntsho Choden who died in 2003 and the first home minister of Bhutan, Lyonpo Tamshing Jakar who died in 1989. I often wish that the people who registered me for school had been more open-minded and let me simply be Jigji. Maybe I could have avoided all the problems I experienced later and continue to experience because of my name, Kunzang Choden.

To begin with, soon after the change in name and only after a few days of being in the boarding school, a nun in the school administration detected that my first name and my father's first name were the same, Kunzang. My father's name was Kunzang Dorji. By her logic she concluded that my father's name must be Dorji Kunzang and mine must be Choden Kunzang. Fortunately, she had the wisdom and the courtesy to confirm what she considered to be an oversight. Employing an interpreter, she told me that she wanted to correct my name according to her deduction because children must take their father's surname. Even after being scolded and humiliated with a cursory slap, I tearfully but bravely defended our names; father remained Kunzang Dorji and my name continues to be Kunzang Choden.

That was not the end of the problems with my name. The irony is that my name can be spelled in diverse ways in English, and my name has been spelled in three ways on three different important documents. The last confrontation I had over my name was in 2008 at the American Embassy in Delhi when I had applied for a visa. Their records showed that I had entered the USA on a previous trip where my name had been written as 'Kuenzang' and now I was holding a passport with my name written as 'Kunzang'. The immigration officer kindly but very sternly warned me, 'For your own good I am telling you this. Only terrorists, murderers, smugglers and bad people consistently spell their names differently. Go home and immediately regularize the spelling of your name.'

I knew I was not a terrorist, murderer or a bad person. I also knew I had juggled names and identities throughout my life. For my own good I wish they had let me be Dorji Jigji, a girl with a boy's name.

7

Reversing Astrological Predictions

THROUGHOUT THEIR LIVES WE referred to our father as *Acho* or older brother and mother as *Nene* or paternal aunt. Following convention, a few days after my eldest brother Rinzin Dorji was born, in the year of the bull coinciding with 1949, his astrological chart was made. One of the findings was that the baby was not compatible with his parents. Father, who was also born in the year of the bull, and mother, who was born in the year of the sheep, were not suitable to be parents to their newborn baby. They were warned that if my brother acknowledged his parents as his parents, it would be harmful to all concerned. In my brother's case the consequences would be dire. If he was to refer to them as his parents, their lives would be shortened. There was nothing alarming about such a prediction; such findings were common, Sometimes, in such cases, other people, relatives or friends are invited to become symbolic parents to babies. In my brother's case, to avert any disaster, he was taught to call his father Acho, or older brother, and his mother became Nene or aunt. As often happens, those of us who followed him in birth also copied him in the way we addressed father and mother. Problems arose again when by custom we began to add the prefix 'Acho' to our eldest brother, Rinzin. To distinguish our two 'older brothers', father was thus referred to as Acho *Gigpala* or Big Older Brother, which alluded specifically to his physical size rather than to his position of birth. Older brother became Acho Rinzin. But even with this rather complicated arrangement, the ominous prediction could not be averted, and our parents died in the prime of their lives.

Mother liked to talk to us about incidents connected with our births. She especially liked to talk about the special signs that accompanied some of our births. She would smile warmly each time she recalled the ragged Tibetan beggar who walked into the room next to where she had just given birth to her eldest son, Rinzin Dorji. The beggar had come in unseen by all, and was loudly chanting the prayer of Sampa Lhendup (the prayer to Guru Rinpoche that spontaneously fulfils all wishes) as he walked in. She marvelled at how he had managed to get past, unnoticed by all the people in the courtyard, the weavers in the loom rooms and the servants everywhere, to come into the private quarters of the family. Although she didn't say it, I think she took this to be an auspicious sign, and I know that she thought her firstborn was special. She maintained her subtle partiality towards him till the end. He was the only one of us who had a chance to be blessed by her own father, our grandfather, Chummey drungpa Gempo Dorji. It was grandfather who had named his grandson Rinzin Dorji.

I heard it often enough to recall that the signs were also very auspicious for my younger brother, Sonam Wangchuk. Not on the exact day of his birth, but on the day that my second brother, who is a year younger than me, was to be taken out of the house for the first time, the signs were remarkably special. The ritual of *lhabsang,* fumigation for purifying the atmosphere and symbolically cleansing the mother and child of the birth pollution, must be conducted three days after the birth of every baby. Only after this ritual are the mother and child allowed to go outside the house. The respected Lopon Tsedarla, a religious practitioner, conducted the ritual. At the conclusion of the ritual, Lopon sprinkled holy water and burnt special incense. As a part of the ritual, all the participants followed Lopon who led the procession circumambulating the house, chanting prayers as he rang the hand bell and sprinkled holy water. Mother and the baby followed as well, accompanied by family members and others who had been involved with the birthing. While the little procession was doing the circumambulation there was a sudden excitement. Phub Dorji, a servant of the household, who had been sent with a parcel to Her Majesty the Queen Mother Ashi Phuntsho Choden some days ago, happened to return just then. He was carrying a big packet wrapped up in his *kabney* (the white shawl men used as a ceremonial scarf) with parcels from the Queen Mother. On top was a large jack fruit. Immediately aware of the coincidence of the timing of his arrival, the jovial parcel bearer swaggered towards the house, and everybody saw the lone peacock feather that stuck out boldly from the top of the luggage. To have the subtropical jack fruit in cool temperate Ogyen Choling, was a rare extravagance that only the royal family could favour us with. Mother probably took this to be a royal blessing for her newborn. The peacock feather, used exclusively during prayers and rituals to sprinkle holy water, was also a very rare item. The coincidence of these two objects coming together was doubly auspicious. My parents were sure that their second son would also be a special child. They probably thought that he was marked to serve the King in the Royal Court.

As Sonam grew older, he was trained by father to wear a small sword in a silver-gilded scabbard. He was taught the court etiquette, and I remember how he was, even as a child, trained to deliver verbal messages from father to the servants. They imagined that he would be required to do that at the court, to carry the King's commands to the courtiers (a task referred to as *kachor*). Father's partiality towards this child was obvious in the innovative toys that he created for him. Once he devised a wooden sheep with wheels and the older children had to pull the sheep for Sonam. The idea of the sheep progressed to a wooden cart. Father fashioned the cart with wooden wheels that was to be pulled by a small mule which he selected from among our horses. Father had probably been inspired by the horse-drawn carts he had seen in India. The use of the cart had to be discontinued after its first trial. My elder brother Rinzin Dorji and our cousin Ugyen Namgyel were made to ride in the cart as a test. There was a serious technical problem in the construction of the cart. As the mule walked, and then galloped, the cart hit the mule's hind legs which frightened it into a wild frenzy. The mule kicked and galloped erratically as the stunned onlookers shouted in panic for the animal to stop. Finally, when the mule could be contained, two very disoriented and slightly bloodied boys got out of the wooden cart. Father considered Sonam Wangchuk too young for this trial run; I think he was considered too precious.

After my parents died, our lives did not play out in the ways they had imagined for us. I think my father wanted to present Sonam Wangchuk to the Royal Court as it was a common family tradition. My grandfather's brother Thinley had been sent to the Royal Court, and then my father's own younger brother Ugyen Wangdi was also sent into the service of the Second King. But father died when my brother was still a small boy. When our parents died, their dream of presenting their son to serve the King died with them.

My youngest brother Ugyen Rinzin was a very small baby, 'just a bundle of wrinkles', so mother spontaneously called him 'Denma' which means wrinkles. It always amused me to hear people guessing the origin and the significance of his name. Many people thought he was named after Denma Tsangma, the commander of the legendary King Gesar of Ling. Little Denma was plagued by serious health problems, and mother did everything she possibly could to save him and help him regain his health. He had such a severe case of chicken pox that his body was covered with sores that festered, and his clothes stuck to his sores. Mother had devised her own method to make sure that his clothing did not stick to his body. In those days plastic sheets were rare, but she found one which she put on a bamboo frame so that the sheet did not come in direct contact with his body, but he was still warmly covered. When he was about three years old, she took him to bathe in Dhur *tsachu*, the medicinal hot sulphur springs in the northern part of Choekor valley. These hot springs at the north end of the valley adjacent to Tang are still very popular for people with all sorts of ailments. Apparently, Denma's health improved immediately. Mother spent her most anxious moments with this baby. She often said that he was her most precious child because life was given to him so hesitantly. Mother told us of an incident when he was a baby and sleeping in a tent, when they were in Lhuentse. The men were playing archery nearby and a stray arrow came through the tent and landed next to the sleeping baby's head, missing it by inches. Denma had a narrow escape. Years later, when as an adult he suffered a bout of ill health, Denma went to bathe in Dhur tsachu because he was convinced of the positive effect of the hot springs. And once again they did not disappoint him.

My mother could not remember any special signs at my birth except that I was the first girl born after several generations of no female children in my paternal house. The anxiety of 'will this girl live past her infancy?' seems to have been the unspoken thought on everybody's mind. She sometimes mentioned that during labour she did not lie down; she walked around the room. Then when she was on her way to the toilet, while crossing the threshold separating her bedroom and the toilet, I was born. I was literally born on the threshold. Not so auspicious or exciting but the story of my birth always ended with the comment, so fortunate that you were not born into the toilet pit. I could have been lost at birth. The long-drop toilet pit, which is several metres long, would have meant certain death for a newborn baby. What mother recalled was that when I learnt to say my first words, they were to ask for very special food. Later, every time a crow cawed, I used to say, 'The crow is saying, "Dorji Jigji coco caw"', which means give Dorji Jigji a fried egg. She teased me, saying I demanded and ate more fried eggs than all her other children.

Mother had a miscarriage after a fall from the stairs in the utse and she also gave birth to another son who died in his infancy. I have a hazy memory of standing at the doorway not knowing what to do as I watched a small reddish baby being bathed in a shallow oblong wooden bowl near a blazing fire in the hearth in the room where he was born. Mother was sitting on the floor, bending towards the baby as she supported him in the tub with her left hand, letting water drops from her right hand dribble on to the baby. It was such a tender, ephemeral picture of mother and child, so delicate and warm. I carry this picture of my little brother. But before we had a chance to get to know him, he was sick, and we could not be with him. In those days it was common for babies to succumb to any one of the many childhood diseases which were rampant and uncontrollable. My little brother died of whooping cough as did many other babies in the village that year. At the time my father was in Tibet on a trading trip, and it would have taken days to reach him. So, my uncle Ugyen Wangdi came from Wangdue Choling palace to help with the death rituals.

After a few days of serious whispers and long silences, one morning, still sleep-ridden and groggy, I woke up early to hear subdued noises and some unusual activity. I stayed at a distance as the men conversed in hurried whispers. According to astrologers, my brother's dead body could not be taken out through the main door. He had to exit the house from the northern side but there were no doors towards the north. So, a wooden wall had to be taken down and his corpse was placed in a wooden box which was lowered to the ground by means of a rope. Babies until the age of eight years cannot be cremated, so their bodies are placed inside boxes or old baskets and then taken to the river. This practice is still common in some rural areas to this day. The boxes and baskets are harnessed to boulders and the river left to consume them. Slowly, over time, the corpses are washed away or eaten by the fish. Diarrhoeal diseases were the biggest killer in those days. Mothers would helplessly watch their babies waste away until 'the cheeks of their bottoms became small circles' on bony bodies. There was nothing to be done to save their babies; neither could anyone ignore the nondescript bundles harnessed to boulders in the river after an epidemic. Long after my brother's death, whenever we went to the river, I always had the uncanny fear that I would come across his body. I never did.

We would have been six siblings but only four of us survived to adulthood.

8

The Family Man

FATHER WAS MORE THAN just the head of the household. As a biased daughter, I will unapologetically say that he was also a loving and caring family man. True, much of his time had to be dedicated to fulfilling his duties as the patriarch of the family and the lord of the estate, but there was one daily routine he would not compromise on for anything. Eating breakfast together with the family was the most important tradition. Our days began only after we had eaten our first meal of the day together. Family members, guests and some of the *kadroepas*, advisors and favoured elderly people who stayed with my father as companions or advisors, gathered in the big east-facing reception room just when the sun's rays spilled into it, casting a warm glow and slowly brightening it up. Father sat on a slightly raised seat in the centre, and we sat on the floor in a semicircle around him. Mother sat in the middle of the semicircle with the breakfast items in front of her. Mother served breakfast every day. We all had our individual bowls, baskets and *toreys*, square cloths for receiving rice. Breakfast invariably consisted of a thick rice soup, *shaythu*, cooked with strands of dried cheese or bones, spiced with ginger and a dash of Sichuan peppers which was barely noticeable – just a hint of its flavourful, woody taste. Mother served as many refills as we desired of the soup. *Suja* or butter tea was served out of a *sujai jamche*, an elegant wooden container. The container was black with delicate patterns in red vermilion around its brim. Tea was served with a round brass ladle with a wooden handle. The ladle had a small hole in it. It was tricky to handle. I used to marvel at how skilfully mother immersed the ladle into the teapot without making a sound and poured out the tea into each individual cup without any spills. It was always white fragrant rice from our estate in Lhuentse that we ate for breakfast. The rice was served out of a brass pot, *soenzar dik*, with a copper lid. There was an established etiquette in eating the breakfast rice. When we were very little, we were allowed to eat the rice from our personal *bangchung*, bamboo basket, but as we got older, father wanted us to learn to eat breakfast rice as it was meant to be eaten. While we were served rice in our individual bangchung at other meals, breakfast rice had to be received in our cupped palms. The mass of rice was brought together into a ball and bits of it had to be broken off to be eaten with condiments such as chilli pastes, fresh chilli salads and, occasionally, roasted and sliced dried meat.

It was during this meal that conversations flowed easily and there was always a sense of congeniality. Yet, a certain decorum had to be maintained. We sat cross-legged on the floor, our backs straight and, even though we were small children, father did not tolerate undue fussing. The breakfast service followed a standard procedure according to the hierarchy. Father was served first, then Lopon Tsedarla, the oldest religious personality in the village, who had been father's teacher, then guests, followed by my eldest brother, then the other children and then finally the kadroepas. We would only start to eat after Lopon Tserdarla had said the *jamchoed*, grace for tea offering. Father kept an eye on how we behaved. I was always seated to the right side of my father, and he watched me especially intensely during a short period of time when I had developed a strange habit of sticking out my tongue to place my food on it rather than putting the food into my mouth, much like a lizard catching its prey. I had once seen our yak herder, a woman, doing this, and was fascinated. I was told that the woman and her family rarely ate rice, so she did not know how to eat it properly which is why she ate the way she did. I tried to copy her and kept trying until it became a habit. My parents were concerned and father thought of a way of stopping this ungainly habit. Without any fuss or drama, he kept a big needle near him. Whenever I stuck out my tongue, he picked up the needle. I don't think he ever pricked my tongue with it even though he threatened to. I was extra conscious of every mouthful I ate and soon stopped sticking out my tongue.

At breakfast, mother had little time for herself as she had to refill everybody's small bowls continually. I can see her sitting in her serving position alert and attentive, making sure she did not miss any empty bowls. When I think of these breakfast sessions, I see my mother with a handful of rice in her basket relishing an avocado which she would have softened by rolling it in her palms to eat the soft pulp. Mother loved avocados and enjoyed them when they were in season. The small native avocados grew in the subtropics in the Lhuentse district, and she got them every year. People travelling through the avocado forests would thoughtfully bring some back for her. This was her one indulgence, rice with avocado. She distinguished two kinds of the fruit, *margoli*, butter avocados, which were bigger and fleshier, and the *prahgoli*, monkey avocados, which were smaller and had very little flesh. She liked both. We could not just get up and leave when we were finished. We had to wait until father indicated that the meal was over. The servants would then come and remove the utensils and sweep the floor, whether it was dirty or not – more a ceremonial sweeping – only then could we leave.

The lunch service was the same as breakfast. We would be seated in the same order in the same room. Our bangchung was generously filled with rice, and our individual bowls would be handed to us. The *tsoem*, vegetable and meat dishes, were brought in pans by the servants, who came in balancing the pans on their upturned palms raised over their left shoulders and served by them. Usually there would be two kinds of tsoem, and buttermilk was rarely missing. We kept some cows near the house to have a constant supply of milk and buttermilk. The main supply came from our two herds of cattle which grazed in the faraway pastures. The herders had *zeuyug*, assistants, who had to bring us timely supplies of dairy products. Again, father insisted on us eating in a particular manner. The bangchung had to be placed on our laps and one bowl of tsoem held level with the bangchung with our left hand. We were all expected to eat with the fingers of our right hands. We were not allowed to pop the rice into our mouth before we made it into small balls; we then had to put it into our mouths discreetly. Father taught us how to do this. As a final touch, we had to close our fists over the rice and move our right ring fingers to gracefully push the balls into our mouth. The bowls of the other tsoems could not be spread out in front of us but kept on our right. We could start eating only after someone had said the *tomchoed*, the meal-offering grace.

We were privileged to eat rice for nearly all our meals. But the servants could eat rice only rarely, so they yearned for it. The servants ate what was left in our bangchung, so we were taught to be careful not to mess up the rice and eat only from one side, keeping the other side untouched. One servant, Sangye, a grumpy, unfriendly man whom I was afraid of, was the one who always brought in my basket of rice. And he would make sure that there was always some rice left for him. On the pretext of checking to see if we needed refills, he would quickly come into the room and make a threatening fist at me to remind me to leave some rice for him at every meal. I dared not to eat more than half of my serving.

Dinners were much simpler, and it was usually only the family eating together. Sometimes, when our parents were preoccupied, we children had our meals by ourselves. Dinners were usually dull. They comprised mostly rice and vegetable or a meat dish and buttermilk. Conversation was uninteresting and we behaved in an unruly, unrestrained and childish way. We ate by the light of flickering oil lamps, and I was often too sleepy to enjoy the meal.

After my parents acquired a radio, our after-dinner ritual was to sit together in our parents' bedroom to listen to it. I recall that they bought it from Dasho Lhunentsepa; it was second-hand. It was a big wooden box with knobs to twiddle and switches to fiddle with and made all sorts of buzzing, twitchy static noises before some audible voices and music came on. It had an aerial. A wire was attached to it and had to be fixed on a tall pole outside the bedroom window. The wire had to be adjusted and readjusted until the radio got reception. What my parents enjoyed was the Tibetan broadcast on All-India Radio, including the programme which taught Tibetans Hindi. The first Hindi word I learnt was *pyala* or cup. The whole family learnt to say pyala for any cup or bowl we had. I used to suffer through the Chinese opera night after night. My parents listened to it because it was the most audible programme – it was clear; there was no static and no disturbance. One night, I was half asleep as usual and my parents were urging us to go to bed, but my elder brother Rinzin wanted to stay and listen to the radio and told me to stay awake. When I couldn't stay awake, he threw a bamboo pen container at me, which missed me but hit my father on his cheek. Against all the clamour of Chinese theatrics, of high-pitched screams amidst clashing gongs and crushing cymbals in the background, my mother calmly treated my father with the indispensable panacea for all wounds, aches and pains – iodine tincture, the miracle medicine – and then rubbed a white cream from a round flat container on the wound. I was fully awake by now and my parents did not scold or punish us. The only concern was that father was leaving for India the next day for his annual trading trip and would he be all right to travel. Everybody was thankful that his eye was spared. He must have been all right because he left for India the next day. The iodine had cured him.

Iodine, which we called '*iden*', had come into our lives curing all sorts of ailments. The black glass bottle, which was within constant reach of my parents, was used for everything that caused pain. Besides all fresh wounds and cuts, bits of cloth soaked in iodine were given to people with toothache; people asked for iodine to apply to their goitres; and my elder brother, who had chronic ear infection, received drops of the tincture in his offending ear. I remember how I cried with him as I watched him stomping his feet in pain. It was the same remedy that was applied to my scraped inner thigh when I fell into a wooden barrel. I had tried to stand on that upturned barrel to look over a fence and watch the forbidden procession of a dead bear being carried into the compound. My father had killed it; its carcass was being brought in to be skinned and the meat cooked to be fed to our ploughing bulls. These bulls needed extra strength and nutritious supplements like the rare bear meat. While my brothers were already part of the procession, I was told not to look at it as it would be polluting for a girl to be exposed to it. But forbidden fruit is always the sweetest and I watched it from behind a fence until the support I was standing on gave way. I screamed into obliviousness when 'iden' was applied to the scratches and deep welts that marked my inner thighs. But I was obviously cured. The iodine could and did cure all sorts of wounds, but not the man who was gorged by a bull. There was panic in the village when a man called Uraipa Nadola was gorged in the stomach by his bull and his guts were spilling out. Nadola was feeding his ploughing bulls with some wild honey for their hard work in the field when the bull attacked him. Pasangla, who was attending to Uraipa Nadola, came to my father for advice when he did not know what else to do. I remember my father telling him to take a clean plank of wood and press it against the wound to keep the entrails from spilling out of the belly and stitch up the gaping hole. I was so convinced of the curative aspects of iodine that I meekly suggested using iodine and received blank and irritated looks from all the adults present. Sadly, the man died within hours.

My parents worked as a team and did all sorts of things together like gardening, listening to the radio, going for walks, but the most important partnership between them developed after they acquired a camera. It was a Leica. Photography became their joint passion, and they would spend hours together processing the films, which we were told was called *par khro ma la*, 'washing pictures'. They had constructed a small yak-hair tent as their dark room in one corner of the altar room – that's how significant their new-found hobby was: it deserved a place in the most sacred room in the house. They would proudly emerge from the tent with long strips of negatives. I think these negatives had to be taken somewhere else to be made into prints. Their initial attempts were wasted, and we often saw blank black strips with no images hanging on the lines in the dark room. We were forbidden to touch anything because there was poison in the chemicals that were used. Over time, some photographs entered our lives; the initial blurry ones were gradually replaced by more defined images. In the early 2000s I collected whatever negatives had survived the ravages of time, neglect and abuse and took all of them to a photo shop in Delhi and had them printed. My daughter printed some negatives while she worked in her college photo lab in the USA, and we now treasure those prints which reveal some historical images. The camera outlived my parents, and we had it in our possession for a while until my elder brother Rinzin took it to a photographer in Thimphu to repair it, but we never saw it or heard about it again.

As long as I can remember, my father was a smoker. His cigarettes came in tins. It was mostly the brand 555. When he ran out of cigarettes, he had prepared tobacco and special papers to roll his own. When his supply ran out completely, I recall mother preparing the tobacco from the dried tobacco leaves that they imported from India. Dried tobacco leaves were always an important commodity that were included in the shopping list for India. Two or three of these brown and brittle dried leaves were given as presents and never failed to bring a smile to the face of the recipients. A bowl of salt and the tobacco leaves seemed like the standard gift my father gave to people when he returned from his trading trips to India. There were more people using snuff than smokers, those days. Older people also used tobacco in their betel quid to give it that extra kick.

My mother was never quite pleased with father's smoking habit, but she let him indulge in this vice and even helped to ensure that he was never out of tobacco, because it made him happy. She used the dried leaves to prepare his rolled cigarettes. She would wet the leaves and then shred them finely. The shredded matter was then mixed with some ingredients. I am not sure what was included but I think ara and sugar were. Then the prepared tobacco was spread out to dry. The pungent smell would waft through the rooms when it was ready for use. I know that father smoked cigarettes from paper packets later. I remember because we children used to fight over the empty packets. It was a small packet with a picture of a man in a top hat looking out of a frame. The packet was purple and black, and we couldn't read the letters on it. The only person who could read English, Jog Phajo, told us that the words written on the packet said, 'Passing show', but we used to exaggeratedly say *passing ga shaaw*, because we liked the sound of the foreign words.

Tobacco gained its hold on some people by about the mid-1950s, when I was studying in the home school my father had already started. We kept losing pages of our books which we kept in the school room. It took some time to find out why this was happening. Eventually, we discovered that one of the horse attendants, Ragola, had found the paper from our books perfect for rolling his cigarettes! To ensure a sustained supply of tobacco, especially between one trading trip and the next, my father even convinced my mother to plant tobacco in Ogyen Choling. Mother did grow some plants in a plot just next to the family's pig sty. She probably thought that the two despicable activities – rearing pigs for slaughter and growing tobacco for smoking – were equally sinful. I remember seeing the patch of lush plants growing near the grunting pigs wallowing in the slushy pen being fattened for slaughter, but I do not know if the tobacco was ever used.

9

Pleasures, Treasures and an Evil Spirit

Some of our favourite childhood games were built around mimicking adults. My brothers and other playmates made imaginary kitchens and cooked meals of mud and leaves. We played house, making shelters with sticks and branches. I remember the cosmos plants, with pink and white flowers, which we called 'Indian flowers', that grew wildly in the compound. By late autumn the plants would dry up, and the dried plants were ideal for constructing our houses. The tall stems were brittle enough to break to size with our bare hands, making them easily usable. Sometimes, we smoked the dried pulps from the stems. We would push out the dried pulp in the stems with a stick and they came out looking like cigarettes. We lit them, sometimes with a match, which were rare and precious, but mostly used a cinder from the kitchen to light them up. We would sit in our houses made of cosmos stalks and smoke these tasteless pulps.

We played with dried beans, imagining them to be cattle and we were the cattle herders. The shiny beans of different colours and sizes could engage us for hours. Any of the stone walls in our compound, with their crevices and bumps, became dangerous and daunting climbs for our cattle, and the cracks between the floor planks became rivers that the animals had to ford. It was not customary for parents or other adults to join in our imaginary games with us. So, unconstrained by adult intervention, our imaginations ran wild.

One of the most enduring themes of our games was performing religious rituals. We saw the adults performing them almost every day, and that was something that we never tired of imitating. It was perhaps the complexity of the activities, where gods and humans interacted and there were standard procedures of chanting litanies, making offerings of food and temple music, that stoked our imagination.

Although I do not remember adults ever joining in our games, we were sometimes invited to join them on their leisure walks. There were days when father and mother would go on *khamsang*. Translated literally from Bumthangkha, 'khamsang' means 'for good health'. The farmers were constantly engaged in physical activities that were strenuous and exacting, and they certainly did not need to go for strolls or walk for 'good health'. A khamsang that required some physical exertion was restricted to those who basically did not have to exert themselves physically. Because mother, as the mistress of the house, was constantly on the move doing numerous chores, climbing up and down flights of stairs and going from one storeroom to another, it was father who needed these walks because he had duties that required him to sit for long hours at a time. In modern terms he did sedentary office work, keeping records, correspondence, and meeting people. He needed some physical exercise, and mother was always happy to accompany him.

But these walks were not private walks where just the two of them went together. These were big events. The children were included, and the servants and often guests were invited to join in. These walks were leisurely affairs and mother often prepared tea and snacks which the servants carried along with carpets which were taken to sit on. On some occasions, the bag with the game of dice was also taken along.

There were regular paths for such walks. When we went eastwards, climbing a gentle slope, it was to the water-run prayer mill that we would go. The water from the spring at this prayer mill was blessed by the deity *Tsepami Amitayus*. This spring was called *Tsepami drupchu* (the spring of the Buddha of longevity). A mere wash in the spring or drinking from it was meant to increase one's life expectancy. On occasion when we did go there, the walks were often khamsang *ning thrue* or a 'walk for health and bath'. On such walks, the big brass and copper cauldrons for heating water were also carried by the servants. There was a small ledge in front of a small *mani* wall (prayer wall) between the prayer mill and a wheat field where a makeshift stove would be lit and water heated in the cauldrons. One cauldron was placed near the waterspout and the hot water from the cauldron on the fire was mixed with the cold water from the spring. We children were made to sit in the bath one after another. The adults would usually just remove the upper parts of their clothing and wash their heads under the cold running water from the wooden spout.

We were made to sit in the cauldrons and soak in the hot water; later, we would be scrubbed hard. Because baths were rare, even for privileged children like us, there was always much to be scrubbed off our bodies. Our hands and legs were pulled out of the water to rest over the rim of the cauldrons and pressed and rubbed so hard we could hear the thumb of the person bathing us pressing and sliding over our bodies. This action, *puta tzer ma la*, or 'pressing for noodles', brought out the dirt and dead skin in rolls. We had no commercial shampoo, so borax soda was used for our hair, and a mock orange (*philadelphus*) bush that grew near the bathing spot was used like a soap. Mock orange bushes grow abundantly in the area and have a pleasantly faint fragrance. The tender stems and leaves from this bush have a slippery feel like soap when rubbed that form a lather. After such a bath you almost felt like a whole layer of your body had been peeled off. I can still feel the lethargic sensation that melted my legs and made them buckle under me after the long soaking baths in the sun. The elders would sit with their backs to the sun drawing up the warmth and chanting prayers quietly or talking and telling stories. Doused by the heat of the water and drenched by the sun, we just lay around until the cold wind drove us home.

This was one of our favourite spots, especially on warm, sunny days. Nostalgia takes me there often, but the place has changed. It saddens me to see how changes in people's mindscape are reflected in how they view and treat the physical landscape. The owners of the wheat field have now dug up patches of unused lands along the sides of their fields to enlarge them. The little patches of natural green are no longer there. Enterprising farmers see no limits to what they can have and have no qualms about how they can get what they want. Even the ledge in front of the mani wall where we used to heat the water is now a very narrow strip barely wide enough for a foothold.

We went for khamsang in different directions from the house. When we went northwards, it was past the small chorten at the end of the village, past the cremation gorge and across to a spot where there were some gigantic boulders stacked together in a curious formation. This spot, *Gor khrak khrok la*, or 'jutting rocks', was considered a nuisance by the elders. Cattle and people carrying their firewood, buckwheat straw and other bulging luggage, found it an especially difficult place to manoeuvre. But this stack of boulders never failed to engage us children, leading us into a fantasy world and stimulating our imaginations. We often found ourselves exploring and scrutinizing the patterns on the rocks. There were footprint-like impressions on the surface of some of the rocks which we believed were those of the heroes of the past. Inspired by the popular folk belief that there were three *kalpa* or aeons in cyclical time, we believed that these rocks existed from the time of the past aeon. According to folklore, time is divided into three segments and sentient life forms appear, manifest themselves and disappear through these aeons. We believed that the first aeon was over, and we were living in the second aeon when people were like we are today. In the past aeon people were colossal in size and lived long lives, hundreds of years, we were told. In the present aeon, human beings had diminished in size and our life expectancy had also lowered. In the third aeon, which would be in the future, the phenomena of *me lo chupa* (life expectancy of ten years) would commence. In that aeon people would live for only ten years and they would be only a foot in height. With unquestioning faith in folklore, we were naturally enthralled by any evidence of the past aeon and terrified of the imminent third cycle.

There were two large boulders at Jutting Rock which really caught our imagination, a big flat piece of stone lying on the ground with another large boulder hanging from a distance above it. The boulder on the ground had a strange shallow depression. Thinking about it now, it did not look anything like footprints, but we were convinced they were made by heroes of the past aeon. We imagined the impressions were made when our gigantic heroes of the past stepped from the overhanging rock on to the rock below and that the smudged impression was created when one of them slipped while landing. There was also what we thought was a footprint on the overhanging boulder from where the hero had jumped. We would place one foot in the footprint in the higher rock and spend hours trying to jump from there on to the one below and trying to land our feet in the depression. This was a dangerous if not impossible endeavour. But we kept at it, encouraged by the knowledge of people whom we believed had succeeded before us. I mostly watched the boys attempt this but occasionally I would summon all my courage, climb on to the overhanging rock and then sheepishly walk away without jumping. The boys challenged each other fearlessly and repeatedly jumped but could rarely land their feet in the depression. People of our aeon were clearly no match for those of the past.

There were also curious cracks in one of these rocks that we would touch in secret wonder. These holes, we were told, were the places where the yetis honed their penises! Yes, they honed them like knives on a sharpening stone. What powerful and mysterious creatures these yetis must be! The Jutting Rocks were the living testimony of the heroes from the past aeon compounded by the mystery of the elusive yetis lurking in the high mountains. Subsequently, many of the rocks were disfigured, blasted and chipped off by enterprising people who collected stones for house construction. More recently the rocks have been cleared away for building a farm road to access the fields in the area. Some remnants have survived, however, as if to remind me of the times gone by.

After passing Jutting Rocks we would pass a formidable place called *Sangdag* where the malevolent, spirit lives. This was another rock formation surrounded by thick forests of blue pine trees, thorny bushes and vines that strangled the trees that they clung to. This spooky place was the territory of a malevolent spirit of the *dued* category. This category of spirits is not only unfriendly but also outright antagonistic to human beings. People who fell ill after passing this place were said to be imprisoned by this spirit and tied up in yak-hair ropes. They were released only after placatory rites were performed. Cattle that sometimes went missing in the forests in this vicinity were believed to have been hidden by this mean spirit. Many people, especially children, are still afraid to go past this place on their own. Had anyone seen the dued? Oh yes! According to Akhu lama, at least two elders from the village who happened to pass the place had seen an enormous man in a black woollen gho with straggly grey hair on his huge head and unruly hair sprouting from his savage face. He was seen sleeping in the meadow nearby, enjoying the warmth of the sun and then walked back into the sheer rock face as if it were an open door. One of the men who saw the spirit said he even saw the beads of sweat on the spirit's face. That is how close he had come to the spirit! At other times he manifests himself as a lone wild boar or a deer which vanishes into thin air when human beings approach.

Today the spirit seems to have lost some of its powers. A few years ago, someone from the village dared to cut down the gigantic and ancient blue pine tree that was said to be the dued's *sokshing* or life force tree (*Sok* refers to life force, *shing* means tree) meaning that the life force of the spirit was attached to the tree. The tree was felled illegally for firewood. Everyone in the village secretly murmured their disapproval but, afraid of offending the tree cutter, nobody said anything outright. But somebody secretly reported the matter to the forestry office. The foresters do not come to check the forests until they are alerted. The forestry officials came, and it was not clear what transpired between the tree cutter and the officials. Maybe it was settled amicably or perhaps there was a fine involved. The tree cutter and his family were unaffected, but for some time there was a frenzy of people making placatory rituals to appease the offended dued who was causing all sorts of illnesses among the villagers. The typical symptoms were aches, pains, sleep deprivation and anxiety. Many elderly women victims showed all these symptoms. They wondered aloud, 'What kind of a dued has he become now? He can do nothing to the actual man who cut the tree, but he discriminates against the weak, frail and especially women in the village?' Gender bias exists in the spirit world too, I thought.

When the dued was still powerful, its power manifested in various ways. I heard with awe and curiosity the story of the hidden treasure. It was said that our ancestors had buried their treasures when they were subjected to *bangche* (raids and plundering) by the strongmen of the country. It was a nasty custom that had prevailed for some time. Although I have never experienced it in my own lifetime, I had heard much about this practice, and it felt like they had taken place recently. People talked about these raids in fear and secrecy. It was said that the more powerful lords could, on very flimsy pretexts, command raids on the homes of those who were seen to possess wealth or were a real or imagined threat to their power. Moveable assets like jewellery, clothes and other precious items were seized. Our ancestors were targets of these humiliating and dehumanizing raids, so they had become experts at hiding their assets on short notice. No maps or written statements of the exact places of buried treasures were kept, in case they fell into the wrong hands. The only record was by word of mouth. Parents told their children, and the children told theirs, so the verbal maps of hidden treasures were passed on from generation to generation. Sometime in the 1950s my father, aided by a team of men, tried to dig up the treasures allegedly hidden near the dued. After digging a few metres into the ground my father broke out in a terrible rash. Immediately he instructed the men to stop the digging and have the hole filled. He was sure that the malevolent spirit had taken possession of the treasures and was manifesting his displeasure. Father's rash was a forewarning of more terrible things to come. What awful things the spirit could do was not hard to guess. These treasures were entrusted to him for safekeeping, not given to him for good. But then the spirits of this category were not trustworthy and not very smart. Father never attempted to get back the goods again. He just said, 'The dued has taken possession of our belongings. Spirits, like humans, also have *doipa* and *dakzin* (greed and attachment).' I wasn't too unhappy about this failed attempt to unearth the treasures in this spot because they were supposed to have been mostly swords and other practical household items and not of particular interest to me. But I often thought about the jewellery and other 'women's things' said to have been buried in another place within the compound of the manor. Even as a small child I felt some sort of claim and ownership over these. If only we could find this treasure, it would be mine! Nevertheless, I still feel a little ambivalent towards the malevolent spirit that lives in Sangdag for stealing from our family. He was worse than the powerful lords! I never liked this spirit, and passing this place always made me feel uneasy, because I was so sure that he knew my thoughts, and these spirits with their supernatural powers could even encroach one's mind!

But during the walks with our parents and the others, I felt safe passing this place; there was safety in numbers. We learnt early in life that every person had different levels of *wangthang* (good presence) and *lungta* (good fortune). Occasionally, the levels increased or decreased. When these decreased for certain individuals, then that person was vulnerable to misfortune and illness. But if there was a group of people together, even if each one had a different level of good presence and good fortune, the accumulative effect would offset those with declining levels. Thus, it was safer to be in big groups. I was reassured, especially because I was with my parents during these walks.

Immediately after passing this dubious place, there were buckwheat fields which were often left fallow for years at a time. The farmers followed a traditional cultivation system which required the buckwheat fields to be cultivated in rotation with fallow periods of up to ten years, after which they would dig up the matured land with a hand hoe. The leftover tufts of soil and vegetation were tediously built into heaps before they were set on fire. The ash enriched the soil. During the fallow periods, the fields would transform into meadows. By July these meadows were full of wild strawberries. The cattle herders from the village would graze their cattle in these fields. My playmates and I used to join them, scrambling alongside the cattle, picking strawberries. The strawberries even made us forget how close we were to the hostile spirit! Armed with our bamboo containers and twigs of dried wormwood, we could spend entire days picking the berries. The bamboo containers were about twenty to thirty centimetres in height; only one side was open, and the base was closed by the internode of the bamboo. A small plunger would be fashioned with another piece of bamboo. We would fill the bamboo with ripe berries and squash the berries with the plunger, sucking the plunger every now and then. We referred to eating the squashed berries as 'drinking berry juice'. On days when we were more patient and artistically inclined, we would choose the most intricate dried twigs of wormwood. We would then clean these twigs of dried leaves and, using the twigs like skewers, we would pierce different-sized berries on different branches, arranging them in intricate ways to make the most beautiful 'coral trees', as we called these delicious works of art. After comparing and showing off our handiworks, we would eat the strawberries slowly by plucking off one berry at a time, or by putting our mouths to the stems and eating them. We did not even mind the slight bitter taste of the wormwood. Throughout the strawberry season most children sported red stains on their faces, fingers and clothes.

The khamsang took us past the buckwheat fields to a small hillock in the middle of two large fields. This hillock was only sparsely forested, with blue pine trees interspersed with a mix of different bushes and plants. This place called *Paropai pong* (the hillock of someone from Paro) was a favourite place for relaxing adults and playing children. It was not so windy, and it caught the last rays of sunshine before sunset. The adults would lay out the carpets, drink tea, sometimes play games of dice or simply chat, as the children were allowed to play in the nearby forest. These excursions were usually uneventful but enjoyable and relaxing for all. But there was a time when something I did made the khamsang a particularly memorable one. Even years later people remind me about it, 'Remember the time when you wanted to be a happy god?'

The forest in the Paropai pong, with patches of bushes and thickets under the blue pine trees, provided the ideal ground for playing hide-and-seek, and we played this tirelessly. On one occasion, we decided to play another favourite game: performing a religious ritual. We all knew what to do for we had often watched the preparations for rituals and seen how they were performed. The ground for an altar was prepared under a tree and a stone seat made with a small offering table in front of it. Then it was decided that I should be the '*Ku*', the statue of the Buddha for whom the ritual and offerings would be made. I was to sit very still, cross-legged on a flat stone in a meditative pose with a downward gaze. I remember even assuming the wish-granting posture, my right hand open, held against my lap and my left hand open, pointing towards the ground. I was offered all sorts of plants and twigs as I tried to hold my pose while the others performed the prayers, imitating the religious chants, '*Oai ya moi ya*.' There was even impressive mimicry of the temple music. My cousin Ugyen Namgyel was the altar attendant, busy collecting and placing all sorts of things on the offering table in front of me. Finally, he came to me and whispered in my ear, 'Show that you are happy with the rituals and offerings and eat one of the offerings.' Saying this, he handed me a beautiful brilliant-red corn-like fruit and, although I recognized the plant as the dreaded *phag dok* or 'pig's poison' (*Arisaema tortuosum*), something prompted me to eat it. Perhaps I figured those gods had powers that no humans had, and that I was a god on this occasion. The other children just looked at me curiously, but nobody said anything. I am not sure how much of the red offering I ate to show my pleasure but soon my tongue was thickening even as the pretend prayers were being chanted beautifully, and the pretend music was being played to perfection. My tongue grew thicker and thicker until my mouth was forced open and breathing was difficult.

The next thing I remember was being put on the neck of Jurmin, one of the servants. 'Hold her legs tight and run as fast you can,' instructed my father firmly to Jurmin, who was to race home carrying me.

'Place your fingers around his head like this,' my mother said as she took my hands and placed them around his forehead. Everybody around had bewildered looks on their faces, but father was in control and trying to keep the sense of panic from growing any further. I could hear all the instructions as if they were coming from a far distance. Jurmin was told to run all the way home, about two kilometres. I managed to hold my hands over his head as he ran, even as I felt myself slumping. I could hear my father whistling loudly and urging him to hurry.

Others were shouting instructions, 'Go straight to the horse stable and let her eat horse dung.' 'Make her drink milk.' 'If there is no milk, buttermilk will do,' added another. But every time my father whistled or shouted out an instruction, Jurmin stopped to listen and this delayed our sprint. But the sense of confidence and authority in each voice was reassuring, even as my face was slowly getting numb. These adults certainly knew what to do when someone was poisoned by this plant. By the time I reached home, I must have passed out because I do not remember a thing. My mother's cousin, uncle Sangye Lhuendup, was home and he took over once we arrived. When I regained consciousness, my parents and the others were hovering around anxiously, and I felt a scratching pain in my throat. I think I had been made to vomit, when the horse dung and milk were forced into my mouth.

I cannot remember anything after that. But I learnt that the plant, 'pig's poison', was one of the deadliest of the poisonous plants in our environs. We had all heard about the potency of 'pig's poison', but now we had witnessed its effect first-hand.

It was feared more than the *Chungkhai* dok, chugh's poison, the *euphorbia* plant that grows abundantly in the summer. The most dreaded was, of course, the *tsen* dok or *aconitum* which was used for lacing arrow tips during wars. Hunters also used this poison when they hunted with bows and arrows or when they placed snares and traps for predators which stole from or damaged their crops.

I came to learn of the power of the deadly poison under the very nose of the Sangdag Dued. I wonder whether he was there watching the whole scenario with malicious pleasure or whether he looked away in cruel apathy. Could I have died from this poison, or did I live through this because he intervened? These days whenever I pass this area, I know he is around, but I do not feel that old sense of awe and fear. For wherever he may be now, his realm is slowly being desecrated, and he does nothing in retribution.

10

The Firecracker

I NEVER SAW MY MOTHER lose her temper or scold anyone. The only time I saw her in her ferocious manifestation was when my cousin, Ugyen Namgyel, and his companion Choktor Gempo blew up a firecracker in their own faces. After my aunt Dechen, my mother's older sister died, my mother invited her son Ugyen Namgyel to stay with us in Ogyen Choling and I soon got used to living with four male siblings. My cousin very quickly became a part of our family. The year that Ugyen Namgyel was with us, he participated in all family events including our annual ritual, the *kangsoi.* The kangsoi, even today, is the most important and exciting tradition that our family observes. During this ritual, that takes place in the tenth month of the lunar calendar, the sword dance was the most anticipated event. A man dressed as a warrior would dance while vowing in front of the family deity to subdue all negative forces. While the sword dance was being performed, the ancient and rusty matchlock gun had to be fired. It was always my father's hunter, Prala, who was responsible for firing the gun. I used to watch with the other children as he set up the stand, loaded the gun with gunpowder, and stuffed the barrel using a metal rod. Then he would lie down on his stomach behind the gun and set fire to the prim of the powder. His goal was to try and synchronize the blast with specific words of the prayers being chanted by the *gomchens*, the lay monks. The synchronization was rarely perfect. The blast from Prala's gun came ahead of the particular words or long after the words had been chanted. The blasts were loud and sharp most of the time but messy and dangerous just as often; sometimes there was just a whiff of sulphuric smoke and a puff. There were times when the ancient machine backfired and sent some of the gunpowder on to Prala, making him look like he had rubbed his face in the sooty hearth. People would cover their ears in anticipation of the sound and the animals in the procession would get highly agitated.

When father realized how unreliable and dangerous the firing was, he got firecrackers from India to replace the matchlock gun. The year Ugyen Namgyel was with us, he noticed that some of the firecrackers had failed to explode. So, he and his friend Choktor Gempo collected them. On a day when the excitement of the kangsoi had died down, the two boys took the unexploded firecrackers and stole a glowing coal from the kitchen hearth. Holding the glowing coal to the cracker, they blew on the spot where the firecracker touched the live coal, their heads huddled together over the deadly fire they were bent on starting. Suddenly there was a loud bang. Everybody stopped what they were doing and rushed to the site of the noise. The two boys, stunned in shock, were lying on the ground amidst bits of paper from the firecracker wrapping strewn everywhere, their faces blackened with gunpowder. When they could finally get up, Ugyen Namgyel ran to hide behind the wooden door to the garden. Some voiced hysterical concerns, but everybody was relieved that the boys were unharmed. My mother was shaking with shock. On seeing the boys were all right, her relief and anger manifested in an unusual gesture. She chastised the boys for their mischief and scolded the men for their carelessness. Overcome by the intensity of her emotions, she made poor Ugyen Namgyel her whipping board. She became a little dramatic. Mother got a bangchung with some rice and chilli. Handing it to Ugyen Namgyel, she said she had failed to live up to the trust of his father, Dasho Sangye Penjor in taking care of him as she had promised. She said he should leave and go back to Chummey before he comes to further harm. The rice and chilli were the ration for his journey home. After some time, the incident was forgotten, but Ugyen Namgyel, to this day, insists that my mother gave him a stinging slap when she found him hiding behind the door.

Even though she did not live a spiritual life engaging in overt acts of religiosity, I remember my mother always being composed and compassionate. The incident with Ugyen Namgyel was the only occasion she lost her composure. Mother did not chant prayers publicly or go around with a prayer wheel and prayer beads. She had a wooden box where she kept her prayer books, which she told me were given to her by her father, and she read her prayers daily. The prayer text container is an oblong wooden box painted with figures of animals and plants in delicate detail. The painting style, I think, is a Chinese rendition of 'the man of long life', a common trope in Bhutanese paintings. I have the joy of owning this box now. I think it was made and painted by her father. My grandfather, whom I never met, was a gifted artist. Now I feel a connection to him through this prayer book box. My mother had a strong bond with her father, and she sometimes talked of him. It was her father's words she repeated to me when she saw how afraid I was of being alone in the dark. What my mother told me about fear when I was a child did not help. I recall her asking me very gently, 'Why should you be afraid of being alone or being in the dark? When you die, you will be alone and maybe in the dark.' She added a third dimension, the fear of death, compounding my fear of darkness and of being alone.

As if to lessen my fears, she told me that her father repeatedly told her we must think of death at least once a day. She said that if we remember the inevitability of death, we will be reminded to live accordingly. I did not understand this rather fatalistic and morbid advice at the time and continued to fear darkness, being alone and death even more. Today I realize that the central message from the most learnt and influential Buddhist teachers is to think of death at least once a day, not in fear but to know that in the fleeting passage of time that is life, the reality of death reminds us to seek liberation. My mother believed in what she was telling me.

My mother faced life and death quietly and fearlessly, all alone. While she lived, nobody knew how special she was. After she died, it was too late. During her cremation, people who were attending to the pyre claimed to have witnessed an unusual sign. At least two or three people vouch to having seen the complete mantra of *Om Ah Hung* embossed on her skull. Maybe being the mistress of a landed household, and all the mundane challenges that came with it, was not her life's call. Maybe she should have practised religion.

11

Protective Deities, Strangers and Fleeting Shadows

As a child, I would often lie in bed in fear, sweating, hot and steamy, my head covered under layers of blankets, heart thumping and ears alert to every noise in the house. Every creak or rattle of a loose bamboo mat in the quiet night would become the ghostly noises that crept into my entire system, and I would tremble in fear and trepidation before falling off to a fretful sleep. This fear intensified and stayed with me for a long time. After the deaths of my parents, I became even more frightened. The empty rooms were now loaded with the mystery of death. I longed to use the rooms that my parents had once occupied to invoke memories of them and perhaps hold on to what I had lost, but they seemed emptier; the spirits haunted me. I grew up in a world that was crammed with the supernatural. Spirits, demons and ghosts crowded my psyche and coloured my life.

Children are not naturally afraid. Fear is learnt, nurtured by the environment they grow up in. I think adults possess the natural flair and a sadistic delight in frightening children, feeding the fear first planted by them in us. Even today, I occasionally see adults mindlessly creating and conjuring characters and images in the minds of their young children in order to discipline them and, worse still, to tease and taunt them. Adults have the power to summarily call upon these 'tools' to force disobedient or wilful children into submission and conformity through fear.

The most common warning being, 'If you don't do what I tell you, so-and-so will come and cut off your ears.' The cutting of the ears was the most dreaded threat that we were subjected to. The source or subject of fear could be a real stranger who might have just passed through the village or a member of the family who was ill-tempered and impatient, especially with children. Sometimes the so-and-so could even be an invisible being conjured up by the adults and made to seem real. Our ears were not the only body parts that had to be protected against pulls and twists, slaps and whacks from impatient adults. The adults sought assistance from the spirits and strangers who were not only capable of maiming us but also taking away our *sog*, life force, and killing us.

My brothers and I cannot recall why we were so terrified of a seemingly ordinary-looking man called Kanjurla. When I was a child, just the mention of his name was enough to make me shiver and take flight. Was he the bogeyman that our parents created to frighten us as a disciplining tactic? The idea more than the man himself was the monster of my childhood days. The elders and my own parents spontaneously transformed this rather harmless-looking man into a mysterious monster. They had succeeded and we were petrified. It was surely not the man but the mystery that they had embellished around him that made him the source of all evil. Unbeknownst to us, there was a conspiracy between him and our parents because he did indulge in some of the very behaviours that our parents had warned us of. Now I cannot remember what it was that this man was supposed to do that was so frightening.

Who was this mystery man? Kanjurla was a servant of Her Royal Highness, Ashi Chokey, and worked in Wangdue Choling palace in Choekor valley, eight hours' walk from our home. He only visited our parents when he was sent on duty by Her Royal Highness to exchange letters and parcels between the two households. So, he would appear suddenly and disappear just as suddenly. Probably the mystery stemmed from the infrequency of his visits. But the frequency of the references to him kept his enigmatic presence alive all the time.

Already on entering the main doorway to the courtyard, he would announce himself loudly, '*Wai, wai Kanjurla wongdu. Dorji Doma chang baghsho*. (Wai Wai Kanjurla is here, Dorji Doma bring me *chhang*.)' This most unusual greeting boomed within the courtyard, then echoed as the words hit against the walls, crept through windows and doors, and every pore in my body tingled with fear. Why did his announcement of his arrival have such a chilling effect on me? Was it the tone of his voice or was it because he dared to address our mother by her name openly and command her to bring him a drink? This was such a blatant breach of etiquette; everybody else addressed mother reverently as 'Ashi' (a form of respect for women of the elite). How dare he address her by her name? What gave him this extraordinary power? He was breaking boundaries by calling mother by her name; if that was the kind of power he had, he could do anything to us small helpless children. The best thing for us to do was to flee from him as far as possible.

On one such occasion, on hearing the dreaded announcement of 'Wai Wai Kanjurla,' I remember running away to the drupchu, about twenty minutes' run up the hill from the house near the prayer mill where the family often went for picnics and baths. There was a forested strip that ran along the entire length of the stream from the source, a spring under a huge peach tree, until it disappeared into a marshy patch a few hundred metres down the hill. This forested patch was our favourite haunt, a secret place hidden away from the adults. Here I felt protected and safe. I climbed up a thorny Sichuan pepper tree among the bushes of wild rose, poplar and willow trees, and stayed hiding among the foliage, carefully avoiding the thorns but almost intoxicated by the pungent smell of the pepper. Somehow in my childish mind I had assumed that Kanjurla would not be able to climb through the thorny branches to come after me. Hours later when mother realized my long absence and asked one of the servants to look for me, he found me in the tree; one of my playmates must have let out the secret. He coaxed me to come home. I remember not daring to mention the name 'Kanjurla'; I referred to him in the third person, 'He will not be able to climb through these branches?' I asked and only after the confirmation, 'Of course not', I went home. Kanjurla was no longer around. There was a quietness about the whole compound although the sound of his voice still echoed in my brain. My father had a strangely amused expression on his face when he heard that I was in a tree but did not say anything. Perhaps he remembered that he too had sought solace and safety in a tree not long ago.

It was during a visit of the third King, His Majesty Jigme Dorji Wangchuck, to Bumthang. He was in Wangdue Choling palace, and my father had gone to pay his respects as he normally did whenever the King came to the palace. We were told that the King was very relaxed and happy during the time of his stay, playing archery for days on end and continuously being entertained by dancers and singers. Everybody was expected to sing and dance. My father, however, who was conversant in literary matters and truly appreciative of the fine arts, could not sing or dance even when a royal command ordered him to do so. When the King commanded him to sing and dance, he hesitated. Then, on some pretext he managed to escape and climbed up an evergreen tree near the palace grounds and stayed hidden among the thick foliage until the singing and dancing stopped in the early hours of the morning. I had inherited his trait of turning to trees in times of distress. Only my choice of tree was more deadly than his. I never found out how my father managed to excuse his absence to the monarch.

The Kanjurla episodes in my life ended anticlimactically many years later, sometime in the late 1970s. While I was on a visit to Thimphu, I saw a strangely familiar man. I could not believe that this diminutive, old, wiry man scurrying down the hillside from his home in Motithang to the town was the most frightening person of my childhood days. He was carrying an empty bag over his shrunken shoulders and scuttling along the footpath in the blue pine forests. Could this be the same man who had created hell on earth for us when we were children in the 1950s? He did not recognize me, and I had to laugh at myself, remembering the terror he had wrought on us.

One of my uncles was the master creator of all evil characters. His creations were so powerful and lucid that I was afraid even during the daytime. I was afraid to walk from one room to another. I would run through the rooms all the time looking back over my shoulders for my invisible pursuers. Some of these were the invisible creatures lurking in the dark passages and rooms, ready to spring at me; then there were the *shinde*, spirits of the dead people who were stuck with human beings because they were stuck with their habits of attachment and greed.

Our minds were loaded with thoughts about the supernatural compounded by the fearsome environment we lived in. We listened in awe when adults talked about subjects that had any reference to spirits, ghosts and the supernatural. At night, with only oil lamps, resin-wood torches and the occasional dry-cell battery flashlights that gave out momentary flickers of light and relief, we imagined all sorts of things could happen, and they did all the time. The stories that were told and retold were not always meant to frighten us children. They were just stories. But every story and incident found its way into our already anxious lives as the truth. One such story was what my father experienced. He said, one late afternoon he was in his bedroom. It was a quiet afternoon and the entire family quarters of the shagkor complex was unusually quiet too. The only sound was the echo of the weavers' beaters as they worked on the looms on the ground floor. All the servants were out in the field engaged in digging the land for buckwheat cultivation. During this digging season the family's male servants had to join the workmen, making the workforce twenty-five to thirty people. They were engaged in *pangola*, the annual activity of digging the dry lands with hoes. The area where these men worked would resound with the earth's vibrations as the thuds of the hoes dug into the hard soil. The task was tough as the land would have been left fallow for several years to mature and replenish itself with the necessary nutrients. This time the men were in a place called Engser, which was about a two-hour walk from our home. So, my father was rather surprised when a man who was supposed to be in Engser looked through the crack in his bedroom door which he pushed ajar and sighed heavily, addressing my father, 'Dasho, *Nyad rasdh*. (Dasho, I have come.)' Father looked up and all at once the man was gone. Father, who was writing a letter at the time, dropped the pen and paper and followed the man. There was an eerie chill as he went through three rooms to the stairs.

At the head of the stairs, he met the village astrologer, Lopon Tsedarla, who, without greeting my father said, 'I have come to report that Ap Dorjila suddenly took ill and died this morning.'

My father said he was seized by a sense of overpowering shock as he said to Lopon, 'Ap Dorjila visited me just now!' Life and death were inextricably connected and so natural. But it was such occurrences that both intrigued and frightened me. I heard father narrate this story several times, not in fear but in appreciation of his faithful servant who felt the relationship with his master even in death.

Ghosts and spirits were one thing, but it was the deities we worshipped who added to the murkiness of the supernatural. In today's lay terms these deities were ultra conservative; they did not like change. Akhu lama, who faithfully followed all the traditional customs and practices and rarely missed a worship dedicated to the deities, said that they resented change. He said that once, the family acquired a gramophone when he was a young child but whenever they played music there were signs of displeasure from the deities. Every time the gramophone was used, strange noises were heard coming from the *goenkhang*, the inner sanctum of the temple, and on occasions even the shutters on the temple could be seen opening and closing noisily. As a result, they could use the machine only outside the house complex, as far away from the temple as possible. Today it appears that the deities have either embraced change or gotten used to the alien noises, or they have abandoned us and relocated somewhere else altogether. The noise pollution that has so invaded our lives is even difficult for human beings to tolerate. There are all kinds of music playing from every cell phone and shortwave radio, and the sounds of efficiency machines that make lives easier for us, such as chainsaws and tractors, drills and washing machines, fill the same airwaves that the deities once tried to protect.

My mother was a staunch believer in the power of the deities, and she did not fear them. She always said, why should we be afraid of anything? Just as we came alone into the world at birth, when we die, we will have to go alone. We may as well practise fearlessness in life in preparation for death, she would say. Without really comprehending the depth of her philosophy, I repeated what she told me. Practising fearlessness was not easy for any of us. But mother practised what she preached. Indeed, she was brave and had no qualms about being alone anywhere, anytime, especially going into the dark utse all by herself to get something she needed, with only a flickering flashlight, and sometimes even without a flashlight, simply by feeling her way through the darkness.

Although we referred to our main deity Maha Kala as Ap Gonpo or Father Gonpo and considered him a common father to all of us, just adding 'father' before his name did not automatically endear him to us unconditionally. He was still a fearsome personality, guarded by two ferocious *kathrabs*, guards, in a dark room where even the paintings on the walls were done in monochrome line drawings on a dark black background. Because he was our protector in life, in death too every dead person's life force had to present itself in front of Ap Gonpo. Although religious personalities explained these fearsome representations to be manifestations of compassion, as children it was almost impossible to separate fear from compassion. The customary summoning of the dead in the presence of Ap Gonpo was not just a belief; it happened all the time. The silence of the dark night would sometimes be punctuated with the muffled groaning of the dead. Whenever somebody in the village or the valley died, the life force was brought in front of the Ap Gonpo by the two kathrabs. These two guards had ropes of serpents and hooks, spears and daggers in their hands, and I imagined that the dead person was bound and pierced with these deadly weapons and brought in front of their master. The adults often talked of the drops of blood that could be seen on the doorsteps of the main temple door, on the stone slabs in the courtyard leading to it and up the wooden stairs all the way into the temple.

I remember my mother sometimes said to the gathered family members and guests at breakfast, 'Last night the groaning from somebody's sog reverberated throughout the courtyard', or asked, 'Did anyone else hear anything?' Nobody would question the fact that she heard the groaning. The only concern was, 'Whose sog could it be?' Chilled to the bones and covered in goose bumps, I could hardly hold the cup of tea to my lips for the rest of the breakfast. Even thinking about it now, I feel my eyes widening with wonder.

Akhu lama often cautioned us, not in a disrespectful way, but rather matter-of-factly, as if speaking of a family member, that the deities could be *kokpa*, rather stupid. They had to be propitiated and appeased all the time, and any failure on the part of the devotee could be met with retribution, even if they were your guardian deities. The image of our common father who was supposed to be protective of our interests and our life was also one who was fearsome, rather stupid, and bloodthirsty. A long time ago, before I was born, live sacrifices of animals had to be offered to the deities. These were later stopped.

The fearsome male deity, our common father, was complemented by the equally, if not more terrifying, common mother Aum Penden Lhamo or Kali. She was often encountered, although only fleetingly, as a woman wearing a blue guzum. Kali wore this shapeless dress, a tunic with a V-shaped neck, just like the women who wore this tunic as an undergarment. I was familiar with this archaic garment as it was still worn by most grown women as an undergarment. Many older women and my own mother wore it as a nightdress. I knew what the garment looked like. Aum Penden Lhamo was to be recognized by the colour of the tunic she wore; she always wore blue. In the dead of night when everything was still, she could be heard dancing, pounding her feet on the slab of stone at the base of the stairs in *sang go*, the 'secret doorway' to the family's private quarters. I was sure that during my sleepless nights it was the muffled, hollow thumping sound which filtered through the stillness of the night and fused with my own heartbeat: thump, thump, thump. Was this universal mother a malevolent or a benevolent being? She could be both, so we were taught to revere her, fear and love her.

Stories of her appearances and disappearances were always kept alive by incidents we so often heard about. One story I remember was about a young man who had disappeared near the Tang Chu river. He was supposed to have stripped naked and folded all his clothes neatly in a pile on the riverbank and then disappeared without a trace. Only a brief glimpse of a woman in a blue guzum was seen by a cow herder in the vicinity of the riverbank around the time of his disappearance. The obvious conclusion was that he had been taken by Aum Penden Lhamo for a reason beyond our questioning. We knew Aum Penden Lhamo could also be a powerful nemesis to those who challenged her. When a part of our temple was robbed and the thieves claimed that they were able to put the stolen goods, mainly *thangkas*, 'on to a road' – meaning that they had sold them profitably – before we even realized that we had been robbed, Aum Penden Lhamo followed the thieves. She made sure that they did not live to enjoy the profits of the stolen goods from the temple she was entrusted to guard. Soon after the robbery, two ring leaders of the thieves fell ill suddenly, and at the moment of their deaths they were both supposed to have uttered, 'A woman in blue guzum has come for me!'

The woman in the blue guzum continues to guard us and all that is entrusted to her. Our house has been the target of repeated thefts, some petty ones, where people just opportunistically helped themselves to artefacts, and even some serious planned robberies over the years. Some of the thieves were caught by the police and some even imprisoned, but the artefacts were rarely returned through official channels. Where justice and police vigilance have failed, our guardian deities have been very effective. Over the years, many articles have been returned, especially to the temple, because of illness in the families where the artefacts ended up. Butter lamps, ritual objects and other artefacts have been surreptitiously brought back. Even as I write about this, a sword, allegedly stolen from the temple, has been returned to us, as well as a copper phallus used during some rituals. What happens is that people fall ill; illness causes them to seek advice from a religious person who specializes in divination; the diviner, after some calculations and readings from the *thamai pecha*, the book of divinations, tells them that they have articles that belong to temples with powerful deities. In many cases we would have not even missed these articles. But the deities take their roles as guardians very seriously.

Several years ago I lost valuables and some family heirlooms from my personal safe, and the suspect, a young man, was caught and kept under police custody for a while but later released for lack of substantive evidence. However, less than two years after the theft, he died suddenly. Barely days after his funerary rituals were complete, the family of the dead man wanted to take me to court, alleging that my deities had killed the man. Indeed, among the valuables stolen was jewellery that had been in the family for several generations. The guardian deities may have had these on their inventory!

But perhaps the stories of ghosts in our midst were the most terrifying because these ghosts were neither protectors nor well-wishers. Once a ragged Tibetan yogin came wandering into our house. Father and mother, who were always kindly inclined towards religious practitioners, invited him to stay. But he immediately declined and said that he preferred to camp out in the open. He put up his small, pointed tent in a field opposite our house at some distance. After spending a night there, he came to see my parents. Again, it happened to be at breakfast that he said, 'No evil spirits will ever harm this village because it is protected by a *godpon*, a strong ghost leader. She is very powerful and has a big following; she lives in this village.' No questions were asked, and everybody held their thoughts to themselves. The yogin continued, 'Last night as I performed the ritual of *choed* (a powerful Tibetan Buddhist ritual in part intended to feed hungry ghosts) the thundering stampede of ghosts joined me in my tent for the feast I was offering, but before them came a young naked man who was born in the year of the horse. He stood at the opening of my tent door weeping silently. It was too late for me to do anything; the ghosts had already eaten him. Then came the ghost leader with a bloodied mouth and hands gleefully celebrating the kill.' What he said next stumped all the listeners. 'As I came for breakfast this morning I met the leader of the ghost. She could not look at me straight and turned away from me.' Everyone present knew who the woman was; they believed that ghosts at night become normal humans in the daytime. Although I was not present at this breakfast, I knew the alleged ghost; she was still alive and actively present in my childhood days. She was reputed to be a ghost, not just a simple ghost but a powerful ghost leader. She lived with her sister in a house close to ours. She looked ordinary like everybody else but there were oddities only ghosts would do or not do. Nobody had ever heard her say a single word of prayer and she never joined in the village's religious congregations. People vouched that her eyes took on a cloudy appearance after sunset and that she never looked at anyone directly. Some people even said that they saw a figure like hers lurking in the shadows at night. She had to be a ghost.

Circumstances that compound the enigmatic atmosphere around the complex encroachment of both the human and ghostly worlds continue to this day. A few years ago, an unusual woman from the village who was mostly in a world of her own was accidentally locked in the utse building for two nights and a day. She had joined a group of visitors to the museum and then lingered on her own and inadvertently gotten locked in. When people asked her how she could stay alone in the building and not be afraid, she calmly said, 'I wasn't alone. There were many people in the building. They were talking among themselves and were busily engaged with all sorts of activities.' She wasn't teasing; she was referring to the normally unseen beings which inhabit the utse, now the Ogyen Choling museum.

12

The Mirror, the Bathtub and the Flask

I HAD NEVER SEEN MYSELF in a full-length mirror. Full-length mirrors were unheard of when I was a child. Like the other children in my village, the only time I could look at myself was when I got my hands on one of those tiny round tin containers like the ones used to hold mint and throat lozenges these days. The ones I am referring to were just the size of an adult's fist and were popular in the 1950s and 60s for they served the dual purpose of being a container for trinkets and a handy mirror. Women and girls carried them in the pouches of their kira like miniature vanity boxes. The tin could be used for storing one's personal and precious belongings: pins, needles, strings, loose beads, pieces of soap, rings and other small mementos. I never owned one of these containers but sometimes I would beg somebody to allow me to look in theirs. This kind of mirror was very different and the image much clearer than what we children used called *duen melong*, the ghosts' mirror. These were flat pieces of shiny mica we sometimes chanced upon in rocks. We were so happy to see the blurry images of ourselves and we fought for every piece. Sometimes I was the proud owner of such a piece until the layers peeled off or the whole piece crumbled away.

These tins with the mirror in its lid, they could not be bought easily. They were only available when the infrequent hawkers came carrying exotic goods that delighted everybody. As soon as the hawkers, who were mostly Tibetans, appeared in the village, the villagers stopped whatever they were doing, and gathered around him and his wares displayed in the steel trunk which he carried. I usually joined the crowd and would stay on looking at the goods yearningly, until all the items were sold off against grain and butter while some actually paid in coins. Some buyers negotiated to pay for their purchases only when they could harvest their crops in a few months or a year. The hawkers were patient, but their mental records were exact and non-negotiable when it was time to pay up. I am quite sure the little mirror containers were the first items they sold.

These small round mirrors allowed us to see only parts of our faces. I remember the first time I looked at myself. A bewildered face with relatively large eyes stared back at me. My lips drooped at the ends of my mouth like a sad fish, my cheeks were flat, and my nose just disappeared between those eyes, hardly any ridge and, therefore, no prominence. I had inherited my mother's nose, a bulge which resembled the snorting angry nose of the ferocious deity Chana Dorji (Vajrapani), as my cousin Ugyen Namgyel teased me. I used to feel sad and a little inadequate when I heard the elders describe beautiful women with noses that resembled the goddess, Tara's. Her nose was straight with just the right ridge to enhance the perfect symmetry of her face. I once heard my mother tell somebody how, as a child, she too was bothered by her flat nose. And that her mother had told her that a cat had sat on her nose and flattened it when she was a baby. I had to turn cleverly, just to the right position to look at my ears in the mirror. I liked looking at my ears, especially after I had heard that my ears had been approved of by Her Majesty the Queen Mother, Ashi Phuntsho Choden. When I was a baby, my mother had paid a visit to the Queen Mother, and she had commented on how pretty my ears were and had kissed them. My ears had been approved of by one of the most important women in the country. Naturally I was rather conscious of them and succumbed to a little vanity. I liked looking at my ears, secretly wondering what was so special about them.

By the time I was about six or seven years old, I had seen nearly all parts of my face and knew how I looked, but the day I saw myself in a full-length mirror I was completely thrown off. How did such a big mirror come into our house? My parents enjoyed the services of a certain *Tsongpon* (Merchant) Yeshila. He was the trader for Her Royal Highness Ashi Chokey of Wangdue Choling palace. Yeshila traded in India on behalf of our family. Every time he came home after a trading trip, he would dazzle us all with some wonderful new items. One year it was a full-length mirror which my parents received happily but were not quite sure where to place. One afternoon I walked into the main room and was suddenly confronted by my own image, all of me. Leaning against the wall was the largest mirror I had ever seen. I fearfully drew back a few paces like a cat on seeing its double. Then I took a few tentative steps forward and looked at the girl with wide eyes, a short fringe, wearing a boy's gho with short white trousers covering her legs. I examined and re-examined myself. I checked my hands and legs and all parts of my body; I was completely transfixed. Suddenly I heard my parents giggling. They had been watching me the whole time I was discovering myself and could not restrain themselves when I touched my groin area in bafflement. I was feeling myself through my boy's clothes, discovering the female part of me in the male dress. I was different from my brothers. Suddenly, aware of my parents' presence, I became self-conscious and shy and walked away in greater confusion.

Tsongpon Yeshila had the knack of surprising us with items that were new to us, children as well as adults. Without any means of communication, we were never sure when he could be expected back from his trips and what he would bring. He would normally return within five or six weeks. We all looked forward to the day he would come home. We could hear his noisy mule train from afar when he approached Ogyen Choling. The bells and gongs that the mules were adorned with were loud, and the sound could be heard over long distances. We children would rush to the end of the plateau and wait excitedly for the caravan of mules to come into view and then repeatedly chant in a sing-song tone, '*kheydrey kheydrey*', the mule trains, the mule trains. We would do the same when the herds of yaks passed through the village, '*Yak yay yak yay.*' Anything that broke the dullness of our mundane lives delighted us into song.

Father and mother would have made their shopping list and, although they never showed any eagerness or excitement, I am sure they too were inwardly eager to see all the items on their wish list. One year the young and the old were gathered on the lookout point, at the edge of the plateau to watch the caravan. There was growing speculation and guesses as to what the large oval metal object which was loaded on a rather small mule could be. Even as the caravan drew closer, nobody could guess what it was. It was really a strange picture as the perky little mule proudly walked into the courtyard with the metal object nearly covering it. Father had a strange expression on his face, but he did not immediately ask Yeshila what it was; he had great control. Even while it was being unloaded and the children gathered around in excited curiosity, father said nothing until Yeshila himself said, 'This is the bathtub you asked for.'

That strange expression on my father's face was one of disbelief. But all he said was, 'It's bigger than I expected.' It was an oval metal bathtub measuring two metres long and one and a half metres wide. It had a depth of more than half a metre. It had been carried by this poor little mule for over twelve days over craggy and narrow paths and finally reached our home. But this was not how my father had imagined a metal bathtub to be.

Soon water was heated in the largest cauldrons in the house and a bath was prepared. But the bathtub was so big that two large cauldrons were not enough to fill it. Based on its size, it would take more than five hundred litres to fill! Water had to be carried from the waterspout which was at least five hundred metres away from the bath house. Poor Chomo, the water carrier, was very unhappy and repeatedly complained, 'Such a tub.' The metal tub did not retain the heat like our wooden tubs; the bath water got cold as soon it was poured in. The bathtub was rejected and lay abandoned in the courtyard until mother decided to use it for storing grain. So, for all these years, from 1960 until 2013, it served as a grain storage container. In 2013 the rejected bathtub found a new use. Piped water filled the tub and was used for soaking the bricks and tiles for the construction projects in Ogyen Choling.

Bringing wonderfully exotic things over long distances was not a new thing for Ogyen Choling. Long ago, glass had been brought for the temple windows and altars. The thin but large glass panes measuring about one and a half metres had been brought from Tibet. How they transported the glass across the high Himalayas over seven to eight days, is a feat. Giving the best to the temple was exemplified by the fact that the glass was used for the temple and not for the home. However, father indulged by having one glass windowpane in his living room.

I can never forget the story of how the first thermos flask reached our home. Phub Dorji was the man who carried it all the way from Tibet. Whenever I think of Phub Dorji, I cannot but recount what a special man he was. He was a young boy of fourteen or fifteen when he was introduced into the service of my grandfather as a tozan or an initiate. He continued to work with my father and stayed with our family for most of his life. My first recollections of him are of an agile young man who accompanied my father on his travels to Tibet and India. He was quick-witted, and competent in handling horses. Later he was sent as a companion to my elder brother Rinzin Dorji when he joined the palace school in Wangdue Choling. There he married one of the royal weavers and embarked on a journey of nomadic life, never staying in one place for more than a few years at a time. Many years later, when he had become an old man and was wandering around looking for a place to settle down, albeit temporarily, my brother Rinzin invited him to stay with him in Thimphu for several years until he moved to Paro for good. By then he had become a recognized quasi-religious practitioner and a healer of sorts. He read scriptures and was especially respected for sucking out poisoned blood. When I asked him how he did that, all he would tell me was that he could do it only through his meditative practice. I persisted and asked how. 'For a start, I have to imagine my tongue to be a golden spoon, scooping up the poison from the blood.' He would not tell me more. He was in demand for his skills as a good healer and had a circle of faithful and generous clients. But we valued him most because he was like a history book for our family. He could tell stories of our grandparents and our parents, having lived with them for many years.

One of the most frequently heard stories was about his last trading trip to Tibet with my father, which may have been in 1957 or 1958. He told us of the wonders of the holy city, Lhasa. Phub Dorji spoke of the Chinese presence in Lhasa and the most amazing goods that one could buy. But he did not tell us about the time he stole some scripture from a shop and the shopkeeper chased him around the Barkor circuit of the Jowo khang. He had to sheepishly hand the text back to the shopkeeper after a long chase and was roundly admonished and called, '*Drukpa Akhen*' or the big thief from Bhutan. Needless to say, we heard this story from his companions and not him.

We could hardly imagine the motor vehicles that Phub Dorji described. Chinese goods were aplenty in Lhasa by then, and my father indulged by buying a Chinese thermos flask. On the homeward journey Phub Dorji was charged with the most precious item. We called this wonder utensil *horbotola* in Bhutanese. It would not take a linguist to trace the Bhutanese term to the English word for 'hot bottle' (*hor* = hot and *botola* = bottle). Phub Dorji was told to protect the precious item with his life. On the day they crossed the Monla Kharchung, Phub Dorji noticed that the saddle on one of the mules had become lopsided so he rushed to straighten it, but the impatient mule would not stop and moved on, pushing against him. Phub Dorji lost his footing and was pushed on to a glacier the size of 'two or more archery fields'. As he went sliding down the glacier, all he could think of was the thermos flask on his back. Phub Dorji recalled that with their 'faces shrunken to a mouthful', everybody looked on in horrified helplessness. He said there was nothing to hold on to; neither was there any object to stop him from sliding all the way down to the end of the glacier. Disoriented and a little dizzy, he fumbled and tried to stand up. By and by, some of the men from the travel team were beside him. In silence they helped him up on his feet. My father, on seeing that he was all right, broke the silence by making a statement that Phub Dorji could not forget for the rest of his life: 'I hope my thermos flask is not damaged.' Phub Dorji used to shake his head incredulously every time he repeated the story and say, 'I could have been lost and dead and all my Dasho was concerned about was his thermos flask!' The flask had survived this adventure and had an added value because of its amazing survival. One of the first things that father did after his arrival was to have the tailor Ap

Ngolay stitch a thick layered cover for the flask. Ap Ngolay made a cover of red blazer material with a fine yellow piping. Even after my parents had died, the flask, easily identifiable by its red-and-yellow covering, stayed on. Then slowly over the years, like many other things, it too disappeared, but its image lingered on as the first horbotola in Ogyen Choling.

13

Visitors

THE MOST IMPORTANT VISIT my parents prepared for was that of the third King, His Majesty Jigme Dorji Wangchuck. I may have been less than six years old at the time, but I remember some of the preparations. I knew something big was to happen. My parents worked for days preparing for the visit. The rooms in the utse were readied in the best way they knew how. I think my mother and her cousin, uncle Sangye Lhuendup, oversaw the internal arrangements, while my father was at the controls, planning, organizing and, literally, transforming even the landscape. The lajab, work supervisor, Meme Balengpa, who had a pronounced limp, hobbled harder than ever, shouting loud instructions tinged with threats to get the workers to work more efficiently. All his commands ended with '*Ya ya*', a mild threat. I remember how the villagers were engaged to fill up the sunken area, the main path, that led to our house. The path was lined with gigantic willow trees, layered with age and scarred by constant lopping, an ancient avenue, but the path was often muddy. Father thought that this was not an appropriate approach to the house for a royal visit. For days he supervised as the workers filled up the area using loads of soil, boulders and the tree trunks of the willows that had been cut down to plug up the depression. They had to raise the sunken area to the level of the adjacent Goenkhang *dumra*, the garden of the deity Gonpo, so named because the area falls near the goenkhang, the chapel of the deity. Once the gap was filled and levelled, a camp was prepared with tents and bamboo mats for the royal attendants, soldiers and porters who would accompany the King. Everything was ready and my parents were waiting with bated breath to welcome their monarch. A few days before the expected arrival, my parents were informed that the King would not come to Ogyen Choling; he would instead travel via the village of Dazur, less than two kilometres from Ogyen Choling, and camp in Phokpai instead.

I wonder how my parents took this. But they were not stumped into immobility. Father immediately shifted the focus of the preparations to Phokpai, the base camp to Rodongla. The King was going to Lhuentse, so Phokpai was on the way. Father, along with all the workers, moved to Phokpai and I vaguely remember people carrying loads of food, cooking utensils and even fodder, grains and hay, for the horses. I clearly remember that there was an unexpected panic about not having enough mustard oil to give the horses. I don't recall how they solved that problem. My father stayed in Phokpai to complete the preparations and to receive the King. By all accounts, His Majesty was pleased and expressed his appreciation for the careful arrangements and reception. Father received generous gifts from him which included a rifle with an inscription on it that stated that the gun had been gifted to the Queen Her Majesty Ashi Kesang Choeden Wangchuck by Pandit Jawaharlal Nehru, the first Prime Minister of the Republic of India.

It was many years later, long after my parents were dead and gone, that I heard the reason for the sudden change in the King's route. It was either a concerned person or more likely a person who was jealous that Ogyen Choling was to be honoured by a royal visit, who informed the King that my parents had had a serious quarrel and that my father had cut my mother's face with a sword. The King, in his concern not to embarrass my parents at such a delicate time, decided not to come. This was an unfortunate missed opportunity for Ogyen Choling's history and reputation, most certainly a source of unhappiness for my parents. My mother did have a scar from a cut on her face starting from her left eyebrow down to the top of her cheek. It was from a fall, not a sword injury. She had fallen when we were in Gorgan, some months earlier. While we were in Gorgan she had work in the grain store, measuring paddy harvested from our fields every day. She had devised a system of keeping the wooden boxes filled with paddy and lining them up against the walls. She used to move from one area of the storeroom to the other by jumping from one box to the next and landing on the soft paddy. One day one of the servants, overzealously, reorganized the grain storage systems, leaving some boxes empty for some reason. Mother jumped from one box to land in an empty box in the dimly lit room. She fell in and banged her face on its edge. Mother told me this story herself. Every time I remember it, I see my mother as a playful, energetic young woman, inventing fun ways to lighten her dull duties as the mistress of a household with many tedious responsibilities.

I have a fuzzy memory of another royal visit, but my brothers and I were hidden away during this one. The two queens, Her Majesty, the Queen Mother Ashi Phuntsho Choden and Her Majesty, the junior Queen Ashi Pema Dechen with her three daughters, Ashi Chokey Wangmo, Ashi Deki Yangzom and Ashi Pema Choden, had come for the sulphur spring baths at Takarla menchu, not far from Ogyen Choling. After their baths they were to visit Ogyen Choling and spend time here. My parents were advised by an uncle who was familiar with the Royal Court to keep us children out of sight to avoid bringing shame upon the family. The reason was that we were not trained to behave properly in the presence of royalty and, moreover, we looked scruffy and peasant-like. For the entire time the royal visitors were with our family we were banished to a part of the house with a trapdoor that was closed; it opened only when our meals were brought in for us.

Perhaps it was well-intended advice to avert shame and disgrace for my parents. For although we were privileged children with more resources and opportunities, our parents were quite laid-back in their parenting style and did not fuss too much over our appearance and hygiene. They let us grow up like the village children. We ate better than the children from the village and may have had more clothes to wear, but we were mostly barefooted, like them, and looked no different. Throughout most of my childhood we had a person to care for us, mainly to make sure that we did not get into serious trouble or cause harm to others. The person who cared for us did give us the rare baths in water so hot that we were nearly scalded and rubbed us so hard that our flesh tingled for hours after. But during the time between the baths, we were crusted with dirt. I clearly recall the reaction of a compounder, Babu Sampa, a medical personnel trained to administer basic medical services. He must have come on some medical duty. When he was leaving, I was playing by the gate, and he wanted to give me something. When I held out my hand to receive whatever it was that he was giving me, he looked shocked at the state of my unwashed hands, crusted with dirt. He asked in a sad tone, 'Don't you ever wash your hands? They look like a pig's trotters.' I immediately hid my hands behind my back. It was the tone of hopelessness in his voice that put me to shame.

I must have been a dirty little girl. My hands were my main source of embarrassment, especially because I had warts on my hands and feet. The warts were so thick and lumpy that the elders compared them to *tokpoi berpo*, a quilt of rags. I got rid of the warts thanks to a Tibetan monk who stayed with us for a while. My parents immediately felt a connection to this raggedy yogin and tried to make him stay with them as an in-house lama. He stayed on condition that my father would give up hunting. Like other aristocrats of the time, my father indulged in the sport of hunting, something my mother never approved of. He had quite a big collection of guns and often went hunting with some servants and his faithful hunter, Prala. They hunted mostly for bears. I wonder if my mother had had an influence on the monk imposing this condition for his stay. My father agreed and the monk stayed with us until my father fell into his sinful indulgence and killed a bear that was damaging our buckwheat crops. The monk did not say anything to anybody but took up his *kesang khurshing*, the cane loops within which he carried his belongings, and left. No number of apologies and pleas could stop him from leaving. He went to stay in Kunzangdrak, the temple associated with the fifteenth-century saint Pema Lingpa. My father went to atone for his sin, and from then onwards they maintained a sort of cordial patron-and-lama relationship, but the lama would not return to live with us. The monk had started a treatment for my warts and agreed to continue the treatment from his self-imposed exile. Every few days drupchu, sacred spring water from Kunzangdrak, which the monk imbued with holy mantras, was brought to our house. I had to wash my hands and feet with the blessed water. I am not sure how long the treatment went on for but one fine morning I got up to see that my warts had disappeared. I was shocked that such bulging appendages could vanish without a sign. I looked for any scabs or skin peelings in my bedding, but there was nothing. They had simply gone without a trace. It was a miracle. Such was the power of this lama whose name I do not even remember.

The visit of the Queens and Princesses was to be a time for celebration and enjoyment. But we, the children, had to be content with hearing the singing and dancing in another part of the house. We peeped through the windows to catch fleeting glimpses of the royal visitors when they moved around. They were staying in the utse. The dancing and entertainment were in the room in the shagkor, the main family room. For this occasion, my parents' gramophone was being used in addition to the dancers and singers who performed continuously. The women dancers, I was told, were dressed up in mother's kiras. All we could do was to strain our ears to listen to the music, songs and laughter of the merrymakers. The only person who showed some concern for us in the 'lock-up' was my aunty Kunzang Wangmo, my father's cousin, who came to us to tell us what was happening. She told us that the youngest princess Ashi Pema Choden, who was known then as Ashi *Bebe*, performed *Chakarpai*, Indian dances. Aunty Kunzang was completely charmed by the princess's performance. The princess could dance to any music playing on the gramophone, and she even danced with phonograph record discs on her palms without dropping them even once.

But my aunty Kunzang herself was the star at that event. Her repertoire of songs was endless, and she never tired from the continuous dancing. Most of all, she beat the court *tsangmo* champion in a competition. Tsangmo is a verse of four lines that can be recited or sung. The singers can recite established verses or spontaneously make up verses following the four-line meter. After the guests had left, I heard with wonder that on that evening my aunt, through her creative verbal mastery, triumphantly packed her opponent in a leather bag and threw him into the river, and that was the end of her opponent.

There is one royal visit that I clearly remember, because Her Majesty the Queen Mother Ashi Phuntsho Choden had asked to see me. I must have washed and cleaned up for the audience. I remember sitting cross-legged in front of her on the shiny floor, so conscious of myself that my knees were not parallel to the floor as they should have been. Instead, I had awkwardly pulled in my knees until they were scrunched up to my chest. The Queen Mother talked to me kindly and asked me some questions. She was sitting with her back to the window from which the brilliant sunlight was spilling into the room straight on to my face. She appeared to me like a dazzling ethereal figure. I remember receiving some gifts from her. I wonder how I behaved. Like a scruffy peasant girl? Nobody said anything as far as I can remember.

There were other visitors who came regularly, mostly our relatives from Lhuentse. Part of my father's family was from Lhuentse, and we seemed to have maintained a thriving relationship with them until my parents died. After they died, most of our connections were lost over time. My brothers and I were still children and away in schools in India, and there were no adults to sustain and nurture these familial connections. A sad reality that I wish had been otherwise. My parents honoured and tried to preserve even ancient relationships. I particularly remember the visits of one of our relatives from Tibet. This relationship went back across several generations to the sixteenth century. The visitor was Guensar lama, Yoeserla. Guensar is in the southern Tibetan province of Lhodark. This was the estate that was once managed by our ancestor, Mogha Drolma, widow of Sangay Thinley, the seventh-generation patriarch who died young. Guensar is close to the Monla Karchung mountain and not far from the Bhutanese border travelling from the north of Choekhor valley. It was not a very large property, with mountains in the background and a river in the foreground. There was a monastery with about a dozen monks, and the family's economic power was based on the herds of yak they owned.

Guensar lama Yoeserla was a tall, distinguished-looking Tibetan gentleman whom I took to be the iconic Tibetan aristocrat. I compared him to my father who was also tall and distinguished-looking. He wore his red brown heavy serge gho in the Tibetan style. The gho fell below his knees (my father wore his just above). Unlike my father's gho, which had a distinctive square pleat in the back, our Tibetan cousin's gho was folded into an indistinguishable bunch of pleats. His was tied at the waist with a red silken belt and the tassels at the end were always hanging down. One sleeve of his gho was off his shoulder and would flap by his side. My father had short, cropped hair while lama Yoeserla had long hair braided with red silk threads and tied on top of his head. He wore knee-length *shutse*, black boots. My father had a similar pair. I think these boots were manufactured in Kalimpong. The most distinguishing aspect of lama Yoeserla's appearance was the big turquoise earring he wore on one of his ears, and I never ceased to admire how it dangled and moved when he spoke.

From my earliest memory, people from Tibet, especially from Lhodrak province, were moving across the border and coming into Bhutan. Historically there was a tradition of Tibetan traders, particularly from the Sey region, moving back and forth across the borders. The rush of Tibetan refugees came towards the end of the 1950s, but our relatives did not attempt to leave their home. My parents always asked after them with every new refugee they met. The last thing we heard of them was that they had tried to escape and hid in the mountains for a while. But when they returned home to take their precious belongings that they had left behind, they were caught by the Chinese and imprisoned. They had to participate in the Chinese re-education classes and were subjected to the humiliation of *thamzing*, denouncements. The final news we received was that our relative, the tall, distinguished aristocrat, was assigned to carry out the night soil. A daughter of the lama escaped and settled in Bumthang and had a daughter who now lives there.

My parents were regularly entertaining monks from Tibet. The visits of monks became even more frequent right before the Chinese takeover and especially after the takeover. It was at this time that we were fortunate to receive many sacred blessings and empowerments. I remember how my parents used to take the lamas into the most sacred part of the house, the family altar, and the lamas would bless us with the most sacred statues and relics there. I think this was the only time we saw these religious treasures housed in our family altars. Among the lamas I remember were Jadrey Jangchuk Dorji, Lama Pelzang, Baza Guru Rinpoche and Beru Trulku. In 1959, one of the most revered Tibetan masters, the sixth Nyamkhai Ningpo Rinpoche of the famous Lhodrak Karchung monastery in Tibet, came to stay with our family for a while. The Rinpoche and his entourage had left the monastery to escape before the actual Chinese invasion of Tibet and had crossed into Bhutan. They crossed through the northern part of Kurtoe, today's Lhuentse district. After spending time in Lhuentse they came to Bumthang. When they arrived the Rinpoche and his entourage came to stay with us as our family had historical and religious links to Lhodrak Karchung.

I remember the lama's arrival as clearly as if it happened a few days ago. My parents, along with family members and many villagers, waited devoutly to receive the Rinpoche and his most impressive entourage. The lama's procession was completely different from the Tibetan refugees who came begging for food and shelter. We had seen Tibetan refugees of every kind; desperate families with hungry children trailing along, mothers with babies pulling at their breasts, and tired-looking men with gaunt and defeated expressions came daily to our house. They all wanted food, and my mother was generous and never sent anyone away without some provisions. The villagers were equally generous, sharing whatever little they had. We were used to seeing these refugees. Even as children we recognized their vulnerability and we internalized a sense that we were the givers and they were dependent on us; therefore, we were better off, higher up. But the lama's arrival changed our perception. The lama came very dignified, riding a horse beautifully caparisoned, and the whole procession was grand by any standard. The lama was followed by monks, loaded horses, porters and some members of his family. My attention was immediately drawn to a girl, some years older than me, who had a youthful and aristocratic appearance. Although she was tired, she smiled at us, and the colourful tassels in her long, plaited hair looked beautiful, (especially since all the girls in the village had short, cropped hair). My hair could also grow long and beautiful, I thought, as I touched my uncombed, stubbly hair. Later I got to know her as Yangdonla, a niece of the lama, with whom I am still in touch.

Although the visitors were refugees, there was a visible finesse and splendour about them. The lama's fine saddle carpets and brocades were not like those of the ragged refugees we were used to seeing. The lama dismounted his horse, helped by attendants from both sides, only when he reached the line of people waiting for him. Through the swirling smoke from the incense of juniper and wormwood, I could make out the lama, a tall, fair and thin man with a beautifully contoured face. As he got off his horse my parents went towards him, holding white scarves and reverently bending their bodies low to receive his blessings. The eager villagers, always hungry for rare and sacred blessings, took advantage of their good fortune and rushed forward to claim their share. I watched as the monk gracefully touched the heads of all the devotees with his hands in in the gesture of *chak wang*, but he honoured my parents with the gesture of *uo thod* (touching their heads with his own).

It was not the ceremony and the pageantry that awed me the most, but a bird cage carried by one of the people in the procession. In it was a green bird perched on a horizontal stick. It looked out at us inquisitively and moved, squawking excitedly. Obviously, the immense religious significance and the important events of history and geopolitics made no sense to the bird or to us children. It was this creature that completely captivated us, and all our eyes followed the bird who recognized our interest and showed off. The dangling cage then disappeared into the utse where the lama was to stay.

There were more surprises in store for us. For it was not just a bird but a talking bird. It squawked and chattered and said some words. It repeated the word 'Truepaiku' referring to the lama and called out the name 'Yangdonla' referring to his niece. We had heard of talking birds. In fact, on our temple wall we had a drawing of two-headed birds that represented the translators of the past. Like all the other pictures in the temple, these birds too had a more superior than human element about them. They were real but beyond the ordinary. And here was a real talking bird without two heads! For some time, we children stayed in the courtyard below the window of the room that the lama had occupied on the second floor of the utse, waiting to hear the words uttered by the bird, while the adults waited to hear the sacred words of blessing from the lama. Perhaps on seeing the eager children hovering in the courtyard, the lama thoughtfully instructed his attendant to hang the bird cage on a nail on the wooden window frame in full view.

The idea that birds can talk left a lasting impression on us and we spoke about it endlessly. That is when Lhamola, a young man appointed by our parents to be our caregiver, had an idea. Lhamola was with us all the time and looked after us day and night. He was full of humour and wisdom and was our guide and mentor. But he was often exhausted by our fidgetiness and having to entertain us and constrain us from our wild roving. He said, 'Of course birds can be taught to speak.' He explained: 'The *junn* (thrush) can be taught to speak very easily. But we must catch it first. The forested strip below the drupchu is home to the junn. Oh, come on, you have all seen the little bird with greyish-green-blue plumage. The one that flits through the forests crying *cheeer cheeer* as it flies up and down. You can easily catch it. Some of you must chase it, and others must wait to catch it as it flies through the trees and bushes into your hands.' He held up his hands over his head, palms facing out. 'Yes, like this. Once you catch it, we will keep it in a basket turned upside down while I heat a frying pan. When the pan gets very hot, you must quickly throw the bird into it and it will say, "*Ma bay* (Don't)." You must immediately take the bird out of the pan before it is scorched to death and then teach the bird to speak. After this the bird's ability for speech will have been stimulated and it will speak just like any one of us.'

Fascinated, we immediately planned how to catch the bird. Lhamola was right. There were several birds in the forest and, disturbed by our presence, they instantly flew up and down the stream as soon as we approached them. Some of us chased them downstream while others waited at the end of the forest with hands raised over our heads, palms opened outwards, waiting for the birds to fly into our hands. After we had chased them several times up and down the stream and we could no longer take another step, the birds tweeted their last goodbyes and flew off. Lhamola encouraged and pressed us on, 'Every day you try harder you will get more practice, and one day you will have a talking bird.' Gradually, we outgrew the hunt for the talking bird and moved on to other adventures, but Lhamola had succeeded in keeping us occupied and out of mischief for several days.

The talking bird incident was not the only consequence of Namkhai Ningpo's visit to our house. Soon after he arrived in Bumthang, his personal physician managed to escape from the prison where the Chinese had him incarcerated and he followed the lama to Bumthang. The adults and children were mesmerized and terrified as we listened to the traumatic tales of his time in the prison, especially his traumatic escape. He told us that he and a colleague had managed to escape after they sawed down a pillar and collapsed a wall with a small penknife. It took them many days to saw down the pillar because it was such a small penknife. Days of persistent hard work were rewarded when they could leave the room they had been locked up in. They crawled through rooms filled with dead bodies. It seemed like the Chinese had forgotten that they locked up these prisoners. The stories sounded like the horror stories of the sinpos who locked up people to be eaten gradually. Were the Chinese like those demons, I wondered.

When the people in the valley heard the new fugitive was a doctor, patients flocked to him with all sorts of problems. He did not mind the audience of children and adults when he treated his patients. The room on the third floor of the utse, where we now have the printing block displayed, was used as the clinic. Patients climbed up three levels of stairs to visit the doctor. The doctor had his implements in a bag and treated the patients with authority and poise. Whenever I got a chance, I too climbed up the stairs and watched with horror and fascination as he burnt spots on people's bodies, inserted needles and cut into parts of the body to let out the 'bad blood'. I remember the day our tailor who suffered from sinusitis came to seek medical attention. I can still see the blood spurting out across the room when the doctor made an incision on the tailor's nose. Another time I saw him making an incision under someone's tongue to cure a stutter; dark black blood oozed out. I think most of the patients believed that these remedies helped them.

After the doctor left, that space was used occasionally to display goods for sale. This merchandise belonged to another regular visitor; a man called Lopon Choeda who was also originally from Lhodrak. He and my family had intergenerational connections. At the time our temple was being painted in the early 1900s by a painter called Ugyen, also from Lhodrak, Lopon Choeda was a child and worked as his assistant. During my childhood, he was a well-respected sculptor and painter. He travelled a lot. So instead of lugging around his belongings, he had arranged to use a room in the utse to store his goods. My parents were fond of this man. They respected him greatly and valued his artistic skills. He stayed with us when my parents had commissioned him to build a life-size Vajrapani, the wrathful form of the meditational deity in blue colour, holding a vajra in his right hand and a scull in his left, and we spent many days watching him as he worked on the statue.

Lopon Choeda had not only managed to avoid the Chinese takeover by leaving Tibet earlier but also brought along some of his belongings which were stored in our house. These goods were exchanged against money as well as grains. Occasionally, when somebody wanted to buy something, the goods were displayed on the floor. People gathered around to buy cloth, prints of scriptures, porcelain and all sorts of other things. I used to hang around and admire the items. As soon as the crowd grew, inevitably there would be chaos with people asking for the price of various items. The negotiations and bargaining, and the person selling the goods would get distracted. That was the time I saw people stealing. For quite some time I had admired a silk scarf and desired it very much. It was bluish green in colour with canary-yellow floral patterns. I had no money. But I wanted it and was encouraged by those who stole and got away with it. After looking at the scarf for days, I had the courage to touch it. It was soft and slippery in my hands. I wanted it more than ever. I had seen a man steal a piece of cloth by putting it between his thighs and casually shuffling out of the room unnoticed. That's what I decided to do. I handled the scarf for a long time, loving it and wanting it badly. Then I placed it between my ankles, visible to all, and tried to shuffle out of the room as the man had done. The person selling the goods was looking at me with an expression of shock and amusement. I felt his eyes follow me until I stepped over the threshold into the next room and was safe. He had watched me passively until I left the room. He was too embarrassed to intervene. After all, I was the daughter of the host who had allowed him to use the space in our house.

I hid the scarf under my mattress for a few days, not daring to even look at it. But I always knew that it was there. I finally had what I had so coveted but now I did not feel any joy in possessing it. Instead, I felt uncomfortable. And it became a source of anxiety and shame. How could I have stolen from a man my parents respected and loved? I never realized until then that stealing had painful consequences. I did not even want the scarf any more. I had not told anyone about it. One day a cousin of mine saw it when I was making my bed and asked me about it. It was a big relief for me to confess that I had stolen it from the lopon's treasury. My cousin brightened up and had the perfect solution: I should give him the scarf, which I happily did, and he would use it as a book wrap for his scriptures. He would not tell anyone about it. If the stolen material was used for an honourable if not religious purpose, there would not be any need for penitence. I was delivered from my sin in giving up my stolen article. I have never forgotten this incident. And even now whenever I go into that room, or see similar blue-green colours, I am reminded of the day I committed larceny.

Another regular visitor was Choeje Rinzinla from Sombrang in Ura. He was related to my mother. My mother appreciated these visits and enjoyed his company. Choeje Rinzinla was a serious man, dignified and calm. Most of his visits were quite uneventful except the one time when he had to lead an elaborate ceremony to propitiate the deity Talo Gyalpo from Punakha. It so happened that Ashi Chokey's daughter, Ashi Deki Choden, who was just beginning to walk, was so ill that the diviners had suggested that a change of residence would be good for her. Ashi Deki Choden was brought to Ogyen Choling, and my parents were charged with looking after her for some time, maybe nearly a year. She had her own attendants – Pasang Dorji, Tshering Lem Lem and Kheng Dorji – who accompanied her from Wangdue Choling palace. My parents were completely wrapped up in ensuring that she was taken care of to the best of their abilities and were ever so attentive to any signs of discomfort or illness. We were on the periphery as passive onlookers in our own house. We saw her regularly but rarely interacted with her. And when we did, it was in a restrained and cautious manner, because she was sick, and she was an Ashi.

One night she got seriously ill and when we woke up in the morning we saw panic everywhere. People were running around in a dazed manner, tired from having stayed up the whole night and at a loss for what to do next. Prayers were going on in the temple. Horses were being saddled and loaded with loads of grains and cloth, and a beautifully caparisoned riding horse was ready for the rider. There was to be a procession to see off an important guest. But who was the important guest? We watched from a distance, trying to keep from getting in the way of the frenzied adults. Throughout the night prayers and rituals had been conducted, while the women had fed food to every *doen*, malevolent spirit, which may have been harming the little Ashi. There was food scattered in the courtyard, so much food that even the crows and dogs were so full they couldn't eat any more. As a last resort, it was decided to try to appease the Talo Gyalpo (the protective deity of Talo), and the only person who knew the appeasement procedure was Choeje Rinzinla. As the Talo Gyalpo was a deity of the highest category, he could not be pacified with scattering food as they had done for the lowly spirits. Talo Gyalpo had to be treated as a royal spirit and seen off in a grand procession. The procession was led by a drummer and a gong beater. To the beat of the drum and the clanging of the gong, the attendants, dressed up as if they were in attendance of a king, followed. A horseman leading the riding horse and the pack mules with the loads of grains and other materials followed. Choeje Rinzinla was walking beside the riding horse on which the Talo Gyalpo was believed to ride away. I excitedly hopped and skipped with the other children, following the procession as they headed west towards the Tang Chu. We were told not to go beyond a certain distance from the house. I am not sure if this extravagant send-off helped the sick Ashi, but soon afterwards she was taken back to Wangdue Choling palace to be with her parents. For my parents, they were freed of a big responsibility. For as long as Ashi was in their charge, our parents had forgotten about their own children.

It was probably because of my father's interest in guns that he became friendly with the commandant of the Bhutanese military border post in Khakthang, in the northern part of Choekor valley. Once when the commandant was on patrol, he came for a visit. He was sitting with my father in the main room, and I happened to be at the far end of the house and looked out of the window. What a shock it was to see an unusual animal grazing by itself in the compound below the old walnut tree. From the descriptions I had heard, I was certain it was a musk deer. It was as big as a young calf and blackish brown in colour. Ah, so this was the animal that people talked about with awe and in secrecy. One part of this animal's body was the coveted musk which was an expensive commodity and a prized medicine. Poachers hunted this animal and sold the musk pod illegally for high prices. There was always secrecy and tension in handling this animal part. My parents had once acquired an entire pod of musk and dried it in secret. They didn't even want the servants to see that we had a musk pod, so they had devised a complicated contraption to dry it in their bedroom. The pod was hung on a long twine from the ceiling directly above the *gochor*, the wooden partition in front of the door. They were drying it over an open brazier with hot charcoals. Someone had to hold the pod over the fire, but any time somebody walked into the room the pod was released, and it would swing back against the screen out of view. I not only saw the musk pod, but I had also touched it. It looked like a leather pouch; it felt rough to the touch and had a very strong smell. On occasions when we were ill and a minuscule amount was administrated to us, it tasted foul even though it was wrapped in butter. We had to swallow it without letting it touch our teeth. We were told our teeth would fall out if the musk came in contact with them.

I had to tell my father that there was a musk deer in our compound, but how could I tell him in front of a visitor who was not just any visitor but a law enforcer? I ran up to him and without saying anything ran back to the veranda to see if the animal was still there. I did this maddening run two or three times until my father followed me and I proudly pointed out the animal. My father took one look and said, 'That is a female musk deer. It has no musk,' and went back to his guest. I learnt an important lesson that day: only male musk deer possess the valuable musk pod.

I had done this wordless running back and forth in front of my parents before and they knew that it was my way of alerting them to something unusual. My mother had a big wooden box in the passageway to keep *tsog*, fried biscuits. These biscuits were offered on the altar and served to visitors. We loved eating these biscuits and could never get enough. My elder brother Rinzin and I used to often help ourselves to them whenever we passed by. Together we would lift the heavy wooden lid, put our hands into the box and bring out as many as we could reach. Over time the level of biscuits went down and finally there was just a thin layer at the bottom. My brother said that I should hold the lid, and he would try and reach into the box. I could open the box only a crack because the wooden lid was so heavy. My brother put in his hands, then his head, then his shoulders and upper body until he was hanging from the edge of the box trying to get to the biscuits. In my attempt to hold the lid, I decided to use a prop because my hands were getting tired. I grabbed a thin bamboo stick from nearby. The stick was what my father used to clean the barrel of his rifles. It was very thin. I was holding up the lid with it when it suddenly snapped, and the lid landed on my brother who was half in and half out of the box. His feet were off the ground and his hands had not reached the bottom of the box. He was trapped, kicking his feet and crying out. I ran into my parents' room and ran out, repeating 'Acho Rinzin, Acho Rinzin.' After I did that twice, both my parents followed me. By then I was crying too. They lifted the lid of the box and freed my brother.

The kind of visitors my parents received and entertained changed over the years. As the district administration began to gain more control and our family gradually lost ground, we had to bear with the visits of the various bureaucrats from Jakar dzong who wanted to assert their influence and power. The new bureaucrats were so different from our most regular visitor, the Tang drungpa, who was the most important government appointee in the valley. The office of the drungpa preceded the dzongkhag administration. His post must have originated during the country's new administration after the death of Zhabdrung. Tang drungpa Tsewang lived in a nagtshang, a two-storeyed manorial house, in the village of Kizom. I have recollections of him visiting us often. He always wore his sword, the badge of his position, rode his white horse wherever he went and was accompanied by an attendant. Although everyone recognized the powers of his position, nobody took him too seriously. Perhaps the office of the Tang drungpa was already losing its importance. His duties were crucial to the existing system which included collecting taxes from the people, settling disputes and granting permission for temporary use of government lands, especially for shifting cultivation for growing buckwheat. He was also responsible for making sure that the *depai choeshing*, the wetlands in the valley, which belonged to the government, were cultivated and that the grains were harvested and stored for distribution to the local population or submitted to higher authorities. He was assisted by the services of two *gups* (village headmen) from the villages of Nurut and Dazur. At the time, the posts of these gups were hereditary. The drungpa seemed to have felt the ensuing changes affecting his office but he mistakenly viewed Ogyen Choling as the main threat to his powers and always asked, 'Who is more important, the Tang drungpa or Ogyen Choling?' He reassured himself by repeating, '*Pon gi jab Pon gi rang bay wong may.* (The powerful will always protect the powerful.)' Ironically, when he fell into the public latrine behind our house, his only support came from his attendant, Sithar, who pulled him out of the mess and gave him a wash under the common waterspout in public view.

My parents were always gracious, kind and correct in dealing with the newly emerging bureaucrats. But from my child's perspective I could see that there were higher authorities of power above my parents. One day our cook Meme Nakzila was agitated because a bureaucrat from Jakar dzong helped himself to drinking water stored in our cauldron and washed his muddied feet in our kitchen at the place where only food and cooking utensils were washed. I saw this as a sign that my parents no longer had the power and respect that they had so far enjoyed.

14

Chasing the Sun

TODAY AS I JOIN the elders circumambulating the temple while taking long breaks to sit in the sun, I am reminded of the sun chasers from my childhood. There was a visible group of older people no longer actively engaged in agricultural work who were always looking for a spot in the sun. As soon as the rays of the morning sun touched certain spots in the village these elders would occupy them, facing the sun like compulsive sunbathers determined to get a tan. But these elders were sun soakers absorbing the sun's warmth. They basked in the sunlight from sunrise to sunset, following the sun and sitting in the spots they knew received the most sunlight at different times of the day. In the freezing morning, they faced the sun; after midday they turned their backs to it before reluctantly but deliberately heading home to sit by their warm hearths, even as the chilly winds whistled and hissed through their poorly insulated houses. As I get older, I find myself chasing the sun too. The bone-nipping chills push me to the very spots in the compound that the sun chasers of my youth used to occupy.

Meme Chowang, a cousin of my grandfather, was one of the most memorable sun chasers. For so large a man, he bounced lightly as he walked. He was always dressed in a faded, red woollen *Nampo* gho and always wore a pair of bobola. He had lived in Lhalung in Tibet for several years and had become more Tibetan than most Tibetans I knew. I used to think that he even smelt Tibetan. I suppose because he had a very different presence compared to the farmers who smelt of the earth and sweat from their daily toil, his smell was different. He smelt comforting; of smoke and butter, which had a sense of quiet calm wealth, since butter was associated with wealth. Because he was of an unusually big stature, I was always surprised when he talked in his high-pitched voice. He had to constantly wipe the corners of his mouth because he was drooling all the time. Long silvery strings of saliva that he tried to noisily suck back into his mouth, as he wiped his mouth with a sweep of his large hands. He often used a thick striped woollen cloth as his handkerchief and was invariably blowing his nose into it, especially after he had had a generous dose of snuff.

He had been entrusted to be the manager to my grandfather's brother, the ninth Lhalung Thugse Thubten Gyeltshen, while he held the post of Thugse. In my earliest memory of him, Meme Chowang was already an old man. He spent much time with my parents, joined us for meals, and I suppose was a kadroepa to my father, one of those who was freed from any specific duties but stayed on to talk with and advise my father. There were several such men with my father. In the absence of a grandfather, Meme Chowang was our surrogate grandfather.

My parents consulted him on many issues, and he was open and loud in his opinions. He was also the most entertaining storyteller for us children. We often found ourselves gravitating towards him whenever he sat down quietly in the sun, especially in the winter. Whenever Meme Chowang was not nodding off to sleep, he would enthral us with stories of his time in Lhalung. Responding to our earnest pleas, we would rouse him from his somnolent state and demand, 'Again!' No story could begin without a good dose of snuff. We were patient as he would take out his snuff horn and go through the elaborate process of preparing a dose. He would first face the sun, and let the warm rays tickle his nostrils and make him sneeze. All the strange expressions on his face, it was like watching a cartoon, the twitching and grimaces before he could get himself to sneeze. After several blows into a thick handkerchief, he would ceremoniously take out the yak horn tip which had been fashioned into a snuff holder. He would carefully unplug the tip of the horn, then pour some of the finely powdered tobacco on to his left hand between his thumb and forefinger. He would divide the powder into two heaps, ensuring that they were of equal quantity. Scrutinizing the heaps, taking a minuscule amount from each, adding, or taking away from each until he was satisfied that they were the same. Then the horn was placed back in his pouch in a reassuring and possessive manner. Now he was ready for the 'fix'. He would transfer the first heap on to the thumbnail of his right hand. When every bit of the powder was on his nail, his nose would twitch in eager anticipation. He would place the nail with the heap close to one of his nostrils and sniff sniff sniff or was it snort snort snort. When every trace of the brown powder was gone, in quick succession he transferred the other heap, and the other nostril received its dose.

After two resounding sneezes he was, finally, happily satisfied, and ready to respond to our petition for a story. His favourite was about his adventure with a bear in Lhalung. The encounter took place while he was squatting on his haunches facing the hillside and relieving himself. As he did not have a secure footing, he was holding on to a small, dried bush. His relaxed and leisurely experience suddenly turned hellish when he saw a big black bear ambling towards him in a resolute manner. He shouted and then screamed but it had no effect on the bear who had decided Meme Chowang was his target. In a sudden reaction he raised his hands to threaten the bear but more so in self-defence. At this moment he let go of the bush and lost his footing. Just when the hot steaming breath of the bear was in his face, he felt something hot and steamy under him. He had fallen in his own defecation and had rolled down the hillside. He rolled down through the rubble and the dried bushes like a 'ball of yak hair thread', down, down, down he went. When he finally stopped against a thorny bush, he was a stinky mess. Slowly he got up and looked up at the bear who looking down at him in puzzlement. Then the bear turned and walked away in the opposite direction.

Later on, the story acquired a pictorial representation. It became more dramatic and exciting and, as he told and retold the story, his drools of saliva hung forgotten and became continuous chains below his chin. Somehow our family had got a picture book that had photographs from all over the world. There was one picture in it that he insisted was a picture of Lhalung. He would roll his fists and put them in front of his eyes like binoculars to help him to identify the place more accurately. Staring at the picture, he pointed assuredly to the parts he recognized as the exact place where he was squatting, and from where the bear came and the trail of his fall. We would crane our necks and push and shove each other to follow his finger moving over the picture. We were transported to Lhalung to the place where Meme Chowang had his bear adventure. Years later, long after he had died and we had learnt to read, we chanced upon the caption under the picture that he had identified as Lhalung in Tibet. It was in reality an ancient monument on a hilltop in Greece!

Another prominent sun chaser was Aie Kesang who may have been around the same age as Meme Chowang. A kindly old woman who held a special status in the village and was always attentive and kind to us was Aie Kesang or Grandmother Kesang, although she wasn't really our grandmother. We could never pass by her house without being invited in for special treats, fruits in season, tea, and even drops of alcohol when she did not have anything else to offer us. She used nice Chinese porcelain bowls, such a rarity in the village in those days, which added to her enigma. There was a certain presence about her that told us that she was special. She wasn't a maid, neither was she a relative, but she stood out from the other villagers. We liked being with her and she was always affectionate and kind to us. Today as I pass the location of her house, I still remember the many times I climbed up the ladder to her house to go into her altar room. After climbing the ladder, we reached a small narrow veranda where her wooden tub of water was placed at one end. It was always wet and dank around the tub. I had once heard a story about a baby dragon that spent some time in a wooden tub of water and one day, when there was a roar of thunder, it responded with a small roar and flew off into the sky. Every time I was on this veranda I used to secretly wonder if there was a baby dragon in her tub of water. The whole place was dark because a huge pear tree literally grew into the space above the ladder. During the season when pears were ripe, we could pluck the fruits from there. It was only in my adult years when everybody of her age group was dead that I learnt what I should have been told a long time ago – that she was my grandfather's mistress and that even my grandmother had accepted her as the junior wife. Aie Kesang had a managerial position in the household during my grandfather's time. My grandmother who, from what I heard, seemed like a rather laid-back person, apparently left all the decisions in the household to her, saying, 'Ask Kesang', or 'Kesang will know what to do.' Why didn't anybody tell us about Aie Kesang's real connection to our family? I would have liked to have had a grandmother, even if she was a step-grandmother.

She was not a beautiful woman. When I think of her now, I see a kindly bundle of a woman in layers of woollen kiras and short toigos. She was fair, had greying hair, and a round face which had deep wrinkles on it. She was the kind of person who you could snuggle up to and feel her warmth and affection. By the time of my first recollection of this woman, both my grandparents were dead, and she no longer held the managerial position in the house. By then, my mother was the mistress of the house. But Aie Kesang still held the seemingly insignificant but in reality, very important position as the *chang nyer* or the mistress of the alcohol. As the mistress of the alcohol, she had access to large amounts of the family's grains, which was the family's wealth. Aie Kesang could have as many measures of grains as she needed. She had two rooms in the structure in front of the shagkor that housed the kitchens. She had the middle rooms demarcated as *changtshang* or alcohol house, enclosed by the public kitchen in the north and the private family kitchen to the south. This was Aie Kesang's domain over which she held undisputed sway. One room had a huge wood-burning stove to cook the grains for fermenting. The next room had a smaller stove for the process of distilling the fermented grains. This room had an additional space partitioned in it for maturing and ageing the fermenting grains in *gartang*. Some of these barrels were taller than six feet in height and had girths that could easily hold up to two hundred kilogrammes of grains. They were kept on wooden shelves off the ground, so they appeared even bigger as we had to look up at them. These barrels were made of wood boards tied with bamboo strips. On the ground, which was made of stone slabs, were lines of bamboo containers called *churmaidung* for storing the ara, the distilled alcohol.

Between her busy schedule of walking from the grain store to her alcohol making house she always took time to sit in the sun with the elders and share a quid of *paan* betel nut (areca nut) wrapped in betel leaf smeared with lime. As the nut which comes from the subtropics was not easily available, paan chewers substituted the nut with the mature bark ripped from peach trees and the roots of the wildflower potentilla. I have eaten so many small quids of this concoction which Aie Kesang lovingly prepared for me and introduced me to the indulgence of chewing pan.

Aie Kesang's responsibility was to ensure that there was always a good supply of alcohol in the house, and that kept her busy. The alcohol was required to serve the family members, given to the workers and visitors, and some of it was needed in the temple for rituals and rites as *duetsi* (ambrosia) and *serkhem* (ceremonial libations). Every time we passed the building, there was either a fire crackling in the stoves cooking grains or the strong pungent smell of the alcohol fumes permeating the air from the distillation in progress. I was often tempted to go and eat the fermenting grains which she used to scoop up with a sturdy wooden ladle and pour on to a rhododendron leaf. I ate the fermenting grains off the leaf. Once in a while she would invite us to taste the ara. She would take us into the storeroom, which was always locked. The key hung around her neck. Every time she locked or unlocked the door, she had to bring her face close to the door because she never took the key chain off her neck. Inside the storeroom she had lined up containers of ara on the stone floor. Each of the containers made of bamboo had a hole on the top for pouring out the liquid. The hole was corked with a folded rhododendron leaf. She not only allowed but encouraged us to taste the ara by removing the folded leaf and tasting the tip of the leaf that was inside the churmaidung, often immersed in the alcohol. For me the thrill was not the taste of the alcohol so much as the fun of seeing how many containers I could uncork.

The ara-tasting ritual took on a dangerous turn one day when Aie Kesang allowed my elder brother Rinzin, who was then about seven years old, to graduate from sucking the tips of the corks to drinking a few drops of the alcohol from his cupped palms. She made him taste the ara from all the containers until he became unconscious! Rather than telling my parents what happened, she simply said that my brother had fallen asleep and that she had carried him on her back in a big shawl. Eventually, my mother became suspicious when my brother was sleeping for very long and insisted on seeing him. What a nasty shock it was for her to see her son completely knocked out. My father was livid and wanted to lock up Aie Kesang, but by and by my brother recovered and she was spared. But from then on, we were absolutely forbidden to go to the changtshang, the alcohol brewing house.

Could my father really lock up people? Did he have the power to do so? Well, in those days my father did lock up people. I remember the case of the Tibetan man who was locked up for a while on suspicion of having murdered one of our family's weavers who was on his way to Tibet on a pilgrimage. Tektong was not just any weaver; he was a very special one, and dear to my parents. He was the only male weaver in the group of weavers my mother employed. He was a transgender and identified with and sought the comfort of being in the company of women. He was accepted by all and respected for his skill as a weaver. I remember spending hours in the loom room where there were always five to seven weavers every day, and Tektong was always among the women, completely comfortable in their warm companionship. He specialized in weaving the thick, elaborately patterned woollen cloths called *yathra.* I would hang around to pick up bits of threads that the weavers discarded so that my friends and I could use them for making rag dolls we called *Tukpui* Ashi or raggedy princess. These were basically stick crosses dressed up with bits of cloth and strings and loaded with lots of imagination.

Tektong wore a man's gho, but he wore it below his ankles like a long skirt. He was a big man, but he was gentle and soft in a deliberate and exaggerated way. He used expressions that were generally considered to be feminine. Men always referred to their friends as *charo* or *tosang*, but he used the feminine term *gonla*. Even children stopped playing to look at him in curiosity when he tried to speak in a high-pitched voice which suddenly dropped to a gruff baritone. At times we used to talk to each other mimicking him. He never minded us imitating him and often laughed at us. Tektong had no inhibitions being in the company of women and regularly joining the sun chasers for a spell of warmth.

Then, one fine day he suddenly decided to go on a pilgrimage to Tibet and never returned. I cannot remember for how long he was gone but there were rumours that he had been murdered by the Tibetans on the way. My father had to act. After all, Tektong was a servant in his household whose welfare was his responsibility. A search team was sent to look for Tektong's corpse. Even if the body could not be recovered, the team was ordered to investigate the crime and arrest the suspect. In those days my father had that kind of power. We had nearly forgotten the whole incident when the search team returned, bringing with them a Tibetan man. We goggled at the young man in a dirty white woollen gho, long hair tied in an untidy braid and a dangling earring in one ear. The search team had arrested him after they had made inquiries in the Tibetan settlements near Mola Karchung. He was the suspect, and they had brought him all the way to Ogyen Choling. I am not sure what was happening among the adults, but the poor man was locked up in one of the empty grain stores in the utse for several days. His hands were tied in front of him, but he was fed regularly and allowed to come out into the sun during the day, ironically becoming another sun chaser. Funny, even while I marvelled at my father's powers, I had an unidentified and lurking fear of a greater power, the *depa zhung* or the government of Tibet. How I even knew the term 'depa zhung' and realized that it was mighty, I don't know. But I felt a real fear over my father's actions. I don't know what happened, but I was very relieved when, after several days, the man was released. I had imagined the Tibetan government responding to my father arresting one of their people. The inquiries based on the information that the prisoner gave led to more searches with the prisoner leading the search, but nothing was ever heard or seen of the remarkable weaver from Ogyen Choling. It was accepted by all that he had fallen into a crevasse and died, which occasionally happened to travellers crossing glaciers. Tektong had died under mysterious circumstances. And because nobody explained how and where and why he died, the mystery of death seemed distant and abstract to us. But there was one man in the village whom we all knew not only defied death but also claimed to have come back from the dead.

Brokpa Dawa did not die, even when attempts were made to kill him. He was an unkempt old man who lived just outside the gate of our house. Despite spending all day in the sun, he was sour-faced and foul-tempered and had little patience with children who teased and taunted him. I never dared to go near him and always watched him from afar as he sat in the sun just outside our fence rolling mud pellets for my father's catapult. Brokpa Dawa would have a large lump of clay beside him and an old piece of cloth on which he placed the clay balls he had rolled. He laid out the marble-sized balls on the cloth to sun-dry and harden.

My father was always bothered by the red-billed chough which nested under the eaves of our house. Bevies of these nasty, dirty birds that numbered in the hundreds came home to roost under the roof every evening, creating a ruckus before they finally settled to sleep. These birds have a sharp, far-carrying, piercing nasal *chung chung* sound that is probably why it got its name, *chungkha*. Many people never got used to their sharp cries and nervous restlessness when they perched on the wooden roof. In addition to which their indiscriminate droppings that splattered the walls and window frames annoyed many, especially my father. He was devising all sorts of methods to chase the birds away. Spiky cotoneaster bushes were collected and filled into the gaps between the roof and the eaves. Unfortunately, the birds found these particularly inviting to roost on. Servants were made to chase them away with long bamboo sticks, but nothing deterred them. They came back again and again. My father's sole mission was to use a catapult to shoot at them every evening. He would shoot into the dark to frighten them but not kill them. But his shots led to more noise and commotion, as the birds' cries became even shriller; they fluttered and fidgeted even more and came back more aggressively to claim their roosting spots. It was for this mission that the old man Brokpa Dawa was employed by my father and given some rations for his services.

Brokpa Dawa lived with two of his nieces who shared the rations he received from our house as *phog* (employment fees) and tolerated him. He had little patience with them, and they had even less love for their unpleasant, foul-mouthed uncle. Once when their endurance was tested to the limit, they decided to kill him by poisoning him with none other than Chungkhai dok. The sisters had cooked the young shoots of the euphorbia for Brokpa Dawa, telling him that they were fern shoots. He ate the meal; the poison in it was not lethal enough to kill him but strong enough to render him unconscious for some time. He not only recovered from this incident but emerged stronger and more powerful. He now claimed that he had died and reached the realms of hell in the transition from life to death. He had met the lord of death, *Shinje Choekye Gyalpo*, during the *bardo* transition and he had urged him to go back to the human world quickly before his crafty wicked nieces were able to burn down the house to claim his land and property.

In another incident he had a fall and became unconscious and again came back with amazing stories of his death experience. Brokpa Dawa continued to sit in the sun and roll mud balls for my father who continued to shoot the birds which never stopped coming to our house. The birds are now such an essential part of the house that we have learnt to live with them. Ironically, it is the memory of the sounds and the sight of these birds that filled my mind whenever I thought of home, even when I was far away for many years. My home was where the red-billed noisy birds came to roost.

15

Sharpening Our Tongues

'AII WA' WAS THE opening expression of deprivation and lament and usually expressed disappointment. As in, 'Aii wa, how can I study religion and choe younton (*choe* = religion, *younton* = knowledge)?', or 'Aii wa, who will teach an unfortunate woman like me?' Religion was supposed to be accessible to all, but women rarely managed to study it. They had all the reason to feel disadvantaged and melancholic. I knew only one other woman besides my mother who could read in the village. I did not realize it then, but I was one of the only girls from among the village girls my age who was being given this rare opportunity to acquire a religious education.

My father had engaged a tutor to teach us to read and write in Choekyed, the classical language of religion. We had regular classes with some boys from the village. In those days I didn't even know that there was a word for school. We talked about the act of learning as pecha *lupkhan,* literally 'learning the books'. I hated this activity and did everything to avoid going to the classes, from begging my mother to assign me tasks to even running away. Rather than seeing this as a privilege accorded to only a few select children, I saw it as a source of anxiety filled with drudgery. It was made all the worse for I was, for a long time, the only girl in a class of five or six older boys eager to learn and advancing rapidly, while I staggered behind, stuck with a text called *Dorji chod pa* (Prajnaparamita). My teacher, perhaps not used to teaching girls, always singled me out and reprimanded and humiliated me, 'You have neither the intelligence nor the diligence to study. Even when you become an old woman with white hair, you will not have mastered Dorji chod pa.' As if in realization of this prophecy, I never did master the text and continue to struggle with it. Although this is a very important Buddhist text that represents the oldest forms of Mahayana Buddhism, it was often used as a primer after mastering the alphabet and considered to be a relatively easy text to read. I read painfully and without any interest or devotion. The teacher had the knack of frightening any intelligence I might have possessed and made me muddle up even the little I knew. I can only remember the quick sharp raps on the knuckles of my trembling hands as I traced the letters, trying to spell out the words. My voice would quiver, and tears would well up, blurring my vision. My first attempts at learning were literally a tearfully painful experience.

The boys in the class were already memorizing their first prayers, while I never got beyond spelling out the text. For a short while, Tshering, a delightfully carefree girl who was infectiously cheerful and bold but decidedly not inclined to learning books, joined the group and I was upgraded to being the second worst in class. She was the daughter of one of my mother's weavers, Pem Zangmo, and was a year older than me. Pem Zangmo was from Chummey, the same village as my mother. According to the prevailing custom, she was chosen to accompany my mother when mother came as a bride to Ogyen Choling. Tshering and I formed a special bond, perhaps because our mothers had a special relationship. From the beginning she just didn't think that learning the alphabet had any relevance to her life, and I felt encouraged. I looked to her for guidance and inspiration. Hers was a short stint of schooling. One day she just said, 'I can't learn,' dropped out of school and moved on with her life. She died of tuberculosis in her mid-thirties. She had lived her life passionately, filled with plucky adventures, verging on risky, and overshadowed later by serious depression. I keep wondering even today whether learning the alphabet would have made a difference. My own life was completely altered by my destiny of having to continue my education.

My father and the generations before him had all been tutored at home. They were not only literate but some of them were even accomplished scholars and religious practitioners. According to family tradition, the start of tutorial classes in our house was not to be taken lightly. The family's astrologer was consulted and an auspicious date set aside. On that date, at an auspicious hour, which happened to be when the first rays of the sun from the top of the mountain on the eastern side of our house emerged and a new day began, was when our first lessons were to begin. We were made to sit in the family's private altar room with our teachers. As we sat in solemn anticipation, father gave us some holy pills to eat, to cleanse our impurities and sharpen our intelligence. After prayers and evocations to Manjushree, the Buddha of wisdom, a formal tea ceremony was conducted. I could barely drink the tea or eat the ceremonial rice prepared with sugar. I was tense and frightened by all this formality. Finally, two teachers, an older man, Lopon Tsedarla, who had taught my own father and his brothers, and a younger man, began to teach us our first lesson. The students sat in a line and each of us was given a sheet of paper with alphabets written on it. I gazed at the letters which seemed to dance and merge into incomprehensible blotches on the sheet.

All the time, I was thinking of a woman in the village who claimed that she had learnt to recognize the alphabets and read texts in a miraculous way. She said that she was in the forest collecting litter one day and the wind blew a sheet of paper with writing on it her way. She picked it up and could immediately recognize the letters and read the whole page. From then onwards she claimed that she could read any text. She held on to her secret but one day her husband, amazed at her ability to read without having learnt to do so, persistently asked her how she could do this. After much hesitation, she told him about her experience in the forest. But the moment she told him, she lost her ability to read. I wished I could have such an experience. I would never tell anyone, I vowed to myself. But the teacher who crouched behind me with his face over my right shoulder was my reality; there certainly was no magic about that. His palm enclosed my hand which held the bamboo pointer; he took me through the alphabets, pointing to each letter and I repeated after him, as I was instructed to do. I trembled and perspired with inexplicable fear. All this time my father stood some distance away, watching us keenly but not really getting involved. I panicked a little when I realized mother was nowhere to be seen. I still recall my teacher's hot breath behind my right ear, his strong body odour that assailed my nostrils and the nausea that stirred in my stomach. It was this younger teacher who would continue our lessons.

The talk of beginning a school for children had gone on for a long time. Days before the lessons were to begin, we repeatedly chanted the mantra *Om a ra pa tsa na dhi*, dedicated to Manjushree. We were told that repeating this mantra would sharpen our tongues as well as our intelligence. We believed that with our sharpened tongues we would be able to pronounce the new and unfamiliar words we had to learn. We loved this exercise, competing to see who could say the mantra faster and for a longer period. We would go on repeating the mantra faster and faster until we grew breathless. Then we would stick out our tongues to see whose had the sharpest tip. We would wag our tongues about and become cockeyed trying to look down at them. But I soon found out that there was much more to education than having a sharp tongue and being able to say the mantras fast.

Once the tutorials began, our days of carefree playing and wanderings were over. We were woken up early every morning to study. In the absence of clocks, father's instruction to the servant was to wake us up when there was 'enough light to be able to read the markings in one's palms'. That was because one's mind was freshest in the early morning and, therefore, able to grasp new knowledge. Either the person who looked after us took a vindictive delight in depriving us of our sleep or because he really cared about our education, I am not sure, but he woke us up very early every morning. In my sleep-drenched mornings I dreaded hearing the impatient bark, '*Da sheng gnay way* (now get up!)' He used the honorific in Bumthangkha even when he was commanding us to get up. We would reluctantly pull ourselves out of our warm beds, fold our blankets, roll up our mattress and often go back to sleep leaning against the mattress while he went to fetch water from the waterspout down in the village. Fresh water was brought in a large aluminium kettle, and we had to wash our hands and faces in a bowl as he poured out the water.

After we had washed, we had to sit near the eastern window to get the maximum light and recite and revise what we had learnt the previous day. Our glum teacher would join us, check our recitations and assign new passages to learn by rote. We were encouraged to recite loudly, perhaps to make sure that father could monitor whether or not we were studying. The whole nagtshang complex would echo with the unenthusiastic and feeble sing-song chant of children's voices repeating lessons every morning. As I sat near the window, I could see directly past the courtyard at my parents' living quarters. I would distractedly watch what was happening there, who was coming or going; there was always a bustle of activity. While mechanically chanting whatever I was supposed to, my attention was totally focused on what was happening there. But the main thing I watched out for was the people carrying *soeja sheythue* (tea and soup), our breakfast, from the kitchen to the living quarters. One would carry the wooden teapot, balanced on the left palm of his hand which was raised over his shoulders. He would be followed by another who carried the brass container for rice in the same fashion. And it was always our cook who would carry the pan of rice soup. This breakfast procession was the most welcome sight for me every morning.

Morning after morning I watched the sunlight dispelling the shadows in the courtyard and knew exactly when it was time to close our books and run to our parents' quarters for breakfast. But there were mornings when nobody would signal us to come and the teacher would not allow us to go, even though he saw the breakfast had been brought in. I would get agitated and impatient at such times. For me these morning studies were useless, and I never learnt anything.

After breakfast we had a break of an hour or so before the bell was clanged, and we had to gather again in the schoolhouse for lessons. I dreaded the ringing of the school bell which was like a death knell for me. I would try to shut it out of my hearing to the point of even running away at times. Every time I ran away the other students were happy to get a break searching for me. They always found me within less than a quarter of an hour. On one occasion, Tshering and I went into the forest below our house. We had no plans beyond simply missing the lessons for the day. But then the teacher began to ring the temple bell which was much louder than the school gong. The *thong thong thong* followed us through the forest. I recall kneeling under a pine tree, the dried pine needles pricking my bare knees as I tried to block my ears. But the sound crept in, and I heard it vibrating in my head, *thong, thong, thong*. Finally, Tshering gave in and said in a hopeless voice, 'Let's go back.' I looked at her in horror and she assured me in gentle coaxing whispers, 'Let's go back, OK.'

'We will be beaten,' I responded.

'Even if we are beaten, it's better to go back.' She was older and wiser, so I agreed.

We went back to the classroom reluctantly and I kept whimpering, 'We will be beaten,' all the way. When we walked into the classroom and took our places, the teacher gave us a disgusted look, making us feel like repulsive vermin. I don't think I was beaten on that occasion. But I was made to report to my father. I cannot recall if he beat me either, but I think he was relieved to see me because it was the height of the bear season, and they had been sighted in the nearby oak forests exactly where we had chosen to hide.

I was never beaten but the sight of other children being beaten in class was traumatic. My skin would tingle in their pain, and I cried with them. Physical punishment was an expected and accepted part of education, and students were beaten on every pretext. The boys were whipped and beaten regularly. In the summer it was branches of stinging nettles rubbed against the tender parts of the body – behind the knees, the calves and the buttocks. In the spring it was the long supple branches of the young willow which made heart-wrenching lashing sounds as the students were struck for the minutest flaws. The most dreaded weapon, however, was the all-season old faithful leather whip that was regularly used. I remember the tension and anxiety when the older boys conspired and tried to sabotage the custom of whipping. They oiled the leather whip and fed it to a hungry dog. The teacher immediately replaced it with a thicker and longer whip. I received countless raps on my head and knuckles and was scolded and humiliated but was never whipped. I was given a special status because I was the youngest, the only girl for most of the time, and I had the habit of telling everything that happened in the class to my parents. But mostly, I think, I was spared because I was the picnic facilitator.

The teacher and the other children loved picnics. We had picnic days very often. It was my job, and I never hesitated, to ask my parents to let us go on picnics and, more importantly, to provide the food for it. Whenever a picnic was approved, which was frequently, mother obliged and always arranged the food. Later I learnt from her that she had never forgotten her sister being the picnic facilitator when she was a child growing up in her own home in Prah. Aunt Dechen could never refuse her friends who wanted picnics quite often and she, unlike me, was quite afraid of asking her parents for the food. These requests caused aunt so much anxiety that it resulted in her sleepwalking. Her own mother had one night followed her into the store where aunt gathered and packed food for her picnic while she was asleep. Naturally my mother was sympathetic to the pressure I was under being the class picnic facilitator.

There were plenty of picnic spots in our vicinity. But our favourite ones were on the banks of the river Sheykhway. This river originates in the mountain called Ayu, and because it is shaped like a *bumpa*, ritual vessel, it is called Ayu Bumpa. The river is regarded to be very special as it seems to flow out of the spout of the vessel. People of Tang take pride that we drink the purest water which comes out of a holy vessel. The river feeds into the Tang Chu and its banks provide wonderful picnic spots. The river flows through a narrow rift and, as the banks widen out, they are ideal grazing grounds for the cattle herds from the locality.

The picnic spots were sheltered from the strong winds and there was always plenty of firewood to cook our meals. The older boys would carry the foodstuff and the pots and pans, and the picnic procession would be led by our teacher. On seeing the procession, villagers would say, 'There they go, again another picnic.' During these picnics there wasn't a single book in sight. Neither was there a single recitation of the prayers we learnt. Some of the older boys would cook and the other boys played games, and I mostly watched or played with some girls who were out in the pastures herding their sheep and cattle. They would shyly join us. Most of the time, the teacher would lie down in a sunny place and soak up the sun.

The taste of food cooked in the open under the direct sun always had what I believed was the sun-drenched taste, something I so endearingly associate with picnics and food cooked on journeys. Sometimes, during a very short season, we collected river algae or just walked along the banks collecting rocks. When in season, we collected wild strawberries and other edible berries such as bearberries, drawing great pleasure from eating directly off the trees and bushes.

Aside from the picnics, I recall the days of my home school as oscillations between hard drills and dulling lazy hours. What did I get out of my days of learning books? Besides a smattering of reading, I learnt little else. The only memento I carry of my school experience is a tattoo of a *yudrung*, a clockwise swastika, a sacred symbol of continuity and stability, at the base of my right thumb. Most of the time I do not even remember that I have this faint and fading tattoo, but whenever I do, I immediately recall my father's reaction on seeing it for the first time. I have rarely seen him so angry. His anger was justified, as he felt that nobody had the right to make a tattoo on his only daughter's hand without consultation or permission. And, most importantly, he said that the symbol was in the wrong place.

The tattooing happened on one of those lazy school days when the teacher yawned louder than the students. At least we tried to stifle our yawns; he did it openly and loudly. Suddenly the teacher had an idea, and we all sat up. He would make tattoos for us. He extracted the needle which he always carried on the collar of his gho and wiped it on his sleeves. Both men and women always carried needles on their clothing. Needles and safety pins were stuck in the thick collar of their garments, handy for repairing and mending clothes, extracting thorns and splinters from our feet and hands, for picking teeth, piercing ears and, in this case, for making tattoos. In case we hadn't heard about the benefits of a yudrung on our body, the teacher explained its importance as a human marker for the afterlife. When a person dies, he said, each must appear in front of the god of death, Yama or Shinje Choekye Gyalpo, who will ask the dead person, 'Where have you come from?'

The dead will say, 'I have come from the human realm.'

The god of dead will then say, 'Show me the proof that you have indeed come from the human realm.' At this time those who have the tattoo of the yudrung will display it as definitive proof in order to be assigned to the next life. Verification would be very difficult without the tattoo. Even as young children we had some idea of the next life, and death was a reality for there were often deaths in the village or in the valley. Being young was a no guarantee that we would live longer than the older people; people of all ages died all the time. We scrambled for tattoos of yudrungs, except for one or two who could not stand being pricked by a needle. Usually blackish-blue iron instruments, needles those days were formidably thick and sturdy. They were, after all, working needles! Having never seen other kinds of needles, I was not intimidated by my teacher's fearsome-looking needle. I wanted a tattoo; I wanted to carry the sign of belonging to the human realm!

A little uneasy but totally determined, I watched with some revulsion as the teacher tied a rag around the wrist of the tattoo seekers. He then dipped his bamboo pen into the soot ink and drew a yudrung on the spot between the thumb and the index finger. Then he tightened the rag around the wrist and began to prick along the lines drawn with ink. Small globules of blood followed each prick until there was a pattern of red jewels sprouting on the hand. Even after having watched the others with fear in their eyes and controlled but apparent grimaces of pain on their faces, I did not change my mind. I boldly put out my hand. Being a girl and perceived as being weaker, the teacher insisted that one of the older students hold me from the back. The teacher cleaned the blood of the previous victim with the rag that was tied around the wrist and was ready to execute my tattoo. A yudrung was drawn on my hand. The rag was tied around my wrist, then prick prick prick went the needle and I made a conscious effort to hold on. I watched the globules of blood blooming. Then the teacher looked at the pattern doubtfully and started reworking it. He said that the ink from kitchen soot mixed with alcohol, cottage cheese and animal glue, was not being absorbed properly. He decided to drain the ink from one prick point to the next by scratching into my skin, from one point to the next. Scratch, scratch, scratch went the needle. I was so glad I had the other student behind me. I fell back and buried my face in his shoulders.

I was so proud of myself, not for the yudrung but for my own courage. I was as brave as the boys, even braver than one or two who had admitted their cowardice. The red swelling of the yudrung was growing and spreading and there was an ache all the way up my arm. I slept during the night but woke up to feel the throbbing. I tried to hide my hand from my father. But the next morning at breakfast he noticed it, as I always sat next to him. I immediately took full responsibility and said, 'I asked Lopon to make the yudrung.' I saw the muscles on my father's face tighten and his face became red as he examined my swollen hand. My mother and he exchanged looks but continued with breakfast. There were guests eating with us that day and breakfast could not be disrupted. As soon as we were done, I had to go into my parents' room and mother took out that dreaded black bottle. She uncorked the bottle of iodine, and I whined and whimpered as father held me, and she poured a drop of the medicine on my tattoo. The undiluted iodine burnt my already smarting hand.

Father was furious. 'This man is supposed to teach the children. Who authorized him to make yudrungs on the children's hands?' He threatened to call the teacher to reprimand and possibly punish him. I had seen father punishing people and I was trembling in fear. As always, mother coaxed and calmed him. My father's anger was bolstered by two fundamental mistakes: first, the yudrung for a woman should have been on my left hand and not on the right; and the teacher had made the yudrung on the base of the thumb when it should have been on the fleshy part in between the thumb and forefinger. I think the teacher heard about my parents' furore and declared himself sick and was absent until my hand had healed. Soon the whole incident was forgotten but the pale blue markings of the yudrung still bring back memories of dreary school days which were temporarily disrupted by my decision to brand myself as being from the human realm.

16

Journey to Our Winter Resort

IT WAS OUR FAMILY tradition to pack up and close the house in Bumthang after the kangsoi, held in October or November, and move to our winter estate in Gorgan in present-day Lhuentse. This migration was referred to as 'going east'. Going east was our ancestral custom to escape the ensuing bitter cold of temperate Bumthang and enjoy the warmth and bounty of our subtropical estate. Caretakers were appointed to stay on to look after the house and the temples in Bumthang. This custom, *jarsa–guensa*, summer–winter habitation, was a luxury for the privileged and a necessity for others who had another notion for this journey *to stuna* (to pursue rice), a gentle term for gleaning and begging. We, like our ancestors before us, would go, following the same trails that our herds of cattle had travelled a week or so earlier when they too had migrated to our subtropical pastures. Father, mother and the older children rode on their own mounts and the younger children were carried on the backs of the servants. The going-east procession included servants, weavers, the pack mules, riding horses and even our dogs and chickens. The chickens were carried in roughly woven bamboo baskets, shut securely and hung on the pack saddles, to sit in between two loads on the horses or mules.

On the first day of the journey, we were able to leave Ogyen Choling after breakfast, quite late because our parents had to attend to many last-minute matters. We travelled rather leisurely to the first campsite at Phokpai, a meadow at the base of Rodongla pass. The large patch of sloping meadow surrounded by fir trees was the usual first night halt on this route. The next day we started early and slowly climbed up towards the 4019-metre-high pass of Rodongla. As we rode through the conifer and rhododendron forests, I continually bothered the elders, asking them, 'Have we reached the porcupine slope yet?' The slope was a small insignificant depression in the track, but there was a story that said that when the porcupine was coming to Bumthang from the east, after having crossed the most arduous Rodongla pass, it was so tired that when it reached this little depression it decided that it could not make another climb and went back east, climbing over Rodongla again. That is why in the days we were growing up there were no porcupines, considered to be creatures of the subtropics, in temperate Bumthang. Nowadays porcupines in Bumthang have become a common menace to the farmers' crops, especially potatoes! Either the porcupines finally succeeded in crossing the porcupine slope or climate change has pushed the animals from the subtropics to the temperate regions.

As we came closer to the top, I could hear and see the breaths of those who walked beside us. The audible gasping and panting of the people and the animals, emitting thick steamy puffs of vapour which hung heavy in the cold grey fog of the mountains. Sitting on my warm and comfortable 'high horse', I watched the whiffs of steam rising from the sweat of the horses and people who walked along. I also noticed the sparse vegetation that had managed to survive, fighting fiercely among the rocks and boulders that dominated the landscape. The low-growing and twisting rhododendrons and juniper became smaller and even more ground-hugging and gnarled as we drew closer to the peak. On occasion, when the pass was already covered by snow, riding yaks would have been arranged for us to travel on.

Father always made sure there were enough riding horses for all. He loved working with animals and would personally break in the young horses and yaks. With my heart in my mouth, I loved to watch him as he worked with these essentially wild creatures. Father imposed one condition – that the children could watch him only from a protected area, either looking out of the windows of our house or from behind the bamboo fences. The animals were agitated and unpredictable, and onlookers could get hurt. In the beginning they snorted nervously and bucked wildly, but over many days they calmed down and allowed themselves to be led. And then, finally, they did not mind being saddled. Eventually, they let us ride them. Father had a way with animals. Thanks to his determined training regime we always had tame and docile mounts. He was firm but patient and asserted his strength and control when it was necessary. Once father was breaking in a young yak which he thought would make a good riding yak, but it refused to be saddled. Its wild instincts got the better of the trainers and it escaped from the compound, jumping over a stone wall nearly two metres high. Of course, father was always assisted by some servants but on the day that the yak escaped, everybody just stood by, gaping in stunned silence.

As young children we were also taught to ride by my father. When I was very young, father allowed me to ride with him on his horses and yaks. He would let me hold the reins and teach me how to guide the animal by loosening or tightening the reins. When I think of these occasions, I can still feel the warmth and security of his arms cradling me as his hand enclosed mine with the reins of our shared mount in my hands. As I grew older, I was allowed to ride on my own but was closely watched by father. There was always an attendant who led the horse. By the time I was nine years old I could ride on my own, and my maiden journey on my own pony was on the three-day trip to Gorgan in 1961. It was my last journey with my parents before my brother Rinzin and I were sent to school in India. My father had chosen a reddish-brown mule for me. She was called Jamu, and she was the gentlest and sturdiest mule.

I have wonderful memories of riding a yak across the Rodongla. Once we were in thick snow, the procession had slowed down to a deliberate pace, as each step was measured and cautious. The yaks would plough through, snorting noisily and moving on but not stumbling and panicking, unlike the horses who panicked as soon as their legs sunk into the snow. Although I felt the chill of the wind bruising my cheeks, I buried my mitten-less hands under the warm woolly mane of my yak and kept them warm. As I kept my hands on the neck of the yak I could feel each rhythmic slow movement of its front legs, so soothing and calming, almost lulling me to sleep. Our parents and the attendants had to continually warn me to stay awake and be attentive. The attendants were always talking to the animals with such phrases as, 'Slow down, there is a drop now.' 'Be attentive, you know how the road is.' 'Be careful, now, there is a climb here.' Once I asked the attendant if the animals understood human language. He smiled and said, 'This animal language is to be understood by the rider and maybe the animal.' We were taught that when there was a climb, we had to bend forward and hold tight, and when there was a drop and going downwards, we had to lean back.

Once we reached the top of the pass, I was not surprised but happy and grateful to see that the panting, sweating men had gone ahead and prepared a welcome tea for us. They must have gone ahead, gasping ever harder to make sure that the tea and the mats were ready for us. We halted and got off our mounts. A fumigation ritual of burning the creeping juniper and aromatic rhododendron branches was conducted along with the ceremony of serkhem, offering libations to the deities of the locality. In the misty fog, we immediately lowered our voices to almost a whisper, lest we disturb the deities who might react by causing the weather to change into fearsome dark clouds. This would make visibility so poor that we would have to feel our way around and might lose each other. We were told that this is what could happen if we did not adhere to the mountaintop customs. Adding to the mystery of the constantly morphing environment was a bigger lurking fear that nobody dared to name. Uttering its name was like calling upon it. This was the place where travellers occasionally encountered the elusive yeti.

In the swirling mists that appeared sharp and crystalline at times, we were served hot tea from thermos flasks that had been carefully carried by the servants, along with food especially made to be eaten in the mountains. The food for the mountain, *lazai*, was usually roasted barley or wheat-flour mixed into a dough with all sorts of goodies, unrefined brown sugar, alcohol, butter, and sometimes bits of crushed dried cheese. The other mountain food was small disc-shaped unleavened buckwheat bread with sugar and some fermented grains. Perhaps it is the nostalgia but, after all these years of travelling and tasting different foods from many parts of the world, nothing measures up to the euphoria of sitting on a small saddle mat among the rocks watching the shape shifting in the dark mist while eating mountain fare at 4019 metres!

Descending the mountain on the eastern side was the most treacherous part of the entire journey. Soon after crossing the pass, on the east side of the mountain, we knew that there was an *iem tsho* or hidden lake, somewhere among the twisting rhododendron bushes and huge boulders, which could be seen only by those destined to see the lake. The colour of the water in the lake augured the future. It was common knowledge that many years ago when one of the young men from the village escaped the drudgery of farm work and ran away to pursue religion, the lake appeared to him as milky white, an auspicious sign. He returned home many years later as a highly evolved monk. I was afraid to look in the direction of where the lake was said to be located, yet my curiosity got the better of me and I could not resist glancing in that direction every now and then. Part of me wanted to see the lake but another part of me said no, no, don't let me see anything. I saw nothing. Years later I heard that my mother, during our last journey together in 1961, saw the lake, which was a blood-red, a highly inauspicious sign. She kept the secret to herself but later told our uncle Akhu lama, who told us after she had died. It was interpreted as an ominous warning. Our father would die in a few months.

As we walked down the mountainside, the heavy fog dissipated gradually, only to be replaced by a thicker invisible tension that descended upon the people and the animals, and everybody became alert and cautious. We had all dismounted our horses and walked along with the adults who insisted on holding us by our hands, just as a precaution. The animals' ears perked up and human eyes dilated with watchful anxiety. It was a steep descent along an extremely narrow footpath which in some places were merely footholds etched into the vertical rock face. There were some rickety planks placed across some crevices and small ravines. Invariably one of the older people repeated the old saying, 'The impartial Rodongla brings all to ground level, the riders and walkers alike.' We repeated this wise saying without realizing that this was meant especially for those who were privileged to ride. The pass was so named because it resembled the outer bend of a yak horn. Even young agile knees would ache from the continuous downhill descent. How the people with huge loads and the aged did this trail is anybody's wonder. During my childhood, this path was used regularly, so the maintenance of it fell on those who used it. Today this path is rarely used and is no longer maintained. Now it is one of the most challenging hiking trails for tourists.

By late afternoon we would be walking through carpets of oak leaves, exaggeratedly kicking through the dried leaves on the ground trying to make the rustling sound, *sok sok sok* for fun, but at the same time looking over our shoulders and all around, in fear of *sok soklai* duen, the rustling ghost who, we were told, inhabited the area. By nightfall we reached flat land in the valley of Pimai. There was a lone house in a small clearing that we referred to as Pimai *neyda*, the host of Pimai.

I always liked to watch the horses as they were unloaded. When the saddles and saddle carpets were removed from the tired animals, they shook their bodies as if dusting off the sweat and rolled in the dirt in relief, neighing. Then they went to graze in the grasses nearby. Only after the horses had gone off did I go into the house to join the others for tea and some snacks. I do not think there was a real host who lived in the house. I think it was an empty house used by travellers. The rooms were empty, and it looked like it had been built recently. The actual hosts were the people from Unger, the nearest village located at some distance, who received us kindly. Many of our pastures were in the vicinity, so the herders came to meet us with hot and cold milk, butter and cheese. Some of the tenant farmers who cultivated land which belonged to our family had already gathered firewood, water, and fodder for our animals. While the adults prepared for the evening meal, father and mother met the local people to discuss land and other related issues.

My brothers and I rushed into the nearby forests, fascinated by the moss-covered exotic vegetation, the avocado trees and giant ferns. For some reason we were in search of a particular creeper called 'monkey's paws'. I don't remember exactly why we wanted it and what we did with it once we found it. But I do remember determinedly climbing up the moss-covered trees to unwrap and break away the finger-like furry tentacles that clasped around the trunks and branches like a monkey's paw.

The next day we followed a path downstream through maize fields, with scattered houses nearby. We finally reached the village of Unger and crossed a bridge. After lunch we were passing through forests of dogwood laden with ripened fruit. Our path was layered with the fruit that had fallen, and the air was suffused with the heady fragrance of the fruit crushed and trampled by the humans and animals in our caravan. The branches hung so low that I could reach out for the hanging fruits while sitting in my saddle. Our parents cautioned us against eating too many of them as it was believed to cause intense headaches. I loved to sink my teeth into the pulpy fruit and feel the seeds in my mouth. The picture of these dogwood trees, full of red strawberry-like fruit in the soft evening light as we rode through the tree-lined paths, is imprinted in my mind. I can understand why artists often chose this beautiful tree to be depicted among the sacred images on the walls of temples. Whenever I look at the mural paintings in our temple, I like to look at the different representations of the dogwood trees, especially in the mural of *Zangdokpalri* (*Zang* = copper, *Dok* = colour) heaven of Guru Padmasambhava painted on an entire wall in our temple. Like other paintings, this one is venerated as a devotional meditational visualization when praying to Guru Padmasambhava.

I think we camped somewhere not far from the dogwood forest. The next day we passed through a place called Khenay lhakhang. I am sure there was a temple somewhere, but it was two tall cypress trees that caught my attention. The glitter of the morning sunlight intensified the brilliant green of these trees. Why would a small girl pay particular attention to trees, one might wonder. My imagination had been stirred by the legend of how these trees came to be there. The trees grew out of the two pegs that fell out of the wooden aircraft that Guru Rinpoche had built to banish Khikha Ratho, the diabolical prince with a dog's mouth and goat's skull, hundreds of years ago. The wooden aircraft flew over the Rodongla, the path we had just passed, and crash-landed in the valley of Tang with a loud '*tang*', which is how the valley where our home was located, was named. Without really understanding the religio-historical underpinnings, I, without a doubt, believed the story to be the truth. And the truth was that an evil queen, Margen, of a good Buddhist king, copulated with a dog and a goat and gave birth to a child with the mouth of a dog and the head of a goat. Even as children we used to clandestinely talk of the descendants of this human–beast king, so sure of who they were because they were supposed to have the same features as their infamous ancestor. It felt so grown-up to be able to tell them apart from the rest of the people, although in truth their physical features were no different from the rest of us. The demon king, however, did leave his mark. Not only was our valley named after his flight but the names of some of our yak pastures were also associated with some of the legendary events during his unhappy stay in Tang. We knew that this king was not immediately taken to his place of expulsion. He had tried to go back to where he had last lived in Khenpalung to fight against Guru Rinpoche who had engineered his final expulsion.

Our journey east was in the opposite direction of the expulsion. The aircraft had entered Tang valley from the north-east. We were going directly east. We reached the final ridge, Takila, before descending to our winter resort, Gorgan. After we were received with a generous welcome ceremony arranged by the manager of our estate and the tenant farmers, we moved on in a leisurely manner to our camp. Once we arrived at the camp, we ran around excitedly looking at all the rooms that had been made ready for us. The camp was a rectangular enclosure made of bamboo stems that were erected to stand tightly together, giving it a natural look while also providing security and privacy. The whole complex looked like a very orderly bamboo grove. There was a large hut for our parents, which included a bedroom, a storeroom and a large open space with an open fireplace to be used as a common room for eating our meals, meeting people and for sitting around and enjoying entertainment.

Over the next few days, the people who farmed our lands came to see father, bringing with them presents – bags of rice, maize, fruits, barrels of fermented grains ready to be distilled for alcohol, vegetables, and even whole pig carcasses. I thought nothing about such presents and, had the social system remained unchanged, I am sure I would have believed that these were given in submission and gratitude to us, and that they were due to us. The social changes that skewed our family's status made me see, today, that such gifts given with sweet words and smiling faces cost the people dearly. That it was the unequal system that legitimized many such injustices in those days.

There was even a compact and efficient pit toilet with a washstand behind a partially closed space. A large brass bowl was placed on the washstand with an enamel pitcher filled with water beside it. There was a thorny pomegranate tree that grew just outside the bamboo wall, and its branches hung over the toilet. This beautiful setting must have had an impact on my young mind because I remember it clearly even after over sixty years. The toilet floor had a layered chir pine-needle carpet. The children's tent was pitched on a small elevation near a giant chir pine tree, a few metres away from our parents' camp. Our tent was near the water channel that fed into the artificial pond. The floor of our tent was also covered with chir pine needles – what luxury! The kitchen was at some distance from the camp, between the camp and the nagtshang. It was housed in an old structure built with stones. It was a single room, narrow and dark. The stove was near the doorway, so it got some natural light, because I think the structure had no windows. The floor was covered with fern leaves.

Our winter camp was located on the flatland just below the chir pine-forested hillside only metres away from the old stately ancestral home, the manor house of three storeys with a small stone courtyard. The compound in front of the nagtshang was enclosed on the north end by a two-storeyed shagkor, the living quarters. The manager of the estate lived in the rooms east of the shagkor. Although the utse appeared intact from the outside, it was thought to be too dangerous to live in, which is why we were camping instead of living in the house. The last known occupant of the manor was our great-great-grandfather Kushu Tsokye Dorji, sometime in the nineteenth century. It is possible that my grandparents used the nagtshang during their stays in Gorgan before the house deteriorated to the state I saw it in the 1950s. We were warned that most of the wooden elements had been damaged by termites. Although it was not visible from the outside, the wooden parts of the building had been eaten from the inside. On occasions when we went into the building, it was not to look at the statues in the temple or at our grain stores on the ground floor but to playfully bang on the pillars that were hollowed out by the termite infestation. We used to curl our hands into fists, hit them against the pillars and listen to the buzzing sound of the angry creatures nesting inside.

The north side of the shagkor was connected to the south side by a continuous wall through which lay the main east entrance. The shagkor structures on the south side were in a poor and dilapidated state, but I still remember row upon row of maize cobs being hung out to dry under the roof. And I think the ground floor was a stable. Most of the village houses were located to the north-east side of the nagtshang. Immediately adjacent to the entrance was an open space. Nothing grew there, where the ground had been compacted by many feet as people used it every day for drying their paddy, where they pounded grains and polished them. This common space was enclosed by a row of dark green *bashakha meto* (*Adhatoda*) bushes, which had edible white flowers. Beyond the row of bushes lay terraced fields of paddy, sugar cane plantations and mandarin groves all the way to the banks of the Kuru Chu. Most of the property belonged to our family. When I recall these scenes, I feel the warm sultry air in my face and the excitement of new discoveries of a subtropical environment. I was fascinated by the light brownish grey, almost translucent-skinned lizards, as there were no lizards in Bumthang. As we watched them, they felt our presence and their colour would change to a darker red, and we were reminded that they had the power to magically suck up our blood through our shadow and that the reddish hue was our blood. When we watched them, we always made sure that our shadows did not fall in their path.

We could go into the nagtshang through a west entrance on the ground floor, which was mainly made of stone masonry, and therefore unaffected by the termites. The ground floor was still being used as a granary. There was a small stone wall of about a metre in height on one side of the path to the entrance, and I remember the red geranium flowers on this wall that hung lazily, drenched by the afternoon sun. Nearby there was a cluster of cacti which we were introduced to as *jewa rignai tsang* or 'thorns of the five-peaked mountain', perhaps referring to the Wu Tai Shan in China. Were there cacti in Wu Tai Shan or did the cactus just look like the five peaks of a mountain? This was a plant I marvelled at but was not very fond of. Instead, I remember fondly the colourful poinsettia bushes adding splashes of red everywhere. But because any plant that exuded milky sap was considered poisonous, we kept away from them. When I think of our family trips to Gorgan, I think of the exotic life forms I saw for the first time in my life.

To the north of the nagtshang was an artificial pond fed by water brought through a constructed channel. Water was scarce, so this pond was created as a reservoir. Even in the winter this pond was full. It was the lifeline for all our paddy fields. I have never seen it, but was told by the last manager of the estate that there is a document that recorded how the water was brought to this reservoir from a water source far away during the time of our ancestor Kushu Tshokye Dorji. The record stated that he paid one silver *Boetang* (a Tibetan coin) to every person for every arm-span of channel that was dug. There was a giant citrus tree near the edge of the pond under which was a *lukhang*, a stone structure, home for a subterranean spirit. The citrus tree was so large that its branches spread over the pond almost covering the entire surface like a giant canopy. The fruits were larger than the normal mandarins, but they were yellow in colour and horrible to eat. It had an extremely bitter taste. But when the fruits dropped into the pond and floated on the surface, we could not resist the temptation of going into the water to see who could collect the most fruits. The subterranean beings we all knew manifested as snakes, and I am phobic about any reptilian creatures. Despite my fears, I could not stop myself from joining in the game with the rest of the children. As my feet sank into the soft squishy soil, my whole body would recoil with revulsion, but I continued to fight over the fallen fruits. Every fruit I collected reassured me of my triumph over the repulsion of the slimy soil on the floor of the pond where the water snakes might have slithered!

A few days after our arrival in 1961, preparations for constructing a new house became the main activity. Father was in a great hurry to construct a new house. Within days beams were being stacked up in the open space, south of the old nagtshang. While the timber was collected and readied for construction, fruit tree saplings were being gathered from everywhere and planted around the compound; father seemed to have all the plans in his head. I could feel the urgency that he felt to build his dream house quickly. He seemed obsessed. It was as if there was a crucial moment and if that moment passed the house would never be constructed. In his tearing hurry he wanted everything to happen immediately.

That was the year when I saw the fields of sugar cane for the first time. Until then I had only seen sugar cane after they were cut into small pieces to be offered in the temple or at other times when it was cut into bite-sized pieces and given to us as a rare, sweet snack. We spent some exciting days in the sugar cane field watching the process of juice being extracted. The sugar cane stems were fed into a wooden press which was rotated by several men pushing a long wooden arm. The men pushed the arm, and the juice came out of the press. The juice was collected and then cooked in cauldrons until it solidified and little round balls were made. We ran around like little crazed creatures not getting enough of this amazing process. But father was busy thinking of how to speed up the process and make it more efficient and less labour-intensive. He figured that if water could run mills for grinding flour and prayer wheels, sugar cane juice could also be extracted using a watermill. Once he decided that it could be done, he proceeded to experiment. I am not sure what exactly they did but again I remember the urgency. Carrying the sugar cane from the bottom of the hill to the watermill on the hillside by one person was too slow for my father. He had men running in a relay as they carried bundles of sugar cane to the experimentation site. Perhaps he was consumed by the premonition that his days were numbered and was compelled to hurry. I cannot remember what the result of the experiment was because I left for India before it yielded results. I heard it being said later that when he returned to Ogyen Choling after some months, even in his ailing condition, he gifted a ball of jaggery to every household in the village!

The dream house could not even be started because father fell ill, his condition worsened and there was nobody to carry forward his dream. After all the energetic and hurried frenzy, when I said goodbye to him a month later, he was ill in bed. The last image of my father was that of a sick man in bed without any apparent symptoms of illness. He died a few months later, and the idea of sugar cane juice extraction using water power died with him. Over the years the nagtshang was dismantled and everything in it was lost. I am not even sure what happened to the statues in the altar. All we got were two large temple bells which now hang in the museum in Ogyen Choling.

Many years later I went to see the space where our old house once stood. There was no trace of the old nagtshang. Using the stones from the old building, a new house has been built by one of the managers of our estate. Overcome with nostalgia and intense emotions, I foolishly begged the manager to sell back my land to me or at least consider exchanging the space for another land; after all, this was my ancestral property! Of course, they would not even consider it. They had colluded a long time ago with the district administration and had legally transferred and registered the land in their name. There was nothing I could do. All I could do was evoke the memories of my whole family living together once, for the last time before everything changed.

17

To the East and Beyond

THE REMINDER THAT MY brother and I were to go to school was received while we were in Gorgan in 1961. Our parents had decided that, as it was to be our first time out of the country to India, we had to begin this important journey in the proper way. Our journey to begin our education and our future was not to be taken casually. We should not start the journey from our temporary home in Lhuentse. We would have to retrace our trek back to our permanent home, Ogyen Choling in Bumthang. We had been at our winter resort in Gorgan for over three months. Just days after the new year celebrations we had to leave our parents. After saying goodbye to them, my elder brother Rinzin and I left our camp in silence despite the cheerful cries of the archers in the background. They were celebrating the new year.

It was a small group of us: two riding horses, four or five pack mules and four men: Tabula, Ragola, Tsundruela and Bumbula. Henceforth, for most our consequent journeys back and forth from home and school over the years, these were the same men who accompanied us. As we climbed towards Takila, riding my mule, following my brother who was riding one of father's own riding horses, I looked back several times until our camp disappeared from my view. Soon after we crossed Takila, we had to dismount because we were descending the hill, and we never rode while going downhill. The three-day journey was uneventful, and I remember little of it. What I do remember so clearly was crossing Rodongla. There had been heavy snowfall the previous day and the foot trails were totally obliterated by a blanket of fresh snow. As we neared the top, the men grew nervous, and we had to dismount our panicky horses who were snorting and fidgety. We had to ford the soft snow, our feet sinking into it. A bitterly cold wind blew incessantly and the whole area was grey and foggy. A steady flurry of snowflakes came down on us. The animals became more distracted and frightened and whinnied softly even as the horsemen guided them, speaking calming words. The men removed the luggage from the packhorses and carried it to a safe distance past the dangerous spots and tried to lead the horses holding on to their harness. Suddenly, the red mule Tsemo fell over the edge of the precipice, and we watched helplessly as she went down the slope. There was a clear track in the snow made by her sliding body. Nobody said a word, as we peered into the distance to see if we could see her. When we thought Tsemo was lost and we would never see her again, there was a loud neighing. Her fall had been broken by some gnarled roots sticking out above the snow and she had managed to find her way back to the foot trail and follow it back to where we were. She climbed back, whinnying softly, shaken but not injured. By then the men had removed the saddle carpets from the horses and made a carpet-covered path across the snow-covered one. The men coaxed the animals to walk on the carpeted path. The horses hesitantly obeyed, their steps measured and tenuous. Finally, we made it through the most difficult bit of the trail. I cannot remember what we did when we reached the top. Perhaps we just continued, relieved to be safe. It was not that long ago, just a few months, that we had stopped on the pass and had tea and mountain snacks with our parents. This time there was no tea or rest; we just pushed on swiftly to safer places. We were fortunate that we had managed to escape the worst of the snow. That same year the snow had continued and blocked the pass, and I heard later that one or two people had died while trying to cross.

When we reached home, mother's cousin uncle Sangye Lhuendup, who had stayed on to look after the house and property during the family's absence, received us. There was no joy in coming home to an empty house. Our parents were missing, and most of the young people from the village had gone in pursuit of rice. Only the elderly and the very young were home. We stayed in Ogyen Choling for a few days and uncle Sangye Lhuendup had been instructed to conduct rituals to our family's deities, to ensure our safe journey. Now our journey began in earnest and uncle Sangye Lhuendup decided to join us for the first part. We spent the first night in Gongkhar in Choekor valley. There was a clearing in the blue pine forests with a spring nearby. This was our usual camping ground. The next day we went to Pangte Gompa in Chummey valley. Uncle Sangye Lhuendup was from Pangte Gompa, and his sister Ashi Kunzang hosted us for the night. There were only two houses in Pangte and Ashi Kunzang's house was just next to the house of Dasho Thinley Namgyel, the retired Zhemgang dzongpon. The next day, we were invited to have breakfast with Dasho. It was our first meeting with Dasho and his wife Aie Pem Doma who was my grandmother's cousin. While we were eating our meal, we heard a loud buzzing and roaring that seemed to come closer. Everybody stopped eating and listened to the sound. All formality and propriety were forgotten as we put down our baskets of rice and scrambled out of the house to the yard when somebody said, '*Namdru*', literally meaning 'ship of the sky'. We were able to see the tiny spot in the sky that soon disappeared over the mountain tops. This was the first time I heard and saw an airplane, albeit only a speck in the sky. Perhaps the airplane signified our long journey into the unknown.

The next day we climbed over the Nangdag La pass and camped near the Nangdag village. Our next stop was Baleng in Trongsa district. Ashi Chokey and uncle Ugyen Wangdi were there spending their winter in the warm subtropical region. They had also come to their winter resort from Wangdue Choling palace in Bumthang. Like us in Gorgan, Ashi and uncle were also camping and in the process of building a new winter house on their estate. They were shocked to see me, with my hair cut short and dressed in a gho like a boy. It was decided immediately that a new set of girl's clothes had to be stitched for me before we could continue our journey. While the tailor stitched my new clothes, a servant was assigned to pick out the lice and nits in my hair. I was infested with these creatures. It had barely been a week since we left home, but it must have been because I was sharing sleeping spaces with the other travellers that I picked up the lice. We must have stayed in Baleng for a few days. All I can remember was me lying down on the floor and putting my head in the servant's lap as he cleaned out the lice. I remember the camp on a hillside facing the west and it was sunny and warm. Having seen this kind of vegetation in Lhuentse, I recognized the groves of banana plants and mandarin trees in the vicinity. By the late afternoon a wind blew hard and raised dust in the newly dug up ground of the camp. The servants came with containers of water and branches of bushes which they dipped in the water and sprinkled on the ground to stop the dust.

With a clean head and new attire, *bhoigho lakdum*, a sleeveless Tibetan dress, I was ready to continue our travel southwards. I had to learn to move in my new dress which was ankle-length, unlike the gho which was knee-length and allowed me more freedom, especially when riding a horse. My horse attendant was always pulling and tucking in my dress because he wanted me to appear respectable. It was in Baleng that our translator was introduced to us. Dasho Gyeltsenla, who was at the time working for Ashi Chokey, was to accompany us all the way to Kalimpong. We could not have travelled on our own as none in the group spoke any other language besides Bumthangkha and none of us had ever travelled to India. Dasho was to be our guide and translator. Even now when I think of Dasho Gyeltsenla, I see him talking like he was eating a delicious meal. He talked slowly and deliberately, savouring each word. We must have travelled for some more days, camping in different places, under trees when the weather was fine, sometimes in caves and, once or twice, we had to use our tent when it rained.

The men who were assigned to us took good care of us and never breached the faith that our parents had placed in them. Each day we travelled for seven or eight hours; we travelled from one established camping place to another at an unhurried pace that allowed for lunch stops where we cooked our meals. Wherever we camped, the comforting sound that lulled me to sleep was the crunch, crunch, crunch of the horses grazing in the night and the soft tinkle of the bells around their necks. In my memory the camp sites were Pangzur, Dangdung, Breti, Tama, and Surrey in today's Sarbang district. Surrey has now been renamed Jigmeling.

There was a definite change in the mood of the travellers when we reached Surrey. The once loud and cheerful group of men became quieter. They lowered their voices when they spoke and were a little restrained. We were going to be spending the night with a Pari family. Ironically, in those days, we highlanders referred to the southern inhabitants of the plains as Pari, which in Nepali and Hindi probably meant *Pahari*, mountain people. We didn't know any better. These people who were of Nepali origin were different from us highlanders. Our guide Dasho Gyeltsenla lost none of his confidence and authority as he approached the hosts, who had come out of their house when they heard us approaching. Dasho talked to them in a language none of us understood. There was no means of informing our hosts in advance, so we had just appeared suddenly and asked them to host us, and they accepted. That was the accepted custom in those days. My brother and I were to sleep inside the house, and the men and the horses could use the space in the open terraced paddy field near the house, which was dry and free of crops. This was the gup's (village headman) family. They had hosted my father in the past; that was enough for our hosts to welcome us.

We were sitting on a mat they had laid out for us and watched them in silence. Our meal was cooked outside by our servants, and we ate outside the house. Dasho had alerted them not to cook beef that day, simply saying that our hosts would be offended. He was aware of and sensitive to Hindu customs. Despite the long, tiring day, I was wide-eyed, alert and observant of everything that I saw and heard in this unfamiliar environment. Everything was new. The houses were built differently, the people were dressed differently, and they spoke a language that was incomprehensible to us. Hurricane lamps were brought into the house when it became dark, and I became aware of the shadowy figures of the women and children who crept in and out of our room on every pretext to look at my brother and me in curiosity. Late into the night I was awake; the newness of the experience overwhelmed me. I was conscious of the smell of the mud-plastered walls and the lingering aroma of the unfamiliar food that the family had cooked for themselves.

Finally, I fell asleep to the sound of the women who were grinding grains by hand.

The second-last halt was Juiligang, the last stop before we finally reached Gelephu which at that time was called Hatisa. Hatisa alluded to the elephants which roamed these areas freely. It was a perfect blend of the two languages, Nepalese and Dzongkha: *Hati* for elephant in Nepalese and *sa* in Dzongkha for land, 'land of the elephants'. Once we were in Gelephu, we stayed in one of the only permanent houses there. It was the Inspection Bungalow, commonly called the IB. Such houses were built for forest inspectors who occasionally travelled to patrol the forests and were sometimes used as a guest house for privileged travellers. We were privileged because our guide was a frequent traveller who knew where to go and whom to meet and negotiate with. I think the concept of having IBs in Bhutan was brand new at the time; it came from the Indian forestry system. We were fortunate to enjoy the facilities of such a place when there was no other lodging. Most travellers camped in the open. Gelephu at the time was just a big clearing in the forest and the settlement was mostly hut-like structures that were still being constructed. The IB building stood out like an imposing mansion surrounded by graceful areca nut palms that swished and shimmered in the tropical sun. Hatisa was a small sleepy place where nothing much seemed to happen. We were to wait here for transport to the train station in Bongaigaon in the Indian state of Assam. We waited to continue our journey in the comfort and safety of a house, unlike at our last camp Juiligang, where we were told that encounters with elephants were common. I could sense the tension although the men tried not to show their anxiety. Throughout the journey they had talked of this place, and I had heard from my mother how during her own journey, they had been terrorized by elephants during their halt in Juiligang.

When I was about a year old, my parents went on a pilgrimage to India and had spent a night in Juiligang. I had heard my mother tell the story of how they had to spend a sleepless night, almost hanging from a precipice, because a herd of elephants had visited their camp. When I understood that we would be camping in the place where my parents had encountered elephants, I was excited but anxious. I had only seen elephants in paintings in the temple: the friendly humble creature in the painting of the four friends or the ferocious raging monsters in the war scenes in the mural of the Shambala in our temple. Thinking of these creatures and wondering in what form they would appear, I fell asleep. We encountered no elephants in the land of elephants that night.

After we had waited for a day or two in Gelephu, Dasho Gyeltsenla found transport for us to go to Bongaigaon. We were to part with our servants with whom we had formed a strong bond by now. They had cared for us, feeding us good food, protecting us from harm and cheering us up with songs and dances in the nights, and regaling us with stories during the day. Now we had to part. They would return to Bumthang, and we would travel farther and deeper into the unknown Indian plains. Although I could not verbalize my thoughts, it was a sad and dreadful parting. I don't think I cried but my heart was wrenched as we lost more and more familiar ground.

For the next leg of our journey, we travelled part of the way in a truck. We sat squeezed in front with the driver. I sat frozen, despite the heat and the sweat, between my brother and Dasho Gyeltsenla on one side and the driver on the other. Every time I had a chance, I looked into the eyes of the driver to see if they were yellow. I had heard that Indians used so much mustard oil in their cooking that the white of their eyes turned yellow. No, his eyes were like ours. Another myth negated; there were no elephants in the land of elephants and Indians did not have yellow eyes. But whenever the driver reached across to pull shut the rattling door of the cabin which kept opening every now and then, I saw that his arms were covered in thick black hair. Yes, they were different from us! We used to affectionately refer to our father as Acho *Posokla* or 'hairy big brother' because he had a few straggly hairs on his face which he plucked with a tweezer. But this man had so much hair that no tweezer would have helped.

I do not know how long we travelled but we had to transfer into a bull cart to reach the train station. It was a surreal, dreamlike experience and I just moved along like a robot. Over the following years, this was to be the travel route for us going to school and coming home for the holidays. I never got used to the noisy crowds, the rush, push and shove that was the essence of the disorienting journey. I feared travelling in these trains, especially after a traumatic encounter I had during one of my later journeys. I may have been twelve or thirteen at the time. It was a hassled nerve-racking entry into a fully packed train compartment. I was literally thrown into the train by the guide–translator and landed on the floor already piled high with luggage. Our own luggage was being pushed through the window and pulled in by my brothers. All the berths and seats were already occupied and all the eyes of the passengers already in the compartment were glaring at us newcomers. My brothers were instructed to squeeze into the crowd, sit on the floor with their luggage and not budge on any account. I stood awkwardly and looked around. I saw an old man sitting on a berth squashed among the other passengers and he motioned for me to come and sit next to him. My brothers and the others urged me to take up the offer. As I headed towards the man, he pushed against the others amidst a chorus of protest from those sharing the space. The man was old, thin and fragile. He was wearing a white dhoti, a brown woollen monkey cap pulled down to his forehead and a sleeveless woollen sweater over his shirt. His dark brown skin was stretched tight over his face revealing his bony structure, a kindly grandfather figure. I heard the others murmuring something that sounded like, '*japarmuk bhotiya*', in disgust. Not knowing whether these were words of welcome or a negative message, I pushed myself forward and sat next to the old man. I sat still, hardly daring to breathe. As the train chugged along some passengers got off and those on the train prevented newcomers from coming on board. As time passed there was more space and people relaxed a little and stretched out their cramped legs. I noticed many passengers nodding off and others trying to sleep.

Once night arrived, the lights were dimmed, and the window shutters were pulled down. I was careful not to touch the others near me. I leaned forward and, putting my head on my knees, I also slept a little, moving to the rhythmic motion of the train. I awoke suddenly when I felt a hand pushing between my chest and my knees, groping and feeling. My first thought was that it was a thief looking for my purse. We had been warned of thieves who employed ingenious ways to steal. I was relieved that I had no money on me; my elder brother Rinzin always kept our money with him. I leaned forward more so that there was no space for the hands to move farther. But the hands came over my neck and he was trying to get under my shirt. I dared to look sideways and realized that the kindly old man was desperately trying to touch me, stealthily but urgently. I could hear his breath hot and fast near my ears and feel his face close to me. I was having trouble breathing. My own breath was sending a steam of hot air into my face, and

I felt suffocated. Nobody stirred and I could hear snoring all around. The whole space was bathed in a deathly dim blue light. I was hot and sweating but I was cold in fear and continued to hold my position into an even tighter grip, tightly hugging my knees. I had no thoughts except to not to allow the hands to grope me further. The old man tried different ways to touch me, but I managed to keep his hands from sliding over my chest and from getting under my shirt. He would not stop, and I held on. What was I to do? I was locked into immobility now.

What a relief it was when daylight broke, and people pushed open the shutters. The sudden daylight and fresh air came into the stifling compartment filled with stale thick air. The old man sat upright and leaned back. I sat up from my bent-forward posture, looked at the other passengers, especially those sitting across from me. I thought they were all asleep but from the teasing remarks they were making to the old man who was now getting more and more agitated, I realized that some of them knew what he had been up to. I felt so ashamed; it was as if I was culpable for the old man's behaviour. I could not understand what the other men were saying but from their gestures, I imagined them asking, 'So what did you get?' I was shrinking in my seat, feeling smaller and smaller, my eyes opened wide in horror and shame. My companions had no idea of what happened, and I never spoke to them about it. This is the first time that I am allowing myself to narrate the encounter. Now when I write about it, I shudder to think that the fellow passengers would not have done a thing if something more serious had happened to a young girl in their midst. They would have watched, laughed and teased the perpetrator for his crime. The man got off the train at the next stop and I could finally breathe. The old man, a seemingly kindly grandfather figure, was a predator preying on vulnerable girls and perhaps young boys too. Through his show of concern and act of kindness he had intended to molest me because I appeared the most vulnerable. In those days I had no concepts to even formulate my thoughts on what had happened to me or articulate my experience in words.

Eventually, we reached our destination, Kalimpong. Dasho Gyeltsenla guided us to Her Majesty the Junior Queen Mother Ashi Pema Dechen's residence. Her Majesty was staying with her children in a big mansion-like house called Lhuendrup Choling. We were received graciously by the royal family and treated with kindness. Before I understood what was happening, my brother and I were separated. He was being sent to a school in Darjeeling, St Joesph's School, North Point. At the time I had no idea of where he was going. All I knew was now I was all alone in a strange place with strangers.

18

Telling Me My Stories

I CANNOT REMEMBER ALL THE details of what happened once I arrived in Kalimpong after more than fifteen days of travel on foot and pony, train and truck. Already during the journey, I was overwhelmed by a lurking fear and disquiet. There was no longer the initial excitement of the new and unexpected. I was being thrust from one unfamiliar situation to another. Everything around me kept changing, causing my apprehensions to grow. In my mind's eye I see myself as a disoriented, out-of-place nine-year-old with a bewildered look on my face with nothing to relate to.

All the talk and discussion about what was to happen to me went beyond me. I moved like a sleepwalker. I sort of floated around, even though I was heavy with unease. Soon after my arrival in Kalimpong, I was taken out of my clothes, a full-length sleeveless Tibetan dress. It was during my journey that I learnt to wear this dress because I was changed back to being a girl, in preparation for school. Now I was made to wear a navy blue skirt and white blouse, my legs exposed with short ankle-length socks and a pair of squeaky black shoes. This was not how I imagined exposed legs would look. Ironically, back home, perhaps a year before I was sent away for school, I had once tried to cut off the legs of the pants that I used to wear under my gho, because I wanted to see what it would be like. Many of the children my age had no pants under their gho and had bare legs most of the time. Maybe because I was a girl, I was made to wear underpants under my boy's clothing all the time. I had taken off my pants in a secret place, all by myself, and had cut off the legs by placing them on a boulder and repeatedly banging on them with a sharp-edged stone. The result was an unusable mess, crookedly cut with jagged edges. One leg was long, and the other was cut close to the crotch. I buried the ruined piece of clothing and kept the secret to myself. Now, under the heavy yet billowy navy blue skirt that felt alien and uncomfortable, I was keenly aware of my spindly legs riddled with scars from the untreated insect bites that plagued us every year.

For several days before I was accepted in the boarding school, I was a day scholar. Dasho Gyeltsenla walked me to school in my new strange outfit every morning.

With a queasy stomach and dread in my heart, I followed him as we walked down the hillside to the school which was not too far from where I lived. For the next few days, I was to walk this path twice a day for as long as I was a day scholar. Dasho and I chatted during the walk. He was natural and open, and I grew closer to him as time passed by. The small steep trail took us along the edge of terraced paddy fields, past a thick grove of bamboo and one or two village houses before we descended on to the road that led to the school. Dasho always told me all sorts of happy and funny things to cheer me up. I can still recall now how he repeatedly said, '*Aiee naie* Ashi Jigji (my poor Ashi Jigji).' He could feel my pain and anxiety and was genuinely sympathetic. I must have been a pathetic sight, an awkward frightened girl. Nearing the school, my heart used to thump in my chest and my palms began to sweat as my confidence dissipated. When we reached the school's grotto opposite the church, I knew I was entering the place of my agony. I would have fled if I could, but I had to join the stream of cheerful girls going to school, laughing and happily carefree. Their unkind stares would bore through me, and I would become self-conscious and feel small. One day a group of girls stopped in their tracks and, pointing at Dasho Gyeltsenla and me, sniggered and said something to which Dasho immediately responded in a cool calm voice. On hearing his response, the girls looked shocked and fled sheepishly. I wondered about their exchange. He said the girls were pointing at his ankle-length socks worn over his knee-length stockings and were making fun of him, laughing at him, saying, 'Look at that man wearing double socks.' He had responded in English, telling them that he would be happy to give his second pair to any one of them if they so wished. They were shocked that this Bhutia man had not only understood but also spoke English. Dasho Gyeltsenla was one of the few men who had been educated in Bhutanese, Hindi and English. That is why he was employed by Her Royal Highness Ashi Chokey Wangmo who had graciously appointed him to accompany my brother and me on our long journey to school and be our guide and translator. Until I was enrolled as a boarder in the school, he stayed in Kalimpong to accompany me to school every morning and come to fetch me from school every evening. He even brought my lunch to school every day. Dasho always reserved a whole table for me in the pavilion where the day scholars ate their lunch. My lunches were always a grand spread with many different dishes from Her Majesty the Queen Mother Ashi Pema Dechen's kitchen. Dasho sat with me and encouraged me to eat while I self-consciously nibbled on a few morsels of the feast.

I learnt that a few years later Dasho Gyeltsenla was appointed to the prestigious position of Royal Advisory Councillor to the King of Bhutan, a position he held until his retirement. He was one of the fortunate few who had studied in the royal tutorial school with the third King of

Bhutan. As for the double socks, in those days it was the height of fashion for Bhutanese men to wear ankle-length socks over their full-length stockings. Those silly sniggering girls had picked on the wrong person to make fun of, and I felt a sense of triumph.

But the reality of my life was that I would have to live with these mean and unfriendly girls.

Over the next days, weeks and months, not a single girl befriended me, and I imagined that they were all making fun of me and laughing at me for being such an oddball. I spoke to nobody for I had no language besides my own, Bumthangkha, spoken by a few thousand people in central Bhutan. Even if they did, I would not have understood a word that they said. Even the other students from Bhutan could not communicate with me because all of them were from Dzongkha-speaking regions of western Bhutan and I did not yet speak Dzongkha. From the day I became a boarder, the noisy and speaking world became silent for me. For the next few months, I was locked in total silence.

As I was an older student, already more than nine years old, I was placed in a special class. This class had an assortment of unconventional students, non-English-speaking students from Thailand, Burma and Tibet. I was the only one from Bhutan. I was the stranger once again. The teacher assumed I knew some English and treated me like the others, continuing the lessons she had begun. I understood none of the instructions or the lessons but diligently copied whatever was written on the blackboard, not having the slightest idea of what it was that I was copying. My exercise book began to fill with squiggly letters that were neither Bhutanese nor English. A few days later, the class teacher and Mother Superior had a solemn discussion. From the occasional glances in my direction and ponderous nods of Mother Superior's head, I knew that they were talking about me.

The next phase of my educational adventure was decided. I was led to what Mother Superior repeatedly called, 'a very nice class for you'. I listened to her carefully as she repeated the phrase again and again and I repeated it in my mind. It was a gesture of sheer kindness on Mother Superior's part to hold me by the hand and take me across the school compound, past the many curious stares to the 'very nice class' for me. We went through the playground and past some classrooms, through a long corridor to my new class. Passing through one of the passages, a fat cockroach scampered in front of us and Mother Superior swiftly stamped on it and squashed it under her shoe. And I wondered, what kind of nun is this? I was placed in Lower Kindergarten, where children aged five and six sat at low pink and pale blue tables and screamed and shrieked. I was the elephant being pushed into a rabbit's hole. I did not fully understand what was happening, but I knew enough to feel the terrible humiliation. I was almost double the age and size of my classmates. Immediately I began to shrink. I could feel my shoulders drooping to become the same size as the rest of my new classmates.

The first name of a classmate that I learnt was Teddy. He was a fair-skinned boy with very short, spiky hair. I think he was a Chinese from Calcutta. I shared the small glossy pink table with him and two others. He was a bright boy who was fast with his work and probably good at it too, but he always had his left arm covering whatever he wrote, so afraid that I would copy from him. I never forgot him. The only pleasant memories of that year were those classes that were conducted out in the garden. They are my only positive memories of St Joseph's Convent. It must have been the early summer months. The weather was wonderful, sunny and warm. The neat hedges of red hibiscus were in full bloom. The rows and patches of pretty flowers and the multitude of butterflies flitting around made me look forward to my classes. I would stand by myself, solemn and silent, away from the rest of my little classmates, and observe them as they ran amok chasing the butterflies and screaming in innocent glee. I was not a part of this class; I did not belong here.

For the rest of the time, I was all alone in the school among hundreds of children and many staff. One of the important routines in the school was the mandatory attendance of Benediction every Sunday afternoon. We had to line up with a partner. This became my biggest problem for the whole week. I was anxious about who would walk with me to the church; would I have a partner? It became a serious obsession, making me so worried that on one occasion I fainted on the way and another time I had a severe nosebleed. My saviour came in the form of an older Bhutanese girl who could be bribed. She demanded and threatened me, 'Give me your biscuits and sweets if you want a partner for church,' she would say, and I gave her all my tuck. By then, I understood enough Dzongkha to comprehend her demands. She also joined me to eat all the picnic meals that my mother's ashang, or uncle Lopon Nado, brought for me on Sundays. The prefix lopon or teacher was added to his because he was a learned scholar. Lopon Nado was my mother's uncle, but everybody referred to him as ashang. He lived in the mansion of Her Majesty the Queen Mother Ashi Pem Dechen. I connected with him immediately because he was familiar to me. He had come to visit my parents in Ogyen Choling. Sunday picnic meals were an important tradition in the school. Every Sunday parents and relatives would bring picnic lunches for the girls in boarding and the whole hillside would be dotted with happy picnickers. My church partner would join the picnic, take the bangchung full of rice, meats and vegetables and eat the whole meal by herself, while I watched, saying I was not hungry. Ashang would just look on with a puzzled and defeated expression on his face. After this happened a couple of times, he stopped bringing me picnics, saying, 'You never eat the food I bring for you, anyway.' But I still needed someone to walk to church with. It would be too humiliating not to have a single friend. Every Saturday when my church partner came to negotiate her 'fee' for going to church with me the next day, I gave her whatever I had.

There were other Bhutanese girls at the school who allowed me to trail them like an obedient and loyal dog, but also at a cost. To them I was the girl from Bumthang who had no rice to eat. In Bhutan rice eaters considered themselves superior. They called me the eater of *bjakhu thungme*, the rice-starch water that is thrown out while cooking. This was the first derogatory Dzongkha term I learnt. I could have told them that my family owned extensive paddy fields and exported excess rice to Tibet and to Tawang in Arunachal Pradesh in India, and that even the people who worked for us were given rice. But I was too afraid to speak up. So, I accepted my new identity in silence.

Somehow my days passed, sitting at the pink-and-blue mini tables in Lower Kindergarten and following the bullies. It was the nights I looked forward to. I slept on a black steel bed placed under the slant of the gabled roof of the dormitory. It was a big dark room with tens of beds placed in lines. There was just enough space between my bed and the slanting wall for a person to pass. But this was the only place of my own, where I could relax, be myself and talk to myself. Once in bed, I would cover myself and talk to myself in Bumthangkha. I whispered so that no one else could hear. Especially not the nun who walked up and down the dormitory 'minding' us until she was sure that everybody had fallen asleep, and all lights were switched off. I whispered to myself all that I had seen and observed during the day and repeated sentences and phrases I had heard. The best part of my nightly ritual was to tell myself the stories I had heard back home. I told myself my stories until I relaxed and fell asleep. It was this part of the night that I looked forward to every day.

Later in the year they shifted me to another, smaller, brighter and airier room with only a dozen or so other girls. The Nepali woman whom we addressed as Ayah *Didi*, who made up our beds and cared for us, immediately took a liking to me and made an extra effort to be kind to me. She became my anchor and source of comfort for the rest of my days in the school. Didi had that rare personality that puts you at ease just by being herself. I remember her roundish face and her fair skin with long dark hair in a thick plait. She had a nose ring, and I was fascinated to see how the gold ring moved and dangled when she spoke. She smelt so clean and now, when I try to visualize her, I see her with a soft worn-out white muslin shawl draped over her shoulders. The ends of her lips were curled upwards, always slightly ready to break into a smile. She spoke to me all the time. She was invariably in the room, making beds, darning our socks, polishing our shoes, and sweeping, and I would sneak into the room during meal breaks and class intervals just to hear her talk to me. She was the only person who spoke to me making sure that I understood what she was saying and repeating new words to me. Then, suddenly one day, I found that I was able to talk to her. Just a few words of Nepali, but I was communicating. What a wonderful feeling it was, a breakthrough from my silent world. I felt like a caged bird taking flight.

Finally, the school year ended, and I was truly free once again. My mother had come to Kalimpong and, together with my brothers, we travelled to Samtse. It was the winter of 1962 and Samtse was the temporary seat of the Government of Bhutan. His Majesty the third King Jigme Dorji Wangchuck and the royal family lived there for that winter. The government offices, I think, were in tents near the royal residences. The carefree and happy days in Samtse ended for me when one of the offices in the tents conveyed to my mother that I had failed Lower Kindergarten in St Joesph's Convent. My mother would not have understood the concept of pass and fail, so someone must have explained. It did not bother me at all because I had already decided not to go back to school, although I had not told anybody yet. But my mother was so distraught that she decided to talk to me very seriously. It was then that I told her that I was not going back. She asked me why and I couldn't articulate a single reason although I knew all the reasons. Mother coaxed me and scolded me, but I stood firm. I had made up my mind. Then finally in desperate defeat mother said, 'All right, come back with me and I will teach you to weave yathra, for that's all I know.' I immediately recalled my childhood caregiver, a young girl who was so eager to learn to weave that whenever a weaver left her loom to do some errand, she would slip the backstrap over herself and start to work on the loom.

One day I heard the old, well-meaning Aie Kesang reprimand her, '*Whay*, girl, why do you want to give up your freedom and get tied to a loom? Once you are tied to a loom you will be stuck.' I am not sure if it was the sudden image of my caregiver tied to a loom or the tone in which my mother said it, or whether it was the images of the weavers I had seen bound to their looms day after day, but I cried non-stop for hours. I cried because I couldn't verbalize my experiences in school. I cried because I had lost my father. I cried because I wanted to be with mother. I cried because I needed to cry. Nobody tried to stop me from crying. I went to the room in which we slept and, leaning against the folded bedding stacked up against the wall, I buried my face in the bedclothes and wept silently. I cried till my face felt taut and stretched with the tears that washed my face again and again. When the tears stopped and the hiccups subsided, I realized to my horror that I had dug my fingers into my chest and ripped my shirt.

The matter of education was at a standstill, and I was quite sure I would go home with mother even if I was tied to a loom. But things were not to be that way because a few days later the Prime Minister of Bhutan, Lyonchen Jigme Palden Dorji, who was also in Samtse at the time, heard about my refusal to continue school. He knew me, as I used to play with the royal children. He was not only responsible for sending Bhutanese children to schools in India but was also the greatest advocate for modern education in Bhutan. One day he approached me as I was climbing up a tree with the princesses. I have preserved this image of the Prime Minister of my country telling me, the miserable girl who had failed Lower Kindergarten, that it is important to go back to school. The image is still very clear in my head as it was a life-changing moment. The Prime Minister stood under the tree which still stands today outside what used to be the Inspection Bungalow. There he stood, this dignified and cheerful man with a kindly smile on his face. After he had greeted and exchanged some words with the princesses, he turned to me and said, 'Education is important. You must go to school. I will send you to a very good new school.' I just nodded. I had been persuaded by just one sentence from the champion of modern education in Bhutan.

By agreeing to go back to school, my educational journey now began in earnest. I knew nothing of the new school. All I knew was that I was not being sent back to St Joesph's Convent in Kalimpong. I had no notion of what school I was going to or how I would get to this new school.

Somebody would have to take me there. Out of the big dark void of uncertainties, there emerged a person who offered to take me. He was Shivraj Gurung, the eldest son of the District Commissioner, Jusraj Gurung. They were from the most prominent family in Samtse. Shivraj's youngest sister Gayatri was also going to start at the same school, so he would take me along with his sister. He drove us in his jeep to a place called Kurseong. By then I knew a few words of Nepali, so I had some limited communication with my co-traveller and her brother. But mostly it was a quiet journey. All the way there I was bothered by a nagging worry that I may have been assigned to a non-English local school because of my poor performance. Despite my tormented year in an English-medium school, I had realized the prestige of such a school compared to a local school. Even if I had not learnt anything in the school, I had succumbed to the Anglophile snobbery – that an English education is superior to a local one. I didn't have the language or the courage to ask Shivraj, whom I had learnt to call *daju*, older brother, about the school. Once we reached Kurseong, we drove through the town, and as we climbed up the hill through a forest area towards the school, I saw an image of Mother Mary standing on a pedestal overlooking a large playground. I recognized her because there had been a similar image of her in the grotto in St Joesph's Convent. This figure conveyed a sense of welcome and I felt naively assured that I was indeed going to an English-medium school. After all, she was not a local divinity; she was foreign and Christian. I say naïve because I later learnt that there were other local schools which were run by Christian missionaries and that Christian images were a common sight.

When we reached the school, we were taken through a beautiful garden to a parlour but there was not a single student in sight and the place was quiet. While at St

Joesph's Convent, I had dreaded the sight of the black-robed, serious-faced busy nuns. On this day, I felt happy and relieved on seeing a foreign nun. I was fully convinced that I was indeed in a superior school. The nun talked with Shivraj daju, and we were told that we were a few days ahead of the first day of school. The other students would come only in four or five days. But it was quickly decided that Gayatri and I should stay on in school rather than go back all the way to Samtse in Bhutan. Both of us were rather shy and frightened, and when Shivraj daju drove off, Gayatri had to be gently held back by the nuns. She clearly was not ready to stay on without her brother. I, on the other hand, had already had a whole year of being in a boarding school and was not too disturbed. In fact, I was happier and more relaxed to know Gayatri was going to be there with me. The nuns looked after us and gave us timely meals, and the two of us spent much of our time in the garden and wandering around the playground. In a day or two, Gayatri became so confident that she said we should go into town; she knew the way. I followed her. We were just at the edge of the forest, past the playground, when we saw two nuns frantically running after us, their long, hurried strides making their skirts swish around their bodies, the long rosary clanging by their sides and their veils fluttering around their faces. They were breathing hard when they caught up with us. They held our hands gently but firmly. They thought we were trying to run away.

By the time the students joined, Gayatri and I were quite at home and familiar with the surroundings. But on the day we were to be assigned classes, I was again in my nervous mode filled with uncertainty. Would they put me back into kindergarten? When I saw the tiny tots in line, some of them crying and frightened, my old fears came flooding back, taunting me. I anxiously listened for my name to be announced. I felt so relieved and happy when I was assigned to class two. But how did this happen? I had failed kindergarten and yet I got a double promotion. Clearly, it was not my academic achievements but my age and size and the nuns' wisdom that secured my allocation. The nuns had taken a risk and made a wise decision. I did not disappoint anybody. I fitted right in and enjoyed my class. Especially because Gayatri was there.

In the three years that I was in St Helen's Convent I was happy, and I found the girls were kinder and friendlier than in Kalimpong. It was while I was in this school that Gayatri's parents took full responsibility for me and became my self-appointed guardians. Gayatri's big family had a big heart, and they welcomed me into their fold as Gayatri's *meti bahaini*, adopted sister, becoming the sixth sister in the family. They invited me for the long weekends to visit their relatives in Kurseong, Siliguri and Darjeeling. During the most important Hindu festival for the southern Bhutanese, the *dasain* celebrations, when most of the children would go home for the school holidays, I was invited by the Gurung family to join them in their home in Sibsoo. Otherwise, I would have had to stay back in school with the few girls whose parents were far away. In Sibsoo I participated in their Hindu rituals: together with Gayatri I sang *Raghupati Raghava Raja Ram*, the daily bhajans, at their altar tucked away in a neat corner, met all their relatives, exchanged *teeka*, received gifts of money, watched the ritual slaughter of an uncastrated goat, ate its meat and blood cooked in all sorts of ways and partook of the wonderful festival foods. They treated me like their own daughter.

Gayatri excelled in her studies and was a star student. She was always at the top of the class, and it was good to have a friend like her who never shied away from assisting others who needed help. By class three, I was fully integrated and happy in school. My only misfortune was to fall ill for a protracted period with a severe case of chicken pox, while the rest of the class was being taught long division. I missed that crucial lesson and the vital building blocks for mathematics and never mastered the essential mathematical understanding which continues to bother me to this day. By class four, I was doing so well that I even received the prize for geography. But at the end of that year, without any warning, I was suddenly told that I was being transferred to Loreto Convent in Darjeeling because my young cousin was starting school there and my uncle thought it was better for us to be together.

I continued to stay in intermittent contact with Gayatri throughout our school days. I had the chance to reconnect with her during our college days in Delhi. I studied in Indraprastha College in Delhi University and Gayatri studied medicine at the All-India Institute of Medical Sciences. Gayatri married an Indian doctor, and they ran a private clinic in Lucknow. Several years ago, I learnt that, sadly, she and her husband had both died, within a few years of each other.

In 1966 I joined Loreto Convent in class five and stayed there until I completed my schooling in 1972. By the time I was in the third convent, I was quite familiar and comfortable with convent ways and did not feel the alienation and confusion I had experienced in 1962. I think in the seven years that I was in Loreto Convent, I became who I am as an adult today. Spending seven years of our lives together, sharing and growing together with the same girls who felt like family to me, I made some close friends whom I am still in contact with, thanks to the internet. Sadly, I was the only Bhutanese girl in my class, so I had no way of fostering close friendships with any Bhutanese during my school days. Even now I sometimes feel a sense of envy for the Bhutanese women who have lifelong friends, their friendships going back to their school days. Many of my friends from school have moved to different parts of the world. How I wish there were at least some of them in closer geographical proximity. My life is poorer for the friends I miss from my school days.

19

A Crippled Family

We didn't know what to make of it when we were unexpectedly summoned into uncle Ugyen Wangdi's bedroom. We were on our winter break, living with our uncle and his family in Kalimpong. It must have been late December or early January 1965. Although we had been in the bedroom occasionally, it was not a place we could enter without a good reason. We had come in from the bright sunshine, and the large room appeared dark and sombre. The curtains had not been pulled back although it was late morning. Yet, the room seemed cool and fresh. Uncle's wife sat on her bed and was preoccupied with writing something. As we entered the room, she acknowledged us as usual and greeted us kindly but continued writing. Every now and then she looked up and gazed at us with a strange expression on her face. Her expression worried me a little. The bedroom was spacious with a sofa and a coffee table. We were asked to sit on the large sofa which was placed against the wall between the beds and the large closets against the adjoining wall. Uncle Ugyen Wangdi walked to his bedside table, picked up something from it and came towards us. We continued to sit quietly, not knowing what to expect. The way he handed each one of us an item in an exaggerated ceremonial fashion unnerved me. I received a small dainty gold Swiss watch. It felt cold and light in my hands. I could hardly breathe. We rarely received presents like this and the way they were being given was very odd. It was my first watch, and I was trembling, not with excitement but with anxious curiosity, for I had never expressed a desire for a watch and never imagined that I would ever possess one. What was happening? I remained controlled and tense, holding the watch in my hands with a mixture of reverence and disbelief. I cannot remember what my brothers received. There was silence in the room and the only sound I heard was the soft modulated flow of our breath. Both my brothers were holding their gifts in their hands, but the hands remained passively on their laps, as if afraid to take possession of what they had just received. As I try to conjure up the image, I am reminded of the game of charades we used to play in school, where everyone had to assume a posture and freeze; we sat frozen in our seats.

Uncle began to talk but I cannot recall what he said. Then suddenly, as if from a far distance, he announced; 'Your Nene is dead.' He referred to our mother as Nene, as we did, but this effort did not lessen the state of shock we were catapulted into. The pain and sense of loss had not yet set in. The cool fresh air in the room now suddenly seemed heavy and claustrophobic. Thinking about it now, maybe it would have helped our later lives if we had cried out loudly, screamed and howled and hugged each other. But no, the three of us sat in stony silence, each of us intensely aware of the other but not even moving. It was as if we were afraid of invading each other's space. There was no touching, no hugging and patting, not even daring to look at each other as we packed our own bereavement inside ourselves. I felt an overwhelming sense of heaviness enveloping me as the dull sensation slowly gave way to a sense of panic. But I continued to sit there on the sofa. Did I cry? No, I did not. My tears fell back into my eyes, stinging, seeping into my body, filling it with the new experience of grief.

I became acutely conscious of my whole being. I felt insignificant and disconnected to everything around me and the world at large. Then with an unintended glance in my elder brother's direction, I noticed a mute teardrop glistening on his cheek. My heart numbed. Sonam, my younger brother, continued to sit in bewildered silence. If there were any words of consolation and assurance from my uncle I cannot remember them, but he continued to talk about his misfortune at having to take responsibility for us, now orphans, and said things that did not make a lot of sense. The words flew past us and stayed suspended in the air, heavy and grave in the darkened room.

Finally, we walked out of the room in silence, as if in a dream, down the flight of stairs and into the ironing room. This was a completely empty room, except for a big table in one corner used for ironing clothes. This was where we ate our meals. The three of us did not eat in the dining room upstairs with uncle's family; neither did we eat with the servants in the kitchen. We ate our meals in this empty room. How this came about I don't recall, but it was the accepted and natural way. There was a door near the table leading to a patio. The sunlight was pouring into the room through the open door, and the polished red cement floor reflected the sunlight. But I felt the overwhelming chill. I still carry the image of the three of us looking like completely wounded beings, suddenly loaded with burdens that were too heavy for us. Our heads hung low, our shoulders slouched, and our limbs clung to us like they did not belong to our bodies as we walked out of the door to the patio for some privacy from the curious and unsympathetic stares of the house servants. We stood there together for a while not saying anything and avoiding even looking at each other until Acho Rinzin shook off the tears coursing down his cheeks and in a gloomy but resolute voice branded us. 'Now we are a crippled family,' he said. We still clutched the presents in our hands, symbols of our new status as orphans in a crippled family. Then we walked away from each other to go and mourn in our own ways.

Our mother had died several months ago, and nobody had bothered to tell us. What had she died of? We didn't know whom to ask and nobody told us. Not that it mattered so many months after her death. Who could we turn to for comfort and consolation? There was nobody there for us. We were orphans and on our own. I will never forget that crippling moment. Throughout my teenage years into adulthood and motherhood, I have mourned my mother's death.

Two years earlier our father had died, and we learnt about it only several months after it happened. In fact, I was made to believe that my father was guarding our northern borders with Tibet against possible Chinese aggressions. I was old enough to understand that there were serious political disturbances with China taking over Tibet. I believed the tale that my father had stayed back to guard the borders because that year, 1962, was the time when Tibetans were fleeing their country in great numbers. And even at that young age, I understood the danger of the Chinese following the fleeing refugees into Bhutan. I cannot recall who had made up this story about my father, but I immediately imagined father riding his black stallion Dranag, pistol in his holster and rifle in his hand, guarding borders, risking his life so that we could be safe. I had watched enough western movies within the year to build up this image of my father as a hero. It was not a totally fabricated picture. Father always rode this horse, and he always carried a pistol. But the truth of the matter was that while I had nostalgically visualized my hero, my father was already dead in the month of May 1962, three months after we had left home for the first time.

By December that same year mother was in Kalimpong with us but silently mourning the death of her husband. Mother had no option but to sell Dranag to a merchant in Gelephu. My imaginary hero and his mount exited our lives. Dranag was a big black stallion my father had purchased in Lhasa during one of his trips. He was a stately, beautifully proportioned stallion that father immediately fell for. He used up several bags of precious rice and some other items to acquire this animal. But Dranag was a nervous creature and quite unpredictable. The boys often said that this was a *mak ta* or a war horse, or perhaps it was how a war horse should be. I still have a vivid image of the horse in my mind and tend to measure every stallion against Dranag. Only my father could handle him and since he had this horse, he rode no other. As none of the horsemen liked Dranag because of his finicky nature, they had persuaded mother to get rid of him, sell him when she travelled to Kalimpong that winter. They had declared that they would not be able to handle such a nervous horse. Some months after her sojourn in Kalimpong and Samtse, on her way back to Bumthang mother saw Dranag in Gelephu with the new owner and she was convinced that he was shedding tears and snorting quietly on seeing her and hearing her voice. He was being used as a draft animal to pull carts. I cried on hearing this. I cried for the horse my father loved; I had not cried at my father's death until then.

By late 1962, as tensions were building up on the northern borders, mother had been advised to flee Ogyen Choling because of possible Chinese inroads into Bhutan. She was not completely aware of the geopolitics of the region but knew enough to know that the Chinese targeted the landlords and the elites, and that she was a likely target for denunciations, torture, imprisonment and even death. The desperate Tibetan refugees coming into Bhutan brought horrifying stories about the atrocities they had experienced. She packed what she could carry, locked up what she could not and, taking her two sons Sonam Wangchuk and Ugyen Rinzin, left Ogyen Choling to its destiny. Because of the difficulty of transporting all that she possessed to Kalimpong, she entrusted some of her belongings in packed boxes to people she barely knew in Gelephu. She sold some of the horses she had brought with her and came to Kalimpong where we were staying at the time. She came to be with us in a safe place even though there was the constant fear of Chinese attacks in Kalimpong and precautions had to be taken. The adults talked constantly about the Chinese, and the new Tibetan refugees continued to tell their dreadful, tragic stories of what the Chinese were doing to Tibet and Tibetans. That was the time I learnt about blackouts. Windowpanes had to be covered with newspapers and curtains had to be drawn to ensure that there were no lights coming out of the houses. Night raids were what we had to be prepared for.

That year His Majesty the third King Jigme Dorji Wangchuck along with the royal family and the entire government were in Samtse. Even the royal family considered the place safe during those uncertain times. Later we all went to Samtse with Ashi Chokey. Uncle Ugyen Wangdi had remained in Bumthang which made the story of my father guarding the borders even more plausible. Mother had a room in one of the guest houses and we all stayed there together. Reminiscent of her pre-marriage days in the service of the Royal Queen Mother Ashi Phuntsho Choden, my mother slipped into her old role. Every day she was with the Queen Mother, but we still managed some precious moments together.

I still smile at the fond memories of the splash baths we used to have together. We were like two little girls playing in the water. Although it was winter, we were still not used to the subtropical heat, and cool baths were a great relief for us. We let the tap run full as we sat under the rush of water. Mother put on a pair of my school knickers. This kind of underwear made from a thick and rather coarse cloth was the total antithesis of lingerie and anything pretty, delicate or feminine. They were navy blue bloomers, balloon-like shorts with elastic bands that hugged the thighs so tightly that even air could not pass through. Probably designed during the prudish Victorian era, these symbols of Victorian primness were still impacting our lives in the Christian missionary schools in 1960s post-British India. We had to wear bloomers over our cotton knickers under our skirts. My mother loved the bloomers as a bathing outfit, although they did not fit her very well. We spent long hours in the bathroom splashing water and rubbing each other's backs.

For my mother, the sorrow symbolized by the fish that she received as a wedding present was trailing her. She had lost her husband earlier in the year, she was still in mourning, and she had to suddenly abandon her home until the political situation cleared up. The Chinese did not enter Bhutan. But in the process of her temporary escape, she lost some of her belongings which were left in good faith with people she barely knew. She did not get back most of the silver which she had been advised to melt and turn into bars, which were easier to transport during her escape. Much, much later I got some of the silver bars which she did manage to retrieve but, sadly, when I tried to use them, I discovered many had been adulterated, mixed with other metals and covered in a coating of silver. The silversmith must have made a fortune!

Coming to Samtse was a sad revelation for mother. We were happy that we could spend a few precious weeks with her before we went back to our schools. She continued to stay on in Samtse with the Queen Mother, but things were not as she had imagined them to be. She later told me that she was at a total loss because there was nobody she could turn to for comfort and counsel. In fact, when the fear of the Chinese invasion subsided, and it was safe to return to Bumthang via Hatisa, she could not get transport to go back. She said Babu Wangchuk, a distant relative of hers from Dagana, was one of the few people who showed some concern, especially for her son Ugyen Rinzin, who was small and weak for his age. Babu Wangchuk introduced her to Horlicks, an energy drink, and insisted that she continue to feed this to him to make him grow. Vehicles were rare and there was no transport service at the time. She had to wait for weeks to arrange a vehicle to go to Hatisa. Finally, carrying her best yathra, she had to go and see Bana Athing, the Sikkimese gentleman working with the Bhutanese government at the time. She begged him to help her to go with her young son to Hatisa.

I think this experience of helplessness and the sense of abandonment she felt in Samtse set the trend for the rest of her life. For the next two years in Ogyen Choling, she was seized by a deep melancholia and despondency. She felt utterly alone, especially after even her third child Sonam Wangchuk was separated from her when he was sent to school in Darjeeling.

It must have been a mirthless journey full of foreboding for mother, with only her youngest son and a couple of male servants, going back to Ogyen Choling. On reaching home, she found that the Chinese had not even come near our house, but that our home had been raided by the locals led by a respected personality from the locality. A year later when we went home for the school holiday, Akhu lama Nuden and she shuddered and shook their heads in disbelief when they told us how the people had robbed the house. They had made torches of wooden splinters and gone into the rooms darkened because all the shutters had been nailed down for security before mother left home. The local intruders were searching for things that they could carry. For some strange reason they did not touch the temples and did not open the sealed boxes, so the religious treasures of Ogyen Choling were spared.

In 1999 when I was in Tibet, while visiting the fifteenth-century Ganden monastery, the tour guide told us that in many instances the destruction and plunder of the aristocratic households and desecration of monasteries and temples during the cultural revolution were carried out not only by the Chinese red guards but that the locals had also joined in the plunder. In fact, the locals were much more ruthless and vindictive. Some of the local Tibetans were fired up by the ideals of communism and were avenging the years of inequality and injustice. But others were impassioned by the animosity and vengeance nurtured over centuries between the landlords and their dependents. Human character is predictable. The everyday displays of mutual respect and duty dictated by the standard norms of society may not always effectively hold back the raw feelings and sentiments that flow underneath like molten lava. In times of chaos, human beings become different creatures all together. I cannot put it past me – I too might have joined the marauding group if I had been from the locality.

All the time that we were together in Kalimpong and Samtse we never spoke about father's death. Mother probably took it for granted that we knew about it or perhaps it was too painful for her to talk about. I think she spoke to Acho Rinzin about it because at some point during the holiday he suddenly transformed into a brooding person. He hunched his back visibly as if the burden of the world had fallen on his shoulders. Sonam Wangchuk had been in Ogyen Choling at the time of father's death, so he had experienced father's passing. I was the only one who had not an inkling of it. It was Sonam who leaked the news of the death to me under an unusual circumstance. When we were back in Kalimpong we had gone to see a movie at the theatre Novelty. There were two cinema halls in Kalimpong at the time, and we went to see every movie that was shown in these halls. We were watching a Hindi movie and when there was a scene of a corpse being cremated on a pyre with the Hindu rituals, Sonam Wangchuk very matter-of-factly blurted out, 'That's what they did with Acho Gigpala.'

In the darkened hall with only silhouettes as my companions in the changing light from the projector, I could hear myself meekly whispering, 'Our Acho Gigpala is dead?'

Sonam was intent on watching the screen as the cremation scene had already changed to some other scene, 'He died a long time ago.' Sitting in the darkness I all at once felt very small and vulnerable. It was then that I became acutely conscious of the fact that even the seat I was on was far too big for me; my feet were dangling from the edge of the seat, and I was literally and figuratively not grounded any more. Slowly I could feel myself shrinking, shrivelling up in my seat and gradually being consumed by the darkness. No thoughts, no feelings, only nothingness. Perhaps it was a death I experienced. Dry-eyed but filled to capacity with inexplicable grief, I emerged out of the dark cinema hall into my now darker new world, deeply conscious of the pain of my silent heartache.

I always felt a little incomplete in my life, lonely and ashamed of not having a father, like it was a failure caused by us children. We were challenged by the fact that we had to use the term 'our late father' when talking about our beloved Acho Gigpala. We consciously refrained from talking about him. He was a sad secret we shared among the three of us. He became a gaping void in our lives that we learnt to carefully skirt around.

With hindsight I realize how important the Bhutanese custom of long-drawn rituals for the dead is for the bereaved family. The rituals that last up to forty-nine days are complicated and expensive and can be financially draining, but it is the best process for healing. They are believed to help the dead travel the path of transition to their next life. For the bereaved family, relatives, friends, well-wishers and sympathizers coming to share the grief in empathy is an amazing experience of comfort and healing. We experienced none of that. There was no healing and no closure.

The schools we attended helped us to temporarily forget our status as orphans, because all the children in boarding schools were away from their parents. It was during the school holidays that we felt the full impact of being orphans of a crippled family, having to be the recipients of the goodwill and charity of others' families. We were completely vulnerable and exposed, and thought of ourselves as intruders who had no rights. School holidays were problematic. Every so often we would momentarily brighten up when we conspired together, 'Let's run away.' But we had no one and nowhere to run away to. In retrospect, I think we were drawing some temporary relief from the fantasy of being able to flee from our plight of being burdensome orphans. We could not run away from ourselves; we could not run away from being orphans.

When we could make the long journey and go home to Ogyen Choling and be with Akhu lama during our holidays, everything was different. We knew he cared for us unconditionally and treated us as 'his own flesh and blood'. For a monk who was never expected to have any parenting skills or experience, he was the only one who helped us restore our dignity and self-esteem. He himself had left his own family before he was fifteen years old to go and live in Mindroling monastery in Tibet. He had lost his own parents while he was away. He too had become an orphan while he was geographically separated from his parents. He never once mentioned that he was burdened by having to care for us. He never declared his love for us openly, but we never doubted it.

He treated each of us as individuals and he had no favourites. In all our conversations he was fully with us. And when he used the terms *nedh* and *neyra*, we and us, we knew we were family.

Today, as I dedicate my life to restoring, preserving and revitalizing Ogyen Choling against innumerable odds, I take consolation in the knowledge that Akhu lama would have approved of all that I am doing. When at a loss for advice or when there is a gap to be filled in the history and traditions of the family, that is the time I lament his absence. I miss his counsel, for he also died before he reached the age of sixty, crippling us further and making us absolute orphans.

20

My Marriage of Choice

MY WEDDING, IN COMPARISON to my mother's, was a humble affair. For a start, in 1948 my mother was just eighteen years old, and her husband was chosen for her by others according to the norms of the time. Twenty-nine years later, in 1977, I was already twenty-five and consciously treading into unknown territory that challenged the norms. And I had chosen the man I would marry. I knew the man I was going to marry for over a year before we decided to get married. Walter came from a Swiss farming family. As is common practice in Switzerland, the parish of every community maintains the family tree of all the church members, so Walter could, if he wished, trace his family tree for centuries. Even without looking at the records, Walter was quite sure that there were no religious personalities or historically outstanding figures in his lineage. His ancestors were all hard-working farmers, proud to farm the lands they lived off.

There were no parents or relatives on either side to plan my wedding. I thought I had nobody who cared about what I did with myself. Walter's parents were far away in Switzerland, and if they disapproved of our matrimony I never knew. Years later, my mother-in-law told me that the day her son decided to leave Switzerland for a place called Bhutan, a country she knew nothing of, she knew that Walter would never be a conventional Swiss man. In other words, she could and would no longer influence his life's choices.

My mother's wedding procession started from a royal palace, Domkhar, and the wedding rituals and celebrations took place in Ogyen Choling, a house of repute and respect. My wedding celebration was held in a simple canteen in the Swiss-funded Rural Development Project (RDP) compound in Choekor valley, where Walter and I were both working at the time. He was working with young boys from the locality, training them in agriculture, and I taught these boys basic literacy and some English. Their canteen which doubled as a classroom was the venue of our wedding party. The canteen was a long narrow room with a long table in the centre and chairs placed against the walls for the invited guests to sit facing the table with the food. The unexpected and uninvited guests (from Choekor and Tang), who were nonetheless welcomed, sat on the lawn outside in two long lines. A monk from the Trongsa *dratshang* (monastic body) who was the *kangjunpa* or ritualist for the temples in the Jakar dzong and who had befriended us, volunteered to be the master of ceremonies. His participation was useful as he had access to the dzongkhag administration, and he borrowed crockery from the dzong's stores because we did not have enough of our own. Within days after our wedding, we had to pay the dzongkhag stores for some broken and missing crockery. There was no procession, almost no relatives came, although my two uncles in Tang sent some food for the party. Akhu lama also sent us a small statue of Tsepadme (Buddha Amitayus) for long life, wrapped in a yellow silk scarf. I still venerate this Tsepadme which is in my altar.

They also sent some of our old family servants to help with the cooking and serving. This turned out to be a bad idea because there was immediate conflict with the young trainees and their canteen cook, Ap Rin Dorji. They did not welcome the old servants from Ogyen Choling. While the old servants were trying to bring in some protocol and old feudal decorum, Ap Rin Dorji and his group had become friends with the Swiss and treated each other like equals. We were fortunate there was no open fighting, and that everybody was fed. The invited guests were our colleagues, the schoolteachers from Jakar high school, the Swiss families who worked at the project and some of the people from the dzongkhag administration. Some people from the valley were joined by people from Tang who had come for the ceremony and lunch. They brought along baskets of eggs, fried biscuits, barrels of fermenting grains for alcohol and containers of alcohol and *khadars*, white ceremonial scarves, to wish us well. I think there were many more people than we had calculated, because at least twice during the party somebody from the kitchen had to rush out and buy more bags of rice from the bazaar.

Our wedding was blessed by the presence of His Holiness the seventh Nyamkhai Ningpo who was a mere eleven-year-old at the time. I can still recall the anxious and shy look on the child's face as the wedding guests rushed to receive his blessings. The attendant who carried him raised him high above the crowd and brought him into the canteen quickly. He blessed us with a khadar and a thangka of Shabdrung. I felt truly blessed by his presence. But I was disappointed and saddened by the fact that Beru Khyentse Rinpoche of Lame Gompa did not come, even though I had sent him a letter of invitation. Later I learnt that he too was disappointed that I had not invited him. In fact, he is supposed to have said, 'I am her only relative here and she did not invite me.' I made inquiries and found out that the invitation we had sent him had not reached him. Alas, in those days there were no telephones, and we could only communicate by shouting out messages across the rivers and valleys or by sending a special courier. Our courier service had lost the invitation and had not told anyone about it.

I had sent verbal messages of invitations to my relatives in Chummey and was touched by the effort Aum Rinchen from Pangte Gompa and a few other women from Chummey valley had invested to walk all the way carrying gifts for us. Aum Rinchen was concerned that I may not have obtained the approvals and blessings of the other relatives to marry a foreigner. Only when I assured her that my marriage had been approved of by the 'concerned authorities' and my relatives, she held my hand, smiled and relaxed. But even today when I think of this, I become a little emotional. She had come to the ceremony even though she was not sure whether I was breaking conventions by marrying a foreigner. I suspect that she may have been advised to attend the wedding by her husband, Dasho Thinley Namgyel of Pangte. To my mind he was one of the most well-informed and progressive persons I knew. A forward-looking man, he faithfully listened to the Tibetan language news on All India Radio and was well informed of current affairs. Whenever I met him, he would discuss world affairs with me. In fact, on one or two occasions he told me to forget the redundant statuses that we were born into. 'These will not help you to go forward,' he said. Once I walked all by myself to Pangte from Choekor valley and everybody was a little surprised and sorry for me, having descended to what they considered such a low state. 'Ashi, you were alone?' 'Nobody to accompany you, Ashi?'

But I seized the moment and joked that I had said goodbye to 'Ashi Kunzang at the bridge and she went in the opposite direction'. I narrated my experience to Dasho Thinley Namgyel, and he was the only one who understood my joke.

He said, 'That is good,' and laughed. I think he was assured that I understood what he meant by forgetting redundant statuses. I think he approved of my marriage.

My assumption that Dasho Thinley Namgyel had approved of my marriage did not mean that there was no resistance to my marrying a foreigner. Had my parents been alive, they may have had only some vague idea of Switzerland. I remember my mother had received a piece of Swiss cheese from Her Majesty the Queen Mother Ashi Phuntsho Choden, and she wasn't sure how to use it. In 1964 when we came home for the holidays, she showed us the small piece of cheese which had by then hardened into an unidentifiable object. Mother put that last piece of Swiss cheese into the dish she cooked for us that day. She had been using bits of it whenever she cooked special dishes in addition to those dishes that were prepared by the family kitchen. She often cooked something on an iron tripod stand placed in the brazier. It amuses me to think that a bit of Swiss cheese had made its presence felt in Ogyen Choling thirteen years before the Swiss man came into the family.

One of the first Swiss men who come to work in Bhutan married a young woman from the locality in 1975. Their marriage was not only approved of but boosted by the personal interest and support from a very highly placed member of the royal family who insured that the first Bhutanese–Swiss marriage was a grand event. Hundreds of people attended the wedding, and dancers had entertained the attendees. It was an occasion to remember, and it was the talk of the valley for many years to come. I had seen pictures of the wedding and was impressed. By comparison mine was modest.

Honestly, I never expected a grand wedding. I just wanted to legalize my marriage and get on with life. But as there was no clear social or legal procedure at the time, I desperately needed some guidance that would take us through the unchartered bureaucratic and legal waters. Finally, by way of verbal consent from the person in the highest authority, came a heaven-sent blessing and there was no looking back. Marriages between Bhutanese and foreigners were discouraged. There had only been three or four cases before me. I had decided that I would marry this man, but at the same time in the back of my mind I knew that I did not want to be a downright social rebel. The verbal approval was imperative.

The reaction to my imminent matrimony was quite unexpected. I had no parents to consult and seek permission from; there was nobody else who would have cared less about who I married. At least that was what I thought. Since the death of my parents, I had literally grown up on my own, making my own decisions about my life. Except for Akhu lama, there were very few adults in my life who had shown any signs of care and concern for me. At twenty-five years of age, employed and earning a respectable salary of 300 ngultrums a month, I was convinced that my life did not matter to anybody, and I felt completely independent. Surprisingly, my two uncles, especially uncle Ugyen Wangdi, were against my relationship with a foreigner. They insisted that I was doing wrong by marrying a foreigner. I had repeatedly asked, 'Why?' each time they tried to dissuade me. They did not outright force me to break up or scold me, and they did assure me that I was independent and free to make my choice. But they gave me all sorts of reasons. Their biggest concern was that he was of a different *rik jue* which refers to race and the purity of bloodlines. Although there is not a strict caste system in Bhutan, most Bhutanese, especially those who considered themselves better than others genealogically and economically, can be obsessive about the purity of rik jue.

The subtle fault lines in our casteless society show up in certain situations and we can become neurotically finicky about the purity of race and genealogy. If I was marrying a foreigner today, I think nobody would bat an eyelid because globalization and economics have obliterated all the concerns in the concept of rik jue. More importantly foreigners are seen in general to be economically better off. But in 1977 rik jue was still a major concern. My uncles in desperation pointed out that, 'Their [Walter's] rik jue allows them to eat horse meat.'

'What's wrong with that?'

'The horse is a hoofed animal. We do not eat hoofed animals.'

'Why?'

'Because we are different.'

My uncles were now confronted with a challenge of dishonouring a long-standing belief and they saw themselves as custodians of this faith that supposedly held together the fabric of their society. But when questioned they could not explain what defined us beyond what we ate. They were not alone in their beliefs. I knew that the concept of rik jue was so widespread and deeply embedded in our conscience that it played out in many ways. In our village of just a few households, rik jue divided the people subtly but brutally. People in Ogyen Choling were keenly aware of the concept and some households were openly discriminated against as being of the *ja rik*, or descendants of Indians who may have come in the 1800s as workers as opposed to us, those who claimed to be the original inhabitants of the place. The idea of rik jue not only covered race but expanded to include hereditary afflictions and beyond.

I had seen my parents and uncles being bothered into anger and become fiercely retaliatory when some people had pointed out that our family had *zepai rik* or a leper rik jue. Tsampa Dawala, a cousin of my grandmother, had a debilitating disease that rendered his limbs immobile and forced him to stay in isolation from a young age. I met him once when he came to visit my parents. I have a fleeting memory of a big man bringing us a basketful of fried cheese wafers coated with sugar, such a rare treat that I remember it. But I cannot remember what he looked like or whether he had eyebrows or not. By all accounts he had been a handsome and capable man who was the overall in-charge of Ogyen Choling during the time of my grandparents, when he was suddenly stricken with this disease. His handsome features became distorted, and his limbs became gnarled like a ginger tuber. Despite these symptoms, my parents claimed that he never lost his eyebrows (which was considered a definite symptom of leprosy) and that the people who stayed with him and cared for him never contracted the devasting symptoms of leprosy, although leprosy was thought to be highly contagious. 'Of course, he did not have leprosy and we are not of the leper rik jue,' they used to argue. Now they were pushing the all-persuasive rik jue argument on me to dissuade me from my resolve to marry a man of my choice.

Within a year of my marriage, I heard a more enlightened view about why I married a foreigner. It had nothing to do with rik jue. Once, on our way from Phuentsholing to Thimphu, my husband and I stopped for lunch in Taktichu canteen. Just as we pulled into the parking lot, a Bhutanese army truck followed and parked beside our car, and I overheard the conversation that ensued on seeing Walter and me together.

'Look, look, she is married to that foreigner,' one fellow pointed out.

'Really?'

'Why do you think she married him?'

'Money, money. Foreigners have lots of money.'

'Ah, yes, if he has money, nothing else should matter.'

A resounding '*Awaw Embay mo*', yes of course, came from the rest of the uniformed soldiers. Although it was humiliating to be talked about so openly on the assumption that I was a fortune hunter, it was in some ways reassuring to hear a truck full of men approving my choice of a partner.

When my uncles realized that they could not make me change my mind, they resorted to more manipulative strategies. Colluding with a well-known and well-respected astrologer, they told me that the birth animal signs according to the lunar calendar for my husband and I were completely incompatible. Walter, born in the year of the metal tiger, and I born in the year of the water dragon, were not only incompatible but would also prove to be harmful to each other to the point of destroying each other. It would altogether be a disastrous match. What I had heard of my parents' marriage was in the back of my mind. A marriage doomed with devastating consequences, because astrological predictions were not followed. But having just graduated with a degree in psychology, I felt compelled to ask for empirical evidence. How many such cases of incompatibility had the astrologer encountered? The astrologer, with great humility and a sweet smile, said, 'I can't remember actual numbers. There were many, but I remember two recent cases. I had advised against two marriages. In one case within the year of their marriage the woman became mad and wandered off into the wild and was never heard of again, and in the other case the husband died within a month of their marriage.' The prospects of death and insanity were causes of great concern to me and I had moments of deep trepidation. I kept thinking of the terrible things that had followed the marriage of my parents. The deaths, sorrow and catastrophes that followed were real and painful. Finally, as if someone was guiding me, I asked the astrologer if there were any remedies to avert the disasters. He agreed to come to our home in Choekor and carry out the remedies. The astrologer was our house guest for a few days and was engaged in rituals as well as in making up some talismans to remedy the terrible consequences of our impending matrimony. After a few days he gave us some cords blessed with sacred mantras as well as tiny wooden *vajras* to wear around our necks for a year. Seeing how relieved I was after this, Walter paid the astrologer well, perhaps far too well. This unexpected generosity opened the astrologer's pact of secrecy with my uncles, and he revealed to us that he had been coached by them to frighten us. But he saw no problems with the marriage. I was shaking in confusion and with the disappointment that my uncles could be so deceitful. For what, I wondered. What did they expect of me? Did they expect me to be a spinster, or if they had a likely candidate for me, I had not been told about him. This was a big turning point in my life. I realized then that only I mattered to me when it concerned matters of the heart. We never wore the sacred cords, neither the wooden vajras, because of what our live-in helper told us. The holy and learnt astrologer who was supposed to be saying his powerful mantras had instead been trying to woo and molest her every night that he was in our house!

While the astrological predications were hypothetical, there was another more real and visible opposition to my marriage. My elder brother Rinzin who was working for the Export Division of the Government of Bhutan in Calcutta at the time, paid a surprise visit in a last bid to stop the marriage. He was very direct and brutal. After one look at Walter, he asked me, 'Have you seen the intensity of his blue eyes? He looks like a maniac.' Yes, of course I had seen those blue eyes. In fact, I was constantly humming the Carpenters' song 'Close to You' which goes 'On the day that you were born the angels got together… and they sprinkled moon dust in your hair … and starlight in your eyes so blue.' My poor well-intentioned brother did not give up. 'Do you want to have weird-looking mixed children with beady eyes?' But I knew better. I had grown up with Anglo-Indian girls in my school and they were, in my eyes, some of the best-looking people I had met. I laughed at his rhetorical question but then he touched on a more serious issue. 'Mixed children will have no national status, and they will never feel that they belong here or there. Look at the plight of the Anglo-Indians in India; they do not feel that they belong here or there.' Perhaps this was a prophetic observation. People who think of themselves as global citizens still must conform to the national legalities of citizenship. That concerned me deeply.

After two days of being with us, Acho Rinzin was drinking beer with Walter, a precious and rare drink that we happened to have a few bottles of – the only available beer in Bumthang those days, Golden Eagle Beer – and they seemed to have accepted each other. Soon after his bid to try and stop the Swiss connection, it was Acho Rinzin who had the opportunity to go to Switzerland on work. During this trip he visited Walter's family and was hosted by Walter's brother. He was a good envoy for me, and Walter's family felt assured that the sister of a nice gentleman like my brother could not be a very bad in-law to have!

Walter had made up his mind to marry me, whatever the costs, and he had anticipated obstacles. In fact, he was already in touch with the Swiss Embassy in Delhi to find out what might happen if he was deported. Ironically, a well-meaning uncle who was in the foreign ministry at the time was considering asking the Swiss Embassy in Delhi to intervene in what he saw was an ill-advised marriage.

It was surely not my culinary skills that endeared me to Walter. Neither did my family background, which he considered to be responsible for maintaining inequality in Bhutan at the time. In fact, when he first heard that I was being assigned to work on the project, he was the loudest voice of opposition, saying that a girl from such a privileged household like Ogyen Choling would not be able to do the kind of practical work that was needed for the project. When he saw that I could roll up my sleeves and was willing to spend my weekends scrubbing the floor and cleaning the windows of the canteen classroom, he let go of his prejudices against me and my privileged upbringing. As for my cooking, having never had a home or access to a kitchen of my own, I had hardly any experience. The first meal I cooked for him using the only available provisions I had, was a soup of cabbage and dried bones. He ate without complaint, remarking that this must be the kind of soup served to prisoners in the Siberian prisons. (He was reading Aleksandr Solzhenitsyn's *The Gulag Archipelago* at the time.) With this statement I knew that Walter was a down to earth and truthful man who did not mince his words.

Perhaps my father's greatest concern at the time of his death about his children marrying outside the community was an uncanny premonition he had that we would, in fact, marry outside our own rik, which both Acho Rinzin and I did. I often wonder, had my parents lived, would I have married Walter?

I wonder if my life's situations would have been different, if my parents had lived. If I had an upbringing with parental care and guidance, if I had not been exposed to other ways of life, and I had been more protected in an inclusive family rather than living an independent life, would I have still married a foreigner? Maybe if my parents had lived, I would not have met Walter at all. I never planned to marry a foreigner; it just happened. But I am convinced that if my parents had the chance to meet and get to know Walter, they would have approved of him and appreciated him as a good human being, like Akhu lama did. It was Akhu lama who referred to Walter as 'Sahib' from the first meeting onwards, a term that was commonly used in respect to refer to Europeans in India. My uncle did not know how to address a foreigner who became a family member. I would like to think that this was a term used to differentiate somebody with deference and not in disdain. Even today many people in Ogyen Choling refer to Walter as Sahib.

21

A Monk's Karmic Debt

After our parents died, the person who filled the role of both parents was the monk Trulku Nuden Dorji, whom we called Akhu lama. He was the only family we knew. However, he did not willingly take on this role. On the contrary, he always saw this unforeseen responsibility as an obstruction in his path to his religious education and practice. I think he finally accepted the role with great trepidation, but in stoic silence, as his karmic debt.

By the time he was fifteen, Akhu lama had chosen religion and convinced his parents to let him go to Tibet. He joined Mindroling monastery where he stayed until the start of the Chinese occupation of Tibet in 1959. His strong attachment to Tibet was, of course, because he, like many others seeking religion, viewed Tibet as the religious and cultural centre. But there was another connection he had to Tibet that was rarely spoken of. He never once mentioned this story to us. He was believed by some to be the rebirth of a Tibetan monk of the Shakya school of Buddhism. It was said that this monk was a highly accomplished yogic practitioner. He came to be known as *Tsa* Trulku or grass Trulku after he demonstrated his feat by sitting on a blade of grass in a yogic posture.

The story goes that my grandmother Keba was a devotee of this master and had received many teachings and empowerments from him. When the lama passed on, she sat devoutly at his cremation among the mourners and prayed fervently as the pyre was set aflame. Suddenly a small fragment, perhaps a piece of bone of the dead lama, fell into her lap. She took this as a sign of blessing from the lama and kept the piece with her as a holy relic. Shortly after this incident she conceived and, when her son was born, he was thought to be the reincarnation of the Shakyapa lama. We have in our family altar a small clay statue of Tsa Trulku.

Already from early childhood Trulku Nuden was different from his two older brothers. While they engaged in common games and activities of other boys their age, Trulku Nuden preferred to read, write, draw and engage in playing the role of a monk. Besides this information, I have not heard anyone talk of any of the usual signs or happenings associated with the behaviours of reincarnated monks. In some cases, enthusiastic parents and relatives recount many signs and behaviours of the child that show that the child is a reincarnation. Sometimes the child is supposed to remember people and incidents from his life. It is also believed that they recognize artefacts and clothing from their past lives and are put through tests. His parents, unlike other eager parents of would-be Trulkus, did not subject him to the usual tests that would prove that he was indeed a reincarnation. If his parents knew anything or had witnessed any paranormal signs, they never talked about it. They instead recognized him quietly and it appears that he was always referred to as Trulku from his childhood. So finally, when at the age of fifteen he declared his intention to join a monastery, his parents were probably not too surprised. I heard that on the day he left the house in Ogyen Choling his mother was bereft. Weeping copiously but quietly, she is said to have stood on the edge of the plateau watching him as he headed towards Phephe la, moving from one vantage to another so that she could see him until he finally disappeared. Perhaps she had a premonition that she would never see him again. She died while he was still in Tibet.

The journey to Tibet was slow. Trulku Nuden's poor health was a disadvantage on the demanding journey. Some years before he decided to undertake the passage to Tibet, he had suffered a terrible debilitating disease that had immobilized him. His joints were locked, and he could not move unaided. How he was cured of this I never found out. But even while they travelled on this perilous journey, his limbs were still swollen, painful and barely mobile.

Some of the men who accompanied him recounted later that when the Tibet-bound travellers approached the pass of Monla Karchung, the weather was dreadful, with heavy mist and a light drizzle. As they breathlessly waded through the slushy slippery path, they were suddenly surrounded by *ja gor gor ma*, circular rainbows. Although rainbows, under normal circumstances, are generally considered an auspicious sign, the rare circular rainbows are considered ominous. It is believed that if a person falls into one of the circles, death is certain. As serious as the situation may have been, whenever I heard about this story I could not help smiling as I pictured the travel-weary, completely weather-beaten men suddenly trying to run, hop, skip and jump, playing hide-and-seek in the precarious terrain covered in thick fog to avoid being trapped in a malevolent circular rainbow.

During the years he was in Mindroling, his family tried to keep in touch with Trulku Nuden by visiting him and exchanging letters. His mother would send him parcels of *tsampa*, roasted barley flour, butter and other foods that she thought he might miss. A man who was once charged with carrying such a parcel recalled how shocked and moved he was on seeing the conditions of deprivation that Trulku Nuden was living in. At the time of this visit Trulku Nuden had probably completed his studies and was in seclusion and engaged in self-study. He was living in a small, almost bare hut with hardly room for two people to sit together. He was sharing the space with another trulku. He was engrossed in his books and quite oblivious of his surroundings. There was an iron brazier with dried yak dung in the room and a tea kettle in the brazier. The parcel carrier immediately stoked the fire and got the dung to burn. Then he made a pot full of fresh tea using the butter he had carried from Ogyen Choling and served the tea with *za phe* (roasted rice flour), dried meat and chilli paste. Although the hermits obviously enjoyed the meal, the parcel carrier was surprised that they did not utter any words of appreciation. Trulku Nuden was keen to have news of his parents in Ogyen Choling and asked about everything and everyone in Bumthang. He was certainly missing home.

My father also visited him in Mindroling shortly before the Chinese occupation of Tibet and they took a trip to Lhasa together. There is a picture of the two of them taken in a studio in Lhasa. Semo Chimmey Wangmo, daughter of the late Dilgo Khyentse, remembers that Trulku Nuden even visited them in Kham Derge and stayed with the family for a while, probably receiving teachings from the Rinpoche. She particularly remembers the trulku from Bhutan with his deep-set eyes and his beautiful raw-silk shawl. A deep bond must have developed with the Rinpoche when Trulku Nuden lived with his family. Trulku Nuden was privileged to enjoy a close guru–disciple relationship and continued to seek advice and confide in Dilgo Khyentse Rinpoche for many years. In the late 1970s when Trulku Nuden was appointed by the Government of Bhutan to become the abbot of Nimalung monastery in Chummey, he immediately consulted Rinpoche. He was hesitant about accepting the appointment, but at the same time it was an honour and a recognition he could not refuse without a good reason. He begged Rinpoche for advice. Dilgo Khyentse Rinpoche encouraged him to take the new appointment. But Trulku Nuden was still apprehensive and hesitated. Then he turned to Rinpoche and appealed to him to intervene so that he would not have to accept the position. The lama said that he could not interfere with the government's command, so Trulku Nuden asked him to say that he had performed a divination which had not been favourable or that he had had an ominous dream. The lama had laughed out loud and said that he had not performed a divination and that he had no bad dreams about this appointment. So Trulku Nuden had no option but to accept the posting. He was the abbot of Nimalung from 1982 until his death in 1985.

I remember only vaguely when Akhu lama came home after he had fled from Tibet. I knew him from the many references made to him – his favourite horse, his room, his drawings, visits by family members and parcels exchanged. He had left for Tibet before I was born, but from my earliest memory I knew that I had an uncle who was a monk in Tibet. It must have been sometime in 1959 when I met him for the first time. How he came home and who was with him, I do not recall. But I do remember the warm welcome he received from his elder brother, my father, his sister-in-law, my mother, and the deference and respect they accorded to him. He only stayed for a while because he wanted to follow his masters who had fled to India. He said that he wanted to go to a place called Kalimpong and continue his religious studies. It was the first time I heard of Kalimpong, where many monks from Tibet had gathered.

As soon as he came home my father gave up his central place in the family meal circle. Akhu lama was given an elevated place and we sat around him. One day I remember watching him make something out of a piece of wood as I sat next to him on the elevated lama seat. I was curious and asked him what he was making. He playfully said that he was making a pointed stick like a toothpick so that he could eat the home-made macaroni-like *laep* (broth) that he was looking forward to eating. That is all I remember of him from our first encounter. I don't even remember whether we did eat laep together. But soon after this meeting he disappeared from our lives; he must have gone to Kalimpong.

Akhu lama must have stayed in Kalimpong for two or three years. But with my parents dying within two years of each other the heavy mantle of Ogyen Choling's legacy was thrust upon him. He was caught up with the extensive death rituals and the building and renovating of chortens and prayer wheels as a means of merit-making for the deceased. Within years of their deaths, he undertook a major project of building an altar dedicated to Dorsem (Vajrasattva) in my parents' memory. He was advised and guided by the master sculptor and painter Lopon Choeda from Lhalung. Akhu lama, a true monk, thought of nothing beyond using the best materials to make the ultimate shrine and used all the resources he had at hand. He sold off many of my mother's heirloom kiras and my father's ghos. He also sold off many of their personal belongings as well as silver jewellery to pay for the project. Akhu lama wanted to offer many of mother's dzi, corals and turquoise to the statue. Lopon Choeda, who was wise and practical, reasoned, why display the jewels around the statue's neck to rouse yearning and greed among the worshippers and, worse still, tempt thieves in the future? His advice to crush, grind and mix them into the clay for the statue was followed. Today people say that the reason why cracks appeared in the statue is because there was a disproportionate amount of clay and other ingredients in the mixture. It seems Lopon Choeda had a prophetic vision of the future. For some decades now, Bhutanese have taken to the despicable practice of robbing temples and statues: they strip the statues of jewellery and dig deep into the figures to search for any precious stones and other valuables.

As the activities around my parents' death eased, the routine and complex intricacies of running a landed household caught up with Akhu lama. Ironically, all that he had abandoned at the age of fifteen hit him like a ton of bricks now. He concluded that these were his karmic burdens and bravely plodded on. Compounding the dire situation was the fact that he was not only alone but that there was also nobody else from the family to help him. He had to take on multiple roles of being a monk, upholding the religious traditions and being the landlord of the estate and overseeing its management. The tasks that were normally done by the mistress of the house, like managing the food and weaving activities, all fell on him. In addition, he had to take on the responsibility of being a parent to four orphans. What really made the situation extremely difficult was that the effect of the social reforms was slowly but surely impacting everybody. Expectations and lifestyles were affected and altered, heralding a bewildering future. The only experience Akhu lama had of running Ogyen Choling was what he knew of the system before the social reforms in the 1930s, when his own parents were still at the helm of the feudal system. He probably had images of the privileged and more laid-back lives of the landed families in those days. In the changing social system, Ogyen Choling, with its huge redundant buildings, was a liability, simply draining his resources and energy when he got nothing in return. It was like a monster, slowly but surely consuming itself. While some similar households as ours were able to plead with the government through connections, to get tax exemptions, he had to pay the full taxes. By today's standards the taxes were not heavy but because of the limited circulation of currency in the country he had no means of getting enough money to pay the taxes. This was a dreadful predicament for him to be in.

The family of Ogyen Choling had no source of monetary income and many of the taxes had to be paid in cash. Akhu lama had to find the money. This was when he surrendered some of the most valuable pieces of our land to the government to lower the tax burden. When the deadline for the taxes drew nearer, Akhu lama fretted and worried endlessly. The only reprieve was the one that he despised most. He asked the alcohol manager in our household to brew some ara. This was filled into bamboo containers and sold in Jakar, mostly to civil servants and businesspeople because they were the only ones who had expendable cash. This was the quick and dirty trick that saved the dignity of our household.

At his lowest moments he told us that he was ready to abandon the house and go live somewhere else. For some reason the place he dreamed of relocating to was Tama in Zhemgang. Our conversations of despair always ended with him joking that there was nothing of commercial value in the house and that the statues in the temple were too big to transport. The only thing we could possibly take with us was the life-sized statue of Dorji Phamo (Vajravahi) in the Dolma lhakhang. This statue is made of silver, and we could sell pieces of it to get by.

As naive teenagers who could not fully comprehend the bleakness of our economic situation, we shared a secret. We wickedly construed a mystery around a black box that Akhu lama had in his room and which was always locked. Our code name, 'the black box', was probably inspired by my brothers having read a series of books detailing the adventures of pilots. We imagined that the box was filled with money and treasures that Akhu lama did not show us. This secret, wrapped in layers of imagination, buoyed our hopes and aspirations of a better life. We were always comforted that there was 'the black box' and that it would save us. We often teased him about it, and he always looked at us in silent bewilderment. On the day we were leaving home for school he would disappear into his bedroom for a while and then hand each of us some cash, never more than fifty or sixty rupees. In those days these amounts were substantial sums of money. I imagined he had taken the money from 'the black box'. Ironically, when he died, we were able to investigate the mysterious box, and all it had in it were correspondence and some of his writing exercises! The money he had been saving was in another box we had never set eyes on. But it wasn't a big amount that would have changed our fortune.

There was yet another box full of Bhutanese currency (ngultrum). None of the notes had a value of more than five ngultrum. This money was what he had received as *gno* from family members and relatives requesting him to do the prayer of liberation for those who had died in their families. He had not used a single ngultrum out of this box; he had planned to use them at a sacred temple for butter lamps for the dead for whom the money was intended. Akhu lama's sudden and untimely death did not allow him to do this. We later offered the money to the tenth Thugse Rinpoche who performed some of Akhu lama's own death rituals. Thugse Rinpoche said, 'You see, the gno money must be used for the dead and not for any other purpose. Late Trulku Nuden followed that code.' Learnt practitioners were also ethical and disciplined in those days, unlike today when some dubious practitioners brazenly bargain and negotiate their fees for religious performances.

With Akhu lama we were a unit bound by history, affection, concern and shared interests. When we came home from school for our holidays, he prepared to receive us by sending horses and provisions to meet us up to the point where the motor roads had reached. Like in the old days, on the day we were to reach home he would send tea and snacks to welcome us at a certain distance from the house. But he was still a distracted parent. One time he forgot to include the cups for the tea. In those days, it was customary for each one to have our own individual cup. Using someone else's utensils was referred to as *kha shrat mala* or 'mixing mouths', a serious taboo. The time we were greeted with tea without cups, I used the old grisly horseman (and my father's former hunter, now the horse man)

Ap Prala's cup for I could not resist the tea from home. Ap Prala went to the stream and washed his wooden cup again and again until I was afraid the last patches of lacquer would come off. For years afterwards he talked about this incident and laughed. Akhu lama was a staunch believer in not 'mixing mouths' and suffered physically. Every time this taboo was broken angry rashes and threatening blisters would appear around his mouth, which is why he always carried his own cups with him.

When we reached home, he received us warmly with the ceremony of welcome tea and *dresi* (sweet rice with butter). Invariably he would have lit one of the precious incenses from Mindroling, and the room would be filled with a wonderful fragrance. I associate this smell with him, the embrace of a warm welcoming home. I have never managed to find any incense even remotely close to the ones from Mindroling, even though many incense manufacturers today claim to follow the Mindroling recipes. We lost our last stock of Mindroling incense to a thief who had robbed our house in the 1970s. The thief clearly knew the value of this incense. Akhu lama would be standing in the middle of the room expectantly, but composed and controlled, and only when we bent down our heads towards him to receive his blessings would he playfully bang his head on ours. That was the only expression of emotion he allowed himself, although sometimes I felt him trembling with emotion.

During our vacations he did everything to make us feel at home and cared for. He instructed our old cook Meme Nagzila to replicate the meals we had when mother was alive. Our meals were eaten with him at the head of the circle in an easy and comfortable atmosphere. It was from him that we learnt some of our history and ancestry. Much more than a storyteller, Akhu lama was a great listener. I think he may have mentioned it in passing, but I heard it from the others that

Ashi Sonam Choden, the powerful sister of the first king of Bhutan, would often invite him to be a kadroepa to her even when he was a mere child. He would just be in her presence mostly listening. Ashi referred to him as Trulku. She is believed to have said that she told him all the '*kha ju, tam ju, lam luk suy* (oral history, sayings, customs and tradition)' because nobody else bothered to listen. I remember him referring to the Kharmsumphe Aum's *gokha* (court) later in life. Although she was alleged to be a tough lady, he remembered her as a very kind person. When he was back in Ogyen Choling he used to receive occasional parcels from her. His listening abilities had forged this unusual bond.

Akhu lama talked contemplatively and yearningly about Tibet and of the time he spent there. He never forced religion on us, but he was concerned that we should know as much as we could. While I was in school in Kurseong and receiving pocket money for the first time in my life, I used to save it and spend most of it to buy Catholic holy pictures and rosaries which I innocently brought home as presents for him and my mother. He was broad-minded and never rejected or showed any disrespect to these objects. Instead, he received them gracefully, saying, 'This is of the *Yeshu* (Christian) religion.'

Often after lunch the boys would romp around and go out to play their games and I would stay inside with Akhu lama. This was the time he dedicated to reading and writing. When I was around, he would read aloud the biographies, especially of the *delogs* (those people who returned from death and served as messengers between the dead and the living). After the heavy meals I ate, I could barely keep awake but he would continue to read aloud because he believed that even if I was overcome with sleep my subconscious would absorb the messages of the stories.

After hearing some of the stories, I was so inspired and moved that I wanted to practise religion and become a nun.

In all sincerity and with full conviction I told Akhu lama that I wanted to become a nun. He looked at me, his eyes dancing with amusement and, laughing uncontrollably, said, 'You don't have to become a nun to practise religion; you already look wild and untamed like Machig Labdron. Be like her.' I had long hair those days and never really took care to groom myself. I probably looked unkempt and dishevelled. I think I cried at his response because I thought he was ridiculing me. Later, when I put things in perspective, I realized the significance of what he had said. At that time, I imagined nuns to be humble and demure women who had retreated from the world and mundane affairs. Akhu lama was telling me to be like the renowned eleventh-century unconventional Tibetan woman Buddhist yogini, Machig Labdron. She was at times a beggar, a committed practitioner, and a brilliant teacher, mother and lineage founder. She is considered to be the lineage founder of the practice of *chod* which literally means cutting through the human experience of grasping of self and self-cherishing attitude. I had seen monks perform the ritual of chod and had a vague understanding that the practitioner had to visualize their own body being offered to feed the hungry ghosts. Because I did not fully understand the significance of the naked dancing woman, I used to be frightened of the temple murals depicting her. His advice shifted my image of women religious practitioners. Whether he intended it or not I will never know. But it was a moment of awakening and empowerment for me. I realized then that to practise religion you did not have to don the garments of a practitioner and, more importantly, women practitioners did not have to be humble or demure; we could be unfettered and different.

Akhu lama sometimes told us that his heart had become weak because of the continuous grief he had experienced in his life. It was a statement without any rancour. His sorrows came one after another. First, he had to bear the grief of the death of his parents while he was still in Tibet, and he could not be present at their cremation and attend to their rituals. Then he had to leave Tibet, abruptly ending his religious studies because of the Chinese takeover. Although it was his fervent desire to continue his studies with his masters in exile in India, he was rudely catapulted into the reality of a lay life following the deaths of my parents. Akhu lama said that his heart was incapable of taking such pain any more. He said he wanted no reminders of the people he had cared for dearly who had died untimely deaths. That was when he began to systematically destroy all the photographs of those who had died in the family. We had a relatively large collection of photographs as my parents had become enthusiastic photographers and regularly took pictures of people and events. Although many of the photographs were the works of amateurs, and the pictures were mostly blurry, they did serve as mementos. Akhu lama only kept the photographs of religious personalities as objects of veneration and meditation.

Even without the help of photographs I remember people who have passed on, and I miss them. Of all the people who are gone I miss Akhu lama the most because I spent the most time with him. Fortunately, we have a collection of pictures of him taken by us after our parents died. Akhu lama the parent, Akhu lama the family man and Akhu lama the monk. Every time I think of him, I am immersed in nostalgia and regret. He was the only parent I knew into adulthood. Every day I regret that I am without his guidance and advice as I try to reconstruct the history and narrative of Ogyen Choling, our common ancestral home, by establishing the family museum.

He was a disciplined and accomplished monk who never asserted himself or engaged in self-promotion. Reading extensively and engaging in religious practice was a part of his daily routine. He instituted a dratshang, with gomchen (lay monks) from the village and the valley, and he was a strict, dedicated and kind teacher. Some of the lay monks today recall how patiently and carefully he taught them to use the religious instruments for temple music. He dreamed of establishing religious performances according to the Dorji Lingpa and Mindroling traditions. Besides teaching the specific mantras, liturgies, chants and mudras, he made sure to have all the accessories, the ritual hats and instruments for all the participants. During the temple rituals he led, the worship was always so dignified and atmospheric, never failing to emanate an intense sense of joyful devotion. Over the years after his death the dratshang disbanded, and although some of the lay monks trained by him still perform the prayers, the atmosphere is totally different.

One of the main reminders of Akhu lama that lives on beyond the sphere of our immediate family is the tremendous effort he invested in collecting and getting all the available manuscripts and prints of the Dorji Lingpa tradition printed and distributed. He was introduced to the legendary Gene Smith of the American Congress Library in Delhi. Gene Smith was well known for preserving and disseminating endangered Tibetan Buddhist texts. Tragically Akhu lama passed away before he could see the fruits of his endeavour.

Akhu lama was a doer. Sometime in the mid-1960s he suffered another attack of the debilitating disease that made him immobile. In a last-ditch effort, he travelled to Dewathang, in today's Trashigang district, because he knew that the Royal Grandmother Her Majesty Ashi Phuntsho Choden was there at the time. He requested her to ask the Indian paramilitary doctors in the Dantak hospital to help him. The Royal Grandmother graciously asked the hospital there to treat him and he was hospitalized for some time. Finally, he recovered enough to travel back to Bumthang, but his fingers were immobile and could not fully function for a while. For a person who was constantly using his hands, always writing, drawing, painting, carving wooden items and moulding clay, it must have been devastating. I was away in school at the time, but my brother Ugyen Rinzin told me how Akhu lama trained himself to reuse his fingers, especially to be able to write again. He forced his fingers to move by massaging them and then held his pen with both hands and literally forced them to write. I saw some of the writing exercises he had done. Ugyen Rinzin said that it was painful to watch as he sweated and cringed in pain during these exercises. He went through this rigorous and unrelenting routine until he finally managed to write again.

I treasure the memories of him coming to live with us in our house in Jakar after I got married. He stayed in the little altar room and quickly adjusted to living with us, a strange Bhutanese–Swiss family. Although he had initially opposed my marriage to Walter, very soon Akhu lama and Walter enjoyed a very close and special relationship. In the beginning of his stay, he laughed at us for eating salad with our meals, saying we looked like rabbits nibbling the greens, but soon he was the one who enjoyed fresh salads with his meals the most. Although my daughters were too young to remember anything of Meme lama, they were blessed to have him around for a small part of their lives. In fact, he was in the house when I delivered my second daughter, and he was as nervous as a first-time expectant father. During a lull in my labour pains, he ran into the birthing room to rub some blessed ointment on my head and say some prayers and ran out again just as speedily as he had come in. After the birth of my daughters, he made elaborate horoscopes with colourful pictures, like children's illustrated books, for both the girls. He even babysat sat them occasionally. I particularly remember one time when he was attempting to change diapers for my second daughter. Because she fussed so much, he rushed around the house in panic saying, 'You have to come.' I was worried something terrible had happened, but it was only because she would not lie still as he tried to put on her diapers. He affectionately named her *Aie Khampa*, or Granny from Kham, because she reminded him of an old woman he had known from Kham. In those days, Akhu lama laughed easily and frequently but always silently. So much of his mirth came through his eyes which danced with joy, wonder and curiosity, as he slapped his thighs in delight and moved back and forth. He laughed with his whole body.

When he took up the post of abbot of Nimalung dratshang, I accompanied him during the elaborate welcome procession that the monks had arranged for him. He lived in the small cottage assigned as the lama's residence near the temple. I think he was happy there. He was fully engaged in improving the monastic standards and educational and social welfare of the monks there. When we visited him, I felt the modest little cottage exude happiness and contentment. I think this was the kind of life he should have had from the beginning. He should not have had to worry about paying taxes on the property and assets he never wanted, bowing down to petty bureaucrats, representatives of the government who excelled in senseless bullying and humiliating others.

In the beginning of the 1980s, Walter and I decided to go to the US for further studies. When we announced our plans, Akhu lama got very anxious. Even though we assured him that we would return after two years, he went about with a concerned look on his face for days. He kept repeating that we must return at the end of the two years. At the end of two years, we received a letter from him in the USA. The envelope had been addressed in his own hand in English, because he was teaching himself English, but he had made my brother Ugyen Rinzin write the letter. In the past I used to correspond with him writing in the Tibetan script but using Bumthangkha, because I had studied some Tibetan in school. This letter was delightful and funny, giving us all the news and telling me all about my house in Jakar and the tenants who were misusing our house and abusing our cows. But the main point of the letter was to ask us when we were returning to Bhutan. There was urgency in that question. But by then we had extended our stay in the USA by two more years to continue our studies. The urgency of this expressed anxiety was to become a tragedy for us. Akhu lama, still the abbot of Nimalung dratshang, suddenly died in 1985. At the time my brother Ugyen Rinzin and his wife Kesang were living with him in the lama's residence in the monastery. On the day he died, he sent both of them out of the house on various errands. Then he locked himself up and died sitting in his bed. He wanted to die alone and undisturbed. The door had to be broken down to enter his bedroom. The monastery took full responsibility to undertake all the death rituals. It took a few days before I could be contacted. But after I was informed of his death, I rushed to Bhutan and reached Nimalung dratshang after a journey of more than thirty-six hours of travel just before his pyre was lit. Completely exhausted and jet-lagged, I managed to stumble through the death rituals. After everything was over, my elder brother Rinzin handed me my vanity box which I had left in Akhu lama's care. He had put some of mother's jewellery in it, including some silver and gold jewellery. Among the contents was a small, tape-recorded message from Akhu lama for me. I think he had prepared for his death. It did not come as a surprise to him. The only surprise was that we had failed to return after the two years, as we had assured him.

It is for him that I have written my memoir. More than the magnetic pull to come back to my ancestral home, it was because I feel Akhu lama would have done the same things I am doing now, had he had the time and resources. The reason that I have decided to come back to Ogyen Choling and undertake the maintenance and upkeep of the property is because I feel in my heart that this is what he wanted for our ancestral heritage. The maintenance of the structural and physical forms through the many transformations and changes are just one way to sustain our religious and historical legacy.

Epilogue

It is springtime as I write this, and I glance at the old oak tree near the temple. The tree seems bare, and the branches appear to be brittle as they have just emerged from the harsh winter cold. The warm south wind blows hard, announcing spring. On closer scrutiny I recognize the unmistakable delicate swell of buds on the tips of its branches. Another year has passed, and a new year has begun, and I feel a sense of gratitude and quiet excitement that I am allowed to witness another cycle of seasons. What will this new year be for me? I do not expect too much. I am blessed that I can continue the life I have chosen: to retire and live in the place of my birth in relative peace and contentment. My days will continue to be devoted to the physical upkeep of the structures that I call home, telling the stories of the place and people to all who care to listen. I will be sharing my stories that I have been telling myself all my life. In the back of my head, I am ever conscious of the Buddhist phenomenon of the impermanence of all things, both the tangible and the intangible. Yet I wish for continuity amidst change to sustain this place and its chronicles that weave through every space and edifice of my ancestral home, Ogyen Choling.

Acknowledgements

Thank you to all whose lives and voices have helped me in the telling of my stories. And thank you to those who spoke to me through their absences and silences and drew me into wanting to know more.

I give thanks to my agent Siyahi for bravely taking on the task of finding a home for my story. I thank my editors at Bloomsbury India for tidying up the mess I offered to them.

Thank you to my family who stands by me and tolerates my long-winded stories. Deepest appreciation to my husband, Walter, for his steadfast support and gentle encouragement. A big thank you to my daughter Dolma who read multiple drafts and urged me to continue writing, saying, 'It's your story, nobody else can tell it for you.'

About the Author

Author of the bestselling and critically acclaimed novel *The Circle of Karma*, Kunzang Choden was the first Bhutanese woman to be published in English. She started her career collecting vanishing Bhutanese folk tales and moved on to novels, a study of food and culture, and children's books. Her works have been translated into many languages including Sinhalese, French, Dutch, Chinese, Japanese, Italian, Turkish and Hindi. A winner of the SAARC Literature Award 2023, she is well known for documenting and reflecting on the experiences of a rapidly changing Bhutan.